Birds in my Indian Garden

MALCOLM MacDONALD

FOREWORD BY BULBUL SHARMA

ALEPH

ALEPH BOOK COMPANY
An independent publishing firm
promoted by *Rupa Publications India*

Published in India in 2015 by
Aleph Book Company
7/16 Ansari Road, Daryaganj
New Delhi 110 002

Copyright © The Estate of Malcolm MacDonald 2015

All rights reserved.

No part of this publication may be reproduced, transmitted, or stored in a retrieval system, in any form or by any means, without permission in writing from Aleph Book Company.

This edition faithfully reproduces the material printed in the first edition (1960) except for the following—a) The photographs by Christina Loke have been omitted. b) Author's Note (called the 'Foreword' in the first edition) has been edited to leave out mention of the photographs; and c) the index has been updated to include the new Latin and English names of the birds referred to in the book.

ISBN: 978-93-84067-40-3

3 5 7 9 10 8 6 4 2

Printed in India

This book is sold subject to the condition that it shall not, by way of trade or otherwise, be lent, resold, hired out, or otherwise circulated without the publisher's prior consent in any form of binding or cover other than that in which it is published

CONTENTS

Foreword ... vii
Author's Note ... xi

One	Delhi	1
Two	January	5
Three	February	17
Four	March	34
Five	Green Parakeets	46
Six	April	65
Seven	The Coppersmith	88
Eight	Two Mynahs	105
Nine	May and June	120
Ten	White-eyes	142
Eleven	Crows and Koels	157
Twelve	The Monsoon—July, August and September	172
Thirteen	Ashy Wren-Warblers	195
Fourteen	Jungle Babblers	215
Fifteen	October, November and December	228

Index of Birds ... 239

FOREWORD

One fine morning in 1916, a bird-watcher wrote in his diary 'Bright sunbirds flit from bloom to bloom, now hovering in the air on rapidly-vibrating wings, now dipping their slender curved bills into the calyces. On the lawns wagtails run nimbly in search of tiny insects, hoopoes probe the earth for grubs, mynahs strut about, in company with king-crows...'

Not much had changed from the time Douglas Dewar wrote about the birds of northern India when almost fifty years later another bird-watcher—Malcolm MacDonald—observed them in his Delhi garden. The birds behaved with the same joyous spirit—singing, carrying out complicated courtship rituals and nesting chores and he noted each task with a keen eye.

Delhi has always been a bird-watcher's paradise and every garden in Delhi has its resident population of birds. A small patch with just a single flower-bed or a vast, rambling garden with old trees or a balcony with a few flowerpots will all attract a large number of birds throughout the year. In my garden, which was as wild and unkempt as a jungle, I could see around 40 species of birds in a week. Not very far from my disorderly garden was a beautifully kept, flower-bedecked garden to which many birds, made their way when they needed a fine dining experience; each one of them was greeted warmly by their host and made to feel very welcome.

Malcolm MacDonald, who was the UK High Commissioner in India in the 1950s, spent more than three years watching birds in this garden which had neatly laid out flower-beds, old trees, vast lawns and a goldfish pond. In 1959, the garden must have been exactly the same as it is today—only the name of road has been changed from King George's Avenue to Rajaji Marg.

The new name of their residence does not seem to bother

the parakeets and they still perch on the old trees; below them energetic mynahs quarrel on the green lawn but they must all miss the presence of their friend who recorded their lives so faithfully in such graceful, witty words.

Bird-watchers are famous for their patience in the field where they often stand in muddy swamps or dusty fields for hours to watch birds, but not many have Malcolm MacDonald's patience to meticulously note each habit, each twist of the wing or turn of the beak. I have been watching birds for twenty years but never noticed how ardently the male parakeet woos and serenades his chosen mate. How many hours of close observation of the courting couple and their nesting site must have been needed to note down all the tiny, interesting details! After reading Malcolm MacDonald's description, I now look at the male parakeet with more respect.

Delhi, with its amazing and varied population of both resident, and migratory birds, has always been fortunate enough in having many keen bird-watchers observing and noting every detail of their nesting, breeding and feeding habits. The keen observations of A. O. Hume, the founder of the Indian National Congress, C. T. Bingham, Douglas Dewar and C. L. T. Marshall formed the basis of several noteworthy books. In 1920, Basil-Edwardes made copious notes about birds he had seen in New Delhi, which was being built at that time. These notes formed the first checklist of birds of Delhi and were published in the *Journal of the Bombay Natural History Society* in 1926. Later, from 1942 to 1948, many other ornithologists, most of them British, made detailed notes about the birds of Delhi. In May 1950, the Delhi Birdwatching Society was formed where enthusiastic Indian and British members exchanged notes and wrote accounts of their field observations. Usha Ganguli, a keen bird-watcher and a friend of Malcolm MacDonald's, writes in her book *Birds of the Delhi Area*: 'Malcolm MacDonald, former UK High Commissioner (is) the author of two delightful books on the birds of Delhi, whose notes on these birds I have freely used.'

As Delhi expands at a breathless rate and green habitats disappear under highways and buildings, the birds have to find new ways to survive. What is very reassuring is that Malcolm MacDonald's observations made over half a century ago have not yet become a mythical story. Hundreds of parakeets still fly to and from their feeding sites, forming green clouds in the skies of Delhi. Gardens and parks, however crowded with people and frantic traffic noise, still offer a safe shelter to many birds, which have now become clever enough to cope with the chaos of the city. Some like sparrows and vultures are having a tough time but they manage somehow to carry on. Like true Delhi residents, birds know where to seek abundant food, cool spots in summer and sunny patches in winter. Fortunately, many of the old neem and tamarind trees planted by the British have survived, and together with the new flamboyant flowering species which flourish next to them, offer safe haven to birds.

Birds are not fussy about which tree they perch on as long it has fruits, buds, flowers and a steady supply of insects. We should all feel grateful that nothing much has changed since the time Malcolm MacDonald sat and watched birds in his garden in 1959, noting that, 'This remarkably assorted company of winged creatures visit the place, and feed, flirt, and rear young families there regardless of the fact that just beyond the garden wall motor-cars, buses, horse-traps, cyclists and pedestrians swarm noisily along the busy thoroughfare called King George's Avenue. Among its other pleasing attributes, Delhi is a naturalists' paradise.'

May it remain like this for many years to come.

June 2015

Bulbul Sharma
New Delhi

AUTHOR'S NOTE

In the perpetual protocol of a diplomat's life, duty (unfortunately) should always take precedence over pleasure; and my work as a High Commissioner in India almost invariably kept me occupied from eight o'clock in the morning until midnight. So my bird-watching had to be confined in time largely to two hours before breakfast each day, and in space mostly to my garden. Luckily, birds are at their liveliest at dawn, so I managed to see some interesting episodes in the careers of many attractive creatures. I watched them through the years 1957, 1958 and 1959. As I wrote the manuscript of the volume in 1959, the term 'this year' in the book represents that twelve months.

I am especially grateful to India's famous ornithologist, Dr Salim Ali, for reading the manuscript of the book and offering some useful suggestions. I also express my thanks to many friends who helped in the spotting of nests, to others who lent me their counsel, to a tireless team of workmen who built countless hides, and to my bearers who often stood guard over those hides day and night. With most painstaking kindness Mrs Usha Ganguli prepared the list of Latin and Hindi names on which the index of the book has been based.

I need only add that this effort does not aspire to be a scientific work on the birds of Delhi; nor is it a detailed reference book. It is a glimpse of a tiny nature reserve in the middle of India's great capital; and I have written only the minimum descriptions of various species that seemed necessary, assuming that readers who are sufficiently interested will refer for additional information to more erudite authors.

March 1960   Malcolm MacDonald
                                    2 King George's Avenue
                                    New Delhi

ONE

DELHI

Delhi is one of the great, historic capitals on Earth. The part it has played in India's long story is pre-eminent. Its geographical position destined it for that role. Strategically situated beneath the Himalayan passes through which invading armies and traders' caravans alike were wont to enter, on the threshold of the vast, fertile plains of northern India, and astride communication routes stretching in all directions, it was a natural seat of government. Whoever commanded it controlled a large part of a subcontinent. The city was already a capital before Alexander the Great intruded into the region; and although its fortunes after that became obscure for a few centuries, more recently through many hundred years it has been the central stronghold of successive kingdoms and empires.

Its historical and cultural interest is enhanced by the fact that not one Delhi, but a series of Delhis, was built on the site: as if Delhi, like some fabulous human being, were a mortal creature doomed periodically to die, yet achieving a certain immortality by its capacity to reproduce in every generation fresh images of itself. Successive dynasties, and sometimes individual rulers in the same dynasty, thought it inauspicious, or beneath their dignity, or unhealthy, to live in the antique home of a predecessor, so they abandoned a previously inhabited capital and built a new one in the neighbourhood. They rarely moved far away, for other places did not possess the strategic and political advantages which seemed to be concentrated at Delhi. Thus when the Great Moguls shifted their court to Agra, only 120 miles off, their occupation of the place was short-lived and they soon returned to Delhi.

So within a radius of a few miles from the modern capital are remnants of more than a dozen ancient capitals. Some of these have crumbled completely to dust, and no recognizable physical manifestation of their existence remains; but others still stand in semi-ruin as grand monuments of earlier Imperial Delhis. The oldest and most lovely of them is the Qutb, with its magnificent Minar, dating from the early thirteenth century; but several others also possess abiding strength, character and grace. Siri, where I have watched wild peacocks dance on broken medieval battlements; Tughlakhabad, whose founder sleeps eternally, like a forgetful sentry, in a massive tomb beside its gateway; Purana Quila, with a handsome mosque still partially bright-tiled in spite of the neglect and storms of centuries; Ferozabhad, inhabited now only by wild animals and tame picnickers; and other similar places, all exhibit impressive evidence of former regal splendour. The Emperor Shah Jehan's Old Delhi is yet another fascinating chapter of history written in stone, now being succeeded by the momentous story of New Delhi. And in the surrounding countryside countless other architectural relics of those vivid centuries linger. In some areas austere, squat-domed Mogul tombs stand in the fields as plentifully as haystacks in an English summer landscape. Even Rome cannot boast a finer collection of noble monuments.

Yet although this ancient, oft-rebuilt capital has been a cultured city for close on two thousand years, in it one is never far from the unregenerate wild, the kingdom of the birds and beasts. I remember my first visit to Old Delhi. As I walked along its crowded main street I suddenly glimpsed, out of a corner of an eye, three small human figures leaping from a roof-top, alighting nimbly on the pavement below, and darting across the roadway, threading a swift, perilous, cunning course through a stream of on-coming traffic. I thought they must be a trio of precocious juvenile delinquents making a getaway from a daring bank robbery, eluding the police by losing themselves in the throng of motor-cars, bullock-carts, bicycles and pedestrians; and I expected to hear whistles blown, horns tooted, and constables alerted to arrest the criminals. But nobody took any notice; everyone proceeded about his business unperturbed; and when the malefactors arrived on the opposite pavement, scampered up a shop wall, settled on its roofs and began to munch bananas, I saw that they were a troupe of monkeys.

The staid precincts of New Delhi, too, have many invasions from such visitors. A stranger would be surprised at the many different forms of wild-life to be met in its prim streets and formal gardens. One of the commonest species is, of course, that to which I have the honour to belong—the members of the Diplomatic Corps. There are forty-one different varieties of Ambassador, eight diverse types of High Commissioner, five sorts of Minister, one Apostolic Internuncio and four Consuls-General. In addition numerous Cabinet Ministers are permanent residents in the capital, while hundreds of Members of Parliament migrate to and fro at certain seasons. It would be improper for the envoy of another State to comment on the strange customs and endearing characteristics of these latter species; so I shall content myself with a passing reference to the Diplomatic Corps. They are all excellent Excellencies endowed with many admirable qualities; but they also betray one odd habit. Between six and eight o'clock every evening for many months in the year they can be seen flocking at a series of tedious, mostly pointless, chatterbox cocktail parties.

Fortunately there are no cocktail parties between six o'clock and eight o'clock in the mornings; so we are free then to pursue more congenial hobbies. Most days I wander round my garden with a pair of field-glasses observing other forms of wild-life in India's capital. It is remarkable to discover how many of them frequent the populous city. My house stands within a few stone's throws of the stately President's House, the busy Government Secretariat and the crowded Parliament Building; yet I have seen eight different species of eagle and buzzard in its garden in broad daylight, and often at nights jackals howl beneath its windows.

Many charming animals live in my small plot of lawns, flower-beds, vegetable patches and shrubberies. Among them are squirrels, flying-foxes, bats, toads, frogs, lizards, mice, and a great assortment of butterflies, moths and insects. Their private lives are endlessly intriguing. Some snakes might well be added to the list, were it not for the presence of mongooses. Several of these potent guardian spirits reside on the property. Sometimes as I sit working in my study a Rikki-tikki-tavi strolls through the French window, ambles inquisitively round the room, sniffs the air suspiciously as it approaches me, takes umbrage at my human smell, and trots quickly out again.

To the garden also come innumerable birds. Some of Delhi's species are as beautiful as any to be found in the world, for they include exquisite creatures like Golden Orioles, Indian Hoopoes, Whitebreasted Kingfishers, Blossomheaded Parakeets, Bluetailed Bee-eaters, Green Pigeons, White-eyes, Yellow Wagtails and Goldenbacked Woodpeckers. Although my garden has no sheet of water except a small goldfish pool, river birds like terns, lake birds like darters and cormorants, and swamp birds like egrets, herons, storks and ibises, often fly above its lawns. My visitors run the whole gamut of sizes from gigantic Sarus Cranes and Griffon Vultures to diminutive Whitethroats and Hume's Leaf Warblers; and they include birds who build many varied types of nest—a slim platform of sticks plaited by Ring Doves, a wondrously suspended globe of grasses woven by Purple Sunbirds, a hole in a wall sparsely furnished by Spotted Owlets, two leaves firmly stitched together by Tailor Birds, or a hammock slung across the forked branch of a tree by a pair of Black Drongos.

The garden does not contain any significant variety of terrain, and covers less than three acres of ground—yet I have seen in or from it in the last three years 136 different species of birds, while in the same period thirty diverse kinds have laid eggs in nests there. This remarkably assorted company of winged creatures visit the place, and feed, flirt, and rear young families there, regardless of the fact that just beyond the garden wall motor-cars, buses, horse-traps, cyclists and pedestrians swarm noisily along the busy thoroughfare called King George's Avenue.

Among its other pleasing attributes, Delhi is a naturalists' paradise.

TWO

JANUARY

I

New Year's Day in Delhi enjoys weather appropriate to the occasion. In the early dawn, wisps of mist loiter over the ground like belated revellers from the old year; but soon they slip away to make room for a clear, bright, promising morning. January is a beautiful month in upper India. At its beginning the days are short, for the sun does not rise until a quarter past seven and it sets again by half past five; but as the weeks pass, daylight gradually lengthens. Usually the sky is blue and the sun smiles benevolently. At midday the temperature sometimes reaches 70 °F in the shade, but at dusk it tumbles quickly and settles low in the forties at nights.

Delhi's gardens are then full of flowers. The varied lovely hues of blooms along herbaceous borders and other flower-beds combine with extravagant splashes of colour on bougainvillaea, poinsettia, bignonia, and varied shrubs and creepers, to make a gay show. By the end of the month the jacarandás, cassias and other trees are shedding their old leaves and preparing to display new foliage and blossoms. Delhi is moving steadily towards its climax of floral beauty some weeks later, as the artists who planned the city deliberately designed. They had an eye not only for imposing architecture, but also for gracious, gigantic landscape gardening.

Bird society round my house is numerous in January, but comparatively inactive and quiet. The mornings are too chilly for sane beings, however thickly feathered, to feel like bursting into song. At 6.30 a silver moon still hangs in a darkened sky, though the gathering hordes of daylight are faintly discernible along the eastern horizon, and night is preparing to retreat as their advance guards start to probe the heavens. But the sun-god in his chariot has more than half an hour's journey yet to accomplish before he arrives; so for a while longer the earth stays silent and still, wrapped in slumber. Not a bird or a beast stirs. The owls have just gone to bed, and other tribes of feathered creatures are not yet risen.

Gradually light increases. At about 6.45 the first birds appear—a few Common Pariah Kites winging noiselessly overhead. Then some House Crows break the silence with harsh caws. Soon afterwards a Green Barbet leaps from a hole in a tree which is its bedroom, perches on a near-by bough and greets the dawn with a subdued yodel. At that, the head of a Green Parakeet pokes through the entrance of its similar sleeping quarters; but it stays indoors for another ten minutes before flying away. In the meantime half a dozen little Crimsonbreasted Barbets, who likewise roost in tunnels chiselled in tree trunks, have peered from their cubicles, hopped out and gathered in a sociable party in a tree-top.

By seven o'clock brief utterances from other species announce that they too are stirring. A staccato call from a Tree Pie, short snatches of a White-eye's whispered soliloquy, tentative chirpings from House Sparrows, and a harsh phrase from a Magpie Robin—which has not yet acquired its beautiful voice of later in the year—issue from the shrubberies. Then a company of noisy Jungle Babblers alight on the lawn to forage for their breakfasts.

Flocks of Blue Rock Pigeons start travelling across the sky towards feeding grounds outside the city, and countless air squadrons of Green Parakeets follow them, shrieking as they go. Night has now almost vanished; the conquering armies of daylight have spread far across the heavens; and the earth is soon fully awake. By the time the sun appears bulbuls and mynahs, wagtails and robins, doves and warblers and other characters are on view to greet it.

In January their greeting is not vociferous. They talk rather than sing, and after a few initial exclamations are more often silent than talkative.

II

The ruins of some of last year's nests linger in the garden. This

January a Little Brown Doves' small stick-platform still lay across the stems of a bougainvillaea outside my study. It had supported two eggs as long ago as the previous June. On the day when the twin chicks hatched they were kidnapped by some piratical animal, and their parents promptly deserted the nest; yet now, more than six months later, its structure remained scarcely disarranged in spite of the prolonged monsoon rains and other elemental chastisements which had intervened. It was notable evidence of the skill with which Little Brown Doves build their homes—contrary to popular belief and even to some professional judgments. A few ornithologists have written sarcastically of the allegedly skimpy way in which doves construct nests, poking fun at their careless throwing together of a few sticks, and comparing the finished work to a loose heap of spillikins or accidentally dropped matches.

If my pair of doves had really been as incompetent builders as that, their cradle would never have sustained two eggs plus a sitting bird for the fortnight during which they occupied it, let alone survived all the harsh climatic tests of the next seven months. The fact is that Little Brown Doves, and other doves, are clever architects. Whatever may be the superficial appearance of their slight creation, it is a careful, painstaking effort which keeps both birds of a pair busy for hours each day through several days. Moreover, to suggest that the nest consists of only a few sticks is nonsense. I have examined several Little Brown Doves' nests after their owners left them, and found that they each contained anything between eighty and 140 sticks. The materials were fine, crisp rootlets and twigs twisted and woven criss-cross into a firm yet flexible pad. Those specimens too could long have withstood the severities of Nature.

All birds are of course competent at building their various styles of nest. Other bits of evidence of their skill in my garden this January were a White-eyes' nest which had harboured chicks in the previous July, a Golden Orioles' nest from which fledglings had flown in August, a Large Grey Babblers' nest which held eggs in September, and several additional relics still more or less intact. The most recent was a Whitethroated Munias' nest from which a young family had departed as lately as Christmas Eve. Built in a thick creeper covering a wall of the house, it was the only egg-holding, chick-producing nest in December.

Many pairs of birds perform strange antics in the emotional excitement of sexual display to each other before mating, but no such acrobatics are more amusing than those of affianced Whitethroated Munias. A hen bird flies gaily across the lawn with a cock bird in hot pursuit, and she settles on a bare branch of a tree. He alights beside her, gazes at her inquiringly, and then jumps rapidly up and down on his perch half a dozen times, rising an inch in the air on each occasion as if he were skipping with an imaginary skipping-rope. While he is thus engaged she crouches and flicks her tail round and round with a circular movement so rapid that its feathers become nearly invisible and seem in danger of falling out. At his next leap the male shifts sideways in mid air and lands on her back. She promptly ceases to twiddle her tail, and their coupling takes place with mutual satisfaction.

III

In January there are not only ruins of last year's nests, but also preliminary constructions of some of the New Year's nests-to-be. As already mentioned, Green Parakeets, Green Barbets and Crimsonbreasted Barbets can be seen at dawn peering from their bedrooms in holes in trees. These retreats are in fact tunnels which they have chiselled during the previous months to use later as nesting places.

Green Barbets and Crimsonbreasted Barbets excavate their tunnels by their own unaided efforts. As early as September they begin to tap and chip at likely areas on tree trunks, and when a bird decides that a particular spot is suitable, it gets to work in earnest. Crouching on the trunk like a woodpecker, it batters and gouges at the wood with its beak so powerfully that gradually a hole is driven into the timber. The labour continues for several weeks, and at its end a shaft about a foot long has been punctured into the tree.

The toil of Green Parakeets making their nests is lighter,

for those beautiful, aristocratic-looking creatures do not usually demean themselves by excavating their own residences. They either select a ready-made natural hole, or else exploit the hard labour of others. Often a parakeet chooses a tunnel built and occupied earlier as a nest by a barbet, and then by a little mild additional chiselling adapts this to its own purpose.

For long periods between one breeding season and the next these holes are used by their owners as bedrooms where they sleep every night. Each accommodates one bird. This January I knew of two Green Parakeets, two Green Barbets and eight Crimsonbreasted Barbets who snoozed snugly in their respective tree-tunnels in the garden. Each evening at twilight I watched them go in turn into their sleeping apartments, the parakeets being the first to retire, followed about a quarter of an hour later by the Crimsonbreasted Barbets, while the Green Barbets stayed up for another twenty minutes after that. In the mornings the order was reversed, the Green Barbets being the earliest risers. Some time after they jumped out of bed I could count on seeing all the eight Crimsonbreasted Barbets pop their heads through their eight separate doorways to survey the prospect for a few moments before flying away; and then I could stroll to the Green Parakeets' quarters and observe their more leisurely departures.

It was a charming beginning to each day.

IV

Other birds who already occupied their nest-to-be in January were a pair of Spotted Owlets. The site of their home was a ventilation shaft in a wall of the house where they lived throughout the twelve months, year after year. Much of each day they spent asleep indoors. With the aid of field-glasses I could spy them peacefully slumbering there. At dusk they would sally forth and pass the nights hunting beetles, crickets, lizards and other small prey from various trees scattered strategically through the garden. Often in the dark I heard them squealing, squeaking and chattering as they enjoyed their sport.

Before sunrise they returned homewards, and in winter they often spent the first few cool hours of daylight snoozing in high branches of an Australian silver oak growing close beside their retreat in the wall. Most mornings I saw them there, for the ventilation shaft happened to be situated just above my bathroom, and the oak tree stood immediately outside the bathroom window. As a result I got on to very familiar terms with those Spotted Owlets—far more intimate than my relations with most of my fellow human beings. When I ran my bath-water the birds on their perches outside the window would open their eyes and watch inquisitively my every movement as I lay soaking in my bath, sat up to lather and scrub my body, and stepped from the tub to dry myself. In return the owlets freely revealed to me all the secrets of their toilets. It was a charmingly uninhibited, neighbourly association.

Spotted Owlets are pretty creatures. Standing only eight inches high, their round heads are covered with soft feathers. Their faces with large, golden-yellow eyes are kittenlike, and the streaked light-and-dark brown plumage on their plump bodies sustain the analogy by markings like those of a tabby-cat. But the wide circles of feathering round their eyes, their sharply hooked beaks and their sage demeanour are unmistakably owlish. When unexpectedly disturbed, they behave in an odd manner, shrieking rudely at the intruder, bobbing up and down on their perches, and glowering threateningly at him in an apparent attempt to frighten him away.

After the first few weeks of our acquaintance they became used to me, and rarely treated me to these demonstrations of disapproval. Nevertheless, whenever I bobbed my head up and down at them they at once returned the compliment by bobbing theirs up and down at me. But they no longer accompanied this action with vocal protests. The gestures seemed to be just a friendly exchange of diplomatic courtesies.

Sometimes the pair would squat outside the window staring at me from separate branches in their tree; but at other times they sat closely side by side, wing to wing, looking extraordinarily like Tweedledum and Tweedledee.

V

There were no nests in active use for reproduction in the garden in January; but elsewhere in and around Delhi certain species were busy laying eggs and hatching chicks. The larger scavenger birds incline to beget their families in winter, though some individuals are still engaged on that happy task well into the summer. Among them are several types of vulture. Occasionally one built its large, untidy nursery in a private pleasance; but unfortunately none ever so favoured me.

However, the birds often soared in the sky above my lawn, and were a magnificent sight. Sometimes as many as fifty Whitebacked Vultures and Neophrons (or Egyptian Vultures) wheeled there, with two or three King Vultures. Once I saw the largest of all the Indian members of the clan, the Griffon Vulture. However ungainly, unseemly and even disgusting vultures may appear on the ground as they squabble over a repast, in flight they have awe-inspiring beauty. Their wing-span is enormous; their movements are easy and graceful; they glide slowly and deliberately in wide circles as they soar; and when dozens of these monsters so manoeuvre together it is a majestic spectacle.

When they cease wheeling at leisure and move off in a set direction, their progress is often slow and sedate, as if they were a procession of official mourners at a State funeral. Nothing could be more appropriate, for probably they are in fact going to a funeral. Indeed, they are almost always attending funerals; vultures must be the most indefatigable funeral-goers in the world. It is therefore apt that most of them are clad in solemn, sepulchral black, like ever-ready undertakers.

It would be no exaggeration to say that they adore a good funeral—or even a bad funeral for that matter. Whether the last rites are about to be performed over the dead body of a dog, a donkey, a buffalo, a camel, or some other mortal being, they are always agreeable to joining in the ceremony. As soon as news spreads that one of these sad events is about to occur—and it is astonishing how swiftly the intelligence communicates itself among the numerous vultures scattered far and wide in the skies—they gather from the four quarters of heaven to pay their respects to the dearly-beloved departed. First a few early birds arrive and stand mournfully round the corpse. Probably they had not far to come, and indeed were loitering near the death-bed for the last hour or two, watching solicitously and speculating expertly on the chances of the invalid's living or dying. Soon many of their brethren fly in from all directions, planing silently earthwards with gigantic wings full-spread and scrawny necks and bald heads craned eagerly to catch a first glimpse of the deceased. Every few seconds a new-comer lands, folds its wings like the sails of a galleon being furled as the ship comes safely into port, and strides towards the body with fond affection gleaming in its eyes. Before many minutes have passed three or four score vultures may have assembled for the obsequies.

As each approaches the body, it reaches forward and nudges the remains with the tip of its beak, as if this were some symbolic, hallowed gesture of respect. Then it withdraws its head, only to stretch it out again a few moments later to nuzzle the corpse once more, poking the carcass this time more inquisitively and perhaps with a touch of unnecessary force. Could it be making sure that life has really departed, and that it is proper for the burial service to begin?

Several of the vultures thus examine the body, and as the crowd of mourners swells a rivalry seems to develop between them to be the most zealous in giving solicitous jabs at various parts of its anatomy. In their anxiety to outvie each other in expressing fondness for the late lamented sheep, horse, cow, or whatnot, the birds begin to quarrel. First one couple and then another, and then several more, snap at each other quick-temperedly, flapping their wings like pugilists exercising their fists, and opening their mouths and calling each other squalid names. The rude noises which they emit are the only hymns sung at that interment, and they compose an execrable dirge.

Soon the excitement spreads, several birds turning their energies against the corpse itself, snapping and biting and tearing at its flesh as if they were grief-stricken souls so distracted by sorrow that they had taken temporary leave of their senses and, in their agony, dishonoured the dead whom they had come to honour. The insane aberration spreads like some infectious madness, and soon all the vultures are climbing over the body, squabbling with each other, and at the same time stabbing, tearing, tugging and ripping at its limbs and entrails in a manner very sad to see. An uninitiated spectator might suppose that the bereaved had been so devoted to the comatose animal that they now wished to detach bits and pieces of it as keepsakes—souvenirs of a highly valued friendship.

Of course he would be mistaken. The mourners' grief is an illusion. Vultures feel overjoyed in the presence of death. For them death means life. The corpse is their dearly-beloved departed in a manner never imagined by the coiners of that sentimental phrase. To them it is desirable meat and intoxicating drink.

I shall not describe further the undisciplined scenes which ensue as the vultures' chaotic ceremonial progresses. The funeral becomes a banquet, and the banquet becomes an orgy. At the end of it the corpse is well and truly buried—inside them.

By these drastic means Nature in some countries provides for the hygienic disposal of diseased and dangerous carrion.

VI

Common Pariah Kites are other useful and plentiful scavengers in Delhi, and they too are already nesting in January. Perhaps because by the end of the month they have ravenous chicks to nourish, they become bold in their search for food. If you leave a plate of buns unprotected for a few minutes on a tea-table in a garden, its contents will all have disappeared by the time you return. Kites have stolen them. Nor are these thieves deterred by the presence of people at the table, for they will hover overhead throughout the meal and swoop down to snatch up a sandwich or a scone from under the eater's very nose, unless defensive measures—like a tactically placed servant armed with a broomstick to beat off their assaults—are taken to deter them.

January

They are superb marksmen. One afternoon I sat alone on my lawn sipping tea and munching delicious cake. As I held a slice between a finger and thumb, and was about to pop it into my mouth, my attention was distracted by two mongooses playing hide-and-seek in a near-by flower-bed. Turning in their direction, I momentarily left my hand upheld in mid air, clasping the cake. Suddenly I felt the food gently extricate itself from my grasp, and a fraction of a moment later my hand was empty. I could no longer feel the cake between my finger and thumb. Then I saw it about twenty yards away, flying rapidly from me in the claws of a retreating kite! Every now and then the bird hesitated in its flight, bent its head, ripped a morsel of cake away in its beak and swallowed it—evidently relishing it as much as I had intended to do. The robber had swooped down from on high, glided above my fist and, as it passed, neatly picked the delicacy from my grip without so much as brushing my thumb or finger or any other part of my hand. It was an impressive demonstration of a kite's sureness of vision, accuracy of aim, precision of movement and delicacy of touch.

Since then other kites have several times repeated that performance, and once a crowd of them gave a demonstration of their skill en masse. When His Royal Highness the Prince Philip, Duke of Edinburgh, visited Delhi last January he honoured me by attending a garden party at my house. Many hundreds of guests were present on a sunlit lawn, and there were also about fifty gate-crashers. None of the gate-crashers was a vulgar human being on the ground; they were all Common Pariah Kites in the air. Nor were they interested in staring at royalty; their entire attention was concentrated on the refreshments. Ceaselessly they glided and swerved overhead, flying low and keeping a keen, hopeful eye on guests with tomato sandwiches or currant buns held carelessly in their hands. And as soon as anyone let slip a titbit of food, a kite swooped down to the grass to grab it, followed at once by others if the first bird got diverted by some movement in the crowd which made it miss its aim.

VII

More than sixty species of birds were visitors in or over my garden this January. Among those who alighted and fed in it regularly were many all-the-year-round residents of Delhi. They included, of course, the ubiquitous House Sparrow; and other every-day callers were Tailor Birds, Purple Sunbirds, White-eyes, Ashy Wren-Warblers, Indian Robins, Redvented Bulbuls, Redwhiskered Bulbuls, Magpie Robins, Jungle Babblers, Large Grey Babblers, Common Mynahs, Brahminy Mynahs, Hoopoes, Crimsonbreasted Barbets, Green Barbets, Little Brown Doves, Ring Doves, Blue Rock Pigeons, Green Parakeets, House Crows, Spotted Owlets and Common Pariah Kites.

In addition a quartet of winter tourists, who summer elsewhere, appeared daily: White Wagtails, Black Redstarts, Lesser Whitethroats and Hume's Leaf Warblers.

Permanent residents in Delhi whose visits to the garden were less frequent included Whitethroated Munias, Small Minivets, Indian Wren-warblers, Green Bee-eaters, Common Wood Shrikes, Yelloweyed Babblers, Koels, Goldenbacked Woodpeckers, Green Pigeons, Tree Pies, Crow Pheasants, Shikras, Redheaded Merlins, Grey Hornbills and Blossomheaded Parakeets. The last-named engaging creatures are described in Delhi's official bird-list as being perhaps only birds of passage; but whatever the truth may have been in earlier years they are now definitely residents, for considerable parties appear in my garden throughout the twelve months. Almost every morning this January a flock of them breakfasted off fruit in the same peepul tree.

Winter visitors who occasionally came to the garden in January were Pied Wagtails and Shortbilled Minivets.

All these forty-four species came down to earth to feed on my lawns, flower-beds, shrubberies or trees. Other species passed overhead. Among them were regular residents of Delhi like Indian Swifts, Redrumped Swallows, Paddy Birds, Little Egrets, Lesser Egrets, Cattle Egrets, Large Egrets, Grey Herons, Neophrons, White-backed Vultures, King Vultures, and Tawny Eagles.

January

In January, too, other attractive species lived in the neighbourhood, and they often flew over my garden. Many times I watched wild duck race across the sky at dawn; but they were usually travelling too swiftly or too distantly for me to be certain of their particular identities. However, I did recognize Shovellers, Pintails, and Common Teal. About fifteen different types of duck are officially recorded as spending the winter on the jheels surrounding Delhi.

Wild geese are a daily sight and sound in January. Two or three times I have spotted Barheaded Geese; but Greylag Geese are much more common. Every evening after dark I heard them calling to each other as they journeyed to their nocturnal feeding grounds, and on moonlit nights their shadowy silhouettes were apparent flying quite low above the house. In the mornings they returned at a greater height. Sometimes soon after sunrise skein after skein of them appeared—hundreds upon hundreds of geese travelling in long, wavering columns or in beautifully symmetrical, wedge-shaped, arrow-headed formations spanning vast areas of the sky. From aloft the exciting music of their trumpeting descended—a truly thrilling sound. There is no more beautiful, exhilarating spectacle in all nature than a multitudinous fly-past of wild geese.

THREE

FEBRUARY

I

Some of Delhi's small winter visitors are strikingly good-looking. The White Wagtail, for example, has daintiness of form, dress and movement. Measuring eight inches long, its figure is as trim as a miniature model of a perfectly streamlined aircraft. The well-poised head, slim body and elongated tail are very elegant, and they are given vivid grace as the bird runs across a lawn, halts for a few moments to glance around and teeter its tail swiftly up and down, and then sprints forward again in search of food. The cock's plumage is a pattern of black, grey and white, and although the hen's appearance is less glamorous—for in bird society the male sex is usually the fair sex—she too is distinctly pretty.

Another handsome creature is the Black Redstart. The cock's head, back and wings are pitch black, his abdomen and rump are orange-chestnut, and the central feathers of his otherwise black tail are brown. The female is mostly brown, with touches of orange and chestnut. Both are roughly the size of an English Robin. They frequent my lawn daily from September until March, but sometimes incline to shyness. At the approach of a monster like a human being they will glance up from their feeding, eye the intruder suspiciously, flicker their tails with a suggestion of nervousness (though the movement is in fact habitual with them) and then skip into the air and flutter a distance away.

Yet another beautiful cold-weather visitor is the Shortbilled Minivet. A wholly arboreal species, it travels through the tree-tops and never descends even to the tallest undergrowth; but its distinctive colouring makes it easily recognizable. The male's upper plumage from his forehead to his throat and middle back is glossy black, the rest of his body is bright scarlet, and his wings and tail are partly black and partly scarlet. The female is greenish-yellow, grey or brown in most places where her lord is black, and yellow in most places where he is scarlet. Incidentally, their cousins, the Small Minivets, are permanent residents in Delhi. Similar to their relations in habits, they are slightly smaller (measuring six instead of seven inches long) and somewhat less bizarre in decoration. Nevertheless, the cock is attractively dressed in black, brown, grey, and flame colour.

This trio of visitors are attractive recruits throughout the winter to Delhi's pleasing company of birds.

II

From early February onwards the sunlight grows gradually warmer, which has its effect on certain species of birds. Spring is in the air, and they respond to its suggestive caress. Indeed, some of them begin to feel like imparting caresses themselves.

Their mood is revealed in both sights and sounds. By February several of them have donned their courtship dresses. The finest of these is perhaps that of the cock Purple Sunbird. Two months earlier he might have been mistaken at a superficial glance for the more modestly-clad hen, since his plumage then was a composition mostly in greenish-brown and yellow; but progressively through December and January dark feathers replace the lighter-coloured ones, and for some weeks his coat is an untidy patchwork of black, green, and yellow. The dark patches spread ever wider and the light patches contract ever smaller until the former entirely displace the latter, and the little four-inch-long bird becomes wholly black except for yellow tufts beneath each wing. Some male sunbirds attain this uniform in January, but the transformation is not complete in all of them until early February.

Their appearance is made especially beautiful by the shining glossiness of their feathers, which shimmer in the sunlight like polished metal. This glitter has the effect of making the birds look purple in certain lights, and their sable brightness is enhanced by the fact that their fine, black, down-curving beaks and dark legs also have a sheen, as if these were wrought of some steely substance. Indeed, the cock sunbirds look as if they were clad from head to foot in armour, and as I watch them flitting through the shrubberies I think of them as small Black Princes. However, the purpose of their brilliant adornment is not war, but love. They are preparing to enchant the ladies of the court, whose plumage remains unostentatiously greeny-brown and yellow.

Other species also begin to exhibit spring fashions. The black, white and chestnut plumage of male Indian Robins, the golden-green mantles of cock Tailor Birds, the white-speckled, verdant capes of Green Barbets, and various courtship costumes of other characters, assume their most fetching hues. At the same time the cockades on the heads of Redwhiskered Bulbuls, the long tail-feathers of Ashy Wren-Warblers, the cockatoo-style crests of Indian Hoopoes, and similarly bold conceits on other dandies, grow to their most seductive dimensions.

Those fresh sights are accompanied by appropriate sounds. Phrases of love begin to echo through the garden. The comparative silence of January is a thing of the past. In the early mornings numerous birds now rehearse snatches of their diverse musical repertoires, like varied instruments in an orchestra tuning up before the performance of a symphony. As February advances the monotonous calls of Crimson breasted Barbets cease to be brief and subdued, and become repetitive and strong; the triple hoot of Hoopoes—which sounds almost exactly like their Latin name, 'Upupa'—is frequently heard; the staccato utterance of Tailor Birds issues with ever clearer confidence from the shrubberies; and the voices of other birds swell a growing chorus. Loudest and most insistent is the yodelling of Green Barbets.

The volume of their choir seems to depend largely on the temperature. If the thermometer suddenly rises a few degrees, there is an equally quick increase in the quantity of singers; and an abrupt drop in the temperature causes a diminution of sound. By the end of the month the temperature is usually well set in the eighties, and the dawn chorus of birdsong is almost as clamorous as its famous counterpart in the English spring. The tuneful yelling of Green Barbets becomes almost ceaseless; Common Mynahs and Brahminy Mynahs often make their less melodious shindy; Purple Sunbirds carol with surprising power for creatures so small; Ashy Wren-Warblers periodically shout their challenging song; Ring Doves murmur repeatedly soft, sentimental serenades; and the gay courtship whistlings of numerous other types contribute their merry discords to the concert.

Nor is it all just talk. Some species soon follow their words with deeds. Before the month is many days old it is not uncommon to see a cock Tailor Bird chasing a hen in and out and round about the flower-beds, passionately desirous of embracing her. Male Little Brown Doves begin to display their charms to the females, each assuming a stance in front of an enchantress and bowing with gallant, old-world courtliness as he coos an invitation to romance. As he does, so he puffs out his throat to exhibit to advantage the patches of black-and-white chequer-board plumage on either side of his neck.

Male Ring Doves, too, become amorous. They are true philanderers, and often their ardour seems more potently developed than that of the members of the opposite sex. Many times in February I watched a cock dove, with rakishly fluffed-out feathers, accost a reluctant hen on the lawn, strut naughtily beside her as she sought modestly to retreat, and pester her with solicitous bows and whispered pleadings which might be interpreted (I suppose) in human speech by the words: 'Dearie, don't you remember me?'

Indian Robins are other birds who start nesting early in the year and therefore begin to engage in flirtations in the first few days of February. Their courtship looks rather ridiculous. Let me describe the spectacle as I first witnessed it.

A hen robin was feeding placidly on the lawn while in front of her a cock indulged in sexual display, making an extraordinary exhibition of himself. His tail stood stiffly erect on his rump, and his neck and head were also craned upwards to their full length and tilted backwards until his crown almost touched the tail. His beak pointed straight towards the sky, his eyes stared glassily into space, and his chest was puffed out like a tiny balloon about to burst. In this uncomfortable posture the bird strutted slowly and deliberately, step by step—backwards! He continued this performance for some time, maintaining an accurately straight line of withdrawal like a pompous court flunkey marching hindwards before royalty.

The hen bird was not impressed and coolly pursued her search for food. Glancing out of the corner of an eye at her, the infatuated wooer noticed this indifference, and promptly relaxed. Running towards her, he began a fresh series of antics. Once more he threw his head upwards, stretching his neck and gazing heavenwards, and at the same time he fluttered his wings, half spreading them and then quickly closing them again, and shivering them a trifle and drooping them whenever they tentatively opened. Simultaneously his tail was alternately tilted in the air and depressed towards the ground, and in both positions it waggled continuously from side to side. No acrobatic clown in a circus ever contrived more absurd contortions. Whenever the female happened to stroll near him, the male's excitement increased. He spread his tail fanwise, lowered it until it touched the grass, and walked a few paces so that it dragged behind him like a train. All the time he uttered small twittering cries.

Even these extravagant expressions of devotion had little effect on the hen. Mostly she hopped around on the lawn, helping herself to titbits of food; but two or three times she did make a mild response, quivering her wings momentarily and elevating her tail coquettishly in the air. That was all; and the reaction lasted only a few seconds. Then she resumed her normal poise and continued her hunt for grubs.

Optimistically the male persevered with his display for ten minutes, but at the end of that time he still had received no further encouragement.

Afterwards the hen flew into a tree. He abruptly ceased his gesticulations, as if their stimulus had been automatically switched

February

off. Hesitating for a while, he then followed her into the arbour and once more assumed a suitor's odd pose on a bough beside her. But she had entirely lost interest, ignored him, and soon sped a distance away.

The frustrated cock relaxed again.

III

Ashy Wren-Warblers are among the most charming birds in the garden, both in appearance and character. A few reside on the property all the year round, and this January I often caught sight of one or another of them fluttering from plant to plant in the flower-beds searching for palatable insects. Each bird was always solitary, unsociable, unaffianced. They never travelled in pairs like the Yelloweyed Babblers, or in small parties like the White-eyes.

This situation continued until mid February. Every Ashy Wren-Warbler kept itself to itself, living and hunting like a lone wolf. The days were cool, and springtime instincts apparently remained dormant in their neat, attractive little bodies.

Then a sudden revolution occurred. On February 12th—which happens to be the official date for the opening of the Indian spring—the atmosphere warmed up and the temperature rose several degrees. The change produced a distinctly flirtatious effect on some species of birds, including the Ashy Wren-Warblers. Indeed, I saw that day what was perhaps the first introduction of a certain cock and hen to each other.

Hitherto these wren-warblers had remained not only solitary but also mostly silent. Occasionally one emitted the succession of nervous, subdued, almost whispered notes which they utter when disturbed by the presence of a strange creature or an untoward event; but that was all. Probably a mongoose, a jackal or some other inquisitive beast was lurking near. For many months I had not heard the wren-warblers' louder calls. Imagine my pleasure, therefore, when I recognized three or four ringing notes, several times repeated, issuing from the top of a small plum tree in the unmistakable voice of a male Ashy Wren-Warbler. I saw the bird perched there, opening its beak wide and singing lustily in tones which sounded like a glad challenge. Sure enough, a few moments later a second wren-warbler appeared and alighted on a stalk in a flower-bed close by. It was a shorter-tailed female. At once the cock leaped into the air and fluttered to and fro, rising, falling and sideslipping gaily as an inebriated butterfly might do, and making every now and then a noise like clapping with its wings (or some other mechanism in its anatomy) which is characteristic of the species' courtship flight. The bird had fallen in love at first sight!

It soon landed near its partner-to-be in the flower-bed, and the two birds chattered and twittered together for a while excitedly and joyfully. At intervals the male rose into the air to show off its aerobatics and to clap its wings once more; and after each sortie he perched again beside the female. But the episode seemed to be only a mild flirtation—an introduction, not a seduction—for after a while their emotions subsided, and they recommenced feeding more or less separately in a casual, matter-of-fact sort of way. Yet from that moment onwards they were in fact to become inseparable companions for several months.

Three or four times in the next half-hour I saw them meet for snatches of further pleasurable conversation, and always sooner or later in its course the cock made a jaunty, wing-clapping expedition into the air above the hen, obviously in a much better mood than he had shown on any earlier morning that year. More than once he alighted on a high twig in the plum tree and gave vent to his feelings in a happy burst of song.

Later that day I heard it several times again—a sweet, enthusiastic proclamation that spring had arrived in Delhi.

IV

Spring was accompanied by other portents of a fresh temper among the birds than these signs of attraction between the sexes. Some of them were less genial. Competition for territory on which to occupy nests, and for the favour of females with whom to share those nests, began to embitter relations between many

February

males. Nor was the consequential quarrelling confined to rival cocks. Sometimes, I think, competing hens also came to blows, and occasionally males and females who perhaps inadvertently trespassed on each other's private property had a sharp tiff. It was not always easy to distinguish the precise nature of the fights, for in some species the two sexes look alike.

I saw a remarkable example of such a conflict between two Green Barbets. Several of these noisy birds were calling vociferously at the time. In February their ejaculations were the most persistent sounds in the garden, the air echoing and re-echoing with their declarations of infatuation.

That morning I noticed four barbets in close neighbourhood in tree-tops above a shrubbery. Suddenly a fifth appeared with two berries stuffed enticingly in its beak, and alighted near one of the quartet who was yodelling fervently. Hop by hop it advanced to the singer, intending (I supposed) to offer the fruit as a token of affectionate, mutually acknowledged partnership. There seemed no doubt that it was a swain wooing his betrothed. The other bird's first action seemed to support this theory, for it stopped calling and leaped to meet the new-comer halfway. Then the affair took an unexpected turn. This bird jabbed its beak at the other's beak, seized hold of a berry and tried to wrench it away. But the first barbet was suddenly unwilling to surrender the fruit, and clung to it obstinately. At that the second bird shook its head vigorously several times from side to side, lugging at the berry in an attempt to capture it—so much so that an extra-determined shake upset the first bird's balance and caused it to fall headlong from its perch. Yet it still clung so firmly to the berry that it hung suspended in mid air, linked to its companion by their mutual grip on the food. Their contest continued, and soon the second bird also overbalanced, with the result that both barbets plunged together towards the ground. As they descended one hit a lower branch in the tree, clutched it with its claws and managed to re-establish a foothold. Yet both birds still retained their grasp on the fruit, and so they remained locked together, one now hanging upside-down from a bough and the other attached precariously beneath it. Their obstinate struggle still persisted, the two combatants shaking their heads and wriggling their bodies violently until the half-perched barbet once more lost its hold on a bough, and both then tumbled into the undergrowth below. There they lay for several minutes sparring like wrestlers. Their fight seemed very vicious. Each kept stabbing its beak at the other, and their bills never loosened their grip on each other (or was it still on a berry?) while their feet clawed and scratched in mutual aggression and their bodies rolled over and over, this way and that, on the ground. Their eyes flashed fiercely; they flapped their wings and occasionally spread their tails in attempts to gain a position of mastery; and neither seemed prepared to yield.

I thought this might all be a spasm of passionate, frenzied love-play, just as I had supposed originally that the berry was an offering brought by a suitor to his favourite. But the episode never reached the climax of mating. On the contrary, after some time one bird broke loose from its opponent and escaped to a near-by bough; the other promptly pursued it and grabbed it once more by the beak; and again they fell struggling to the ground. Three times in as many minutes that happened. There could be no mistaking the duellists' anger and enmity—but I did not fathom the cause. Could it result from a misunderstanding—a cock bird having offered its bribe of fruit to the wrong hen by mistake, and realized its error too late? Or were the combatants just rival males? I did not see what happened to the berry, the original apple of discord—whether one or the other bird swallowed it, or whether it got torn to pieces in the melee, or whether it was quietly dropped in the heat of conflict. In the end the contest remained undecided, the barbets seeming to part by mutual consent. Each flew into a separate shrub and instantly started yodelling defiantly.

Often I saw similar contests between two Crimsonbreasted Barbets, except that in their cases no fruit was involved. The pair would meet in a tree, and immediately one would flutter its wings and at the same time jab its beak viciously at the other. The second would stab back. For a while they thus fenced without either scoring a hit—until suddenly one gripped the other's bill in its own. The couple would then sway their joined heads in apparent attempts to upset each other, like two competitors in water sports trying to tip each other off a greasy pole; and in due course one would succeed in tumbling its rival from their perch. Completely undeterred, the capsized barbet would maintain its hold on its opponent as it hung in mid air. Eventually the upper bird would also be dislodged, and both then fell to the ground, where they lay side by side scuffling violently.

Probably these were skirmishes between rival males or rival females trying to establish rights to nesting territory; or again, the conflicts may sometimes have resulted from mistaken identity. A cock may at first glance have taken another for a hen, and come with intent to make love—only to stay, when it learned its error, to make war. Whatever the explanation, these little battles were not infrequent, and they had their counterparts in the lives of other species. Often in February I saw two male Indian Robins, two Tailor Birds or two other types bickering. As among the human species, love among birds has its unpleasant and even tragic side.

V

The first birds in the garden to press their suit to the point of mating were (so far as I could observe) a pair of Green Parakeets. I had already kept an eye on this particular couple for several months. Ever since the previous August they had maintained a close and faithful but platonic friendship beside a potential nest-hole in a jacaranda tree. On February 1st their companionship became more intimate.

I noticed them perched side by side on their favourite branch. The cock was standing placidly, but the hen's attitude seemed less passive. She crouched low across the bough with her feathers fluffed out and her head held upwards and backwards in the poise of a flirtatious young lady tilting her face to be kissed. There was something extraordinarily suggestive about her demeanour.

Her technique was successful. After a few moments the male

parakeet sidled up to her, lifted a foot towards her with a coy gesture and then bent his head, touched the back of her neck with his beak and nibbled affectionately at the soft plumage there. She closed her eyes dreamily and turned her face sideways in an invitation to him to extend the area of these operations. He readily obliged, nuzzling first one side of her neck and then the other. After an interval in which he looked cautiously around as if to make sure that no stranger was watching, he tickled the top of her head with the tip of his bill. She seemed well pleased, and indeed enticed him by little co-operative shifts of her body. So his next movement was bolder. Raising one leg, he stretched it across her back and placed his foot on her further wing, with the gesture of a man putting an arm round the waist of his beloved; and again he gently scratched the crown of her head. Then he hesitated, removed his foot from her back and withdrew a pace away. He seemed suddenly diffident, as if lacking confidence in the propriety of his conduct. At that the hen stood upright for a moment, but soon squatted again in further solicitation of him. He stepped to her side once more, stroked her cheeks tenderly with his bill, and stretched a foot again across her body. He clasped her so for a while, fondling her neck with his beak, and then slowly and deliberately he placed his second foot on her nearer shoulder and climbed on her back. She crouched lower to give him firm support.

At first he merely stood there scratching and nibbling at various parts of her head. Presumably this was an instinctive preliminary to the fuller arousing of his physical desire. The wings of both birds were now stretched slightly away from their sides, with a sensuous kind of air. Gradually his nuzzling became more eager, and his scratches turned to pecks, and then he started a series of frenzied, passionate thrusts with his beak at the nape of her neck as he lowered his hindquarters until they rested on hers. For a while his vent settled there, but then it descended further, twisting round the side of her body and seeking to make intimate contact with her. It seemed a difficult contortion, for the birds' two tails were apt to get in the way, and he kept shifting his position, trying to achieve his purpose first on one flank of her posterior and then on the other, so that his long, fine tail-feathers kept flicking from side to side in a somewhat impotent manner. The stabs of his beak on her neck now became quite violent. But she did not mind. Those thrusts of his head moved in unison with the equally vigorous jerks of his rear as he sought to make union with her. They were probably necessary to enable him to keep his balance in his precarious stance on her back.

The action continued for more than half a minute. Then she turned her head and pecked at his beak—a signal, apparently, that he should desist, for he opened his wings, fluttered awkwardly off her back and perched on the bough beside her. She stood up and stretched herself; he drew away from her; and they both folded their wings and shook their feathers into place—like two lovers putting on their clothes after a stolen embrace. Then he flew from the tree, and a little later she departed in the opposite direction. He promptly reappeared and chased her; but she sped to their nest-hole-to-be, alighted at its entrance and disappeared indoors. He took up the position of a sentinel outside.

I watched with deep interest these auspicious goings-on. The nesting season in my garden had begun in earnest, ushered in with appropriate ceremony by the Green Parakeets.

Although the ceremonial was impressive, I do not think it was successful—but that is a matter which I shall discuss when I write in a later chapter the love story of those two parakeets.

VI

A pair of Green Barbets were interested in another nest-hole in the same jacaranda tree where the parakeets proposed to produce a family. It was one of the tunnels into which I had watched a barbet—presumably the hen of this pair—disappear to roost every evening throughout the winter. No doubt the couple also contemplated rearing youngsters; but I think this was still only a vague, intuitive notion at the end of February, for I saw no sign of the birds flirting until early March, and they did not start carrying food to chicks in their nest until a month after that.

Nevertheless, in February their instinct about events to come was so compelling that they developed a strong sense of property rights in the neighbourhood, and would not let any strange creatures venture near their prospective nest. Frequently they shooed the Green Parakeets as well as other birds away from the vicinity. Indeed, they seemed never to become reconciled to the fact that the parakeets were legitimate, law-abiding fellow residents in the same tree. The parakeets did not retaliate, always giving way gracefully, though temporarily, when one of their short-tempered neighbours gave forceful expression to its resentment at their presence. The barbets seemed to have more offensive natures than the genteel parakeets.

Several Crimsonbreasted Barbets likewise became self-conscious property owners in the garden as February advanced. Each hen having tunnelled her nest some months earlier, only the final touches were still required to make its internal accommodation suitable for the reception of eggs. The quarrelsome rivalries concerning the selection of particular females by particular males—or of the males by the females—gradually sorted themselves out; and before the end of the month several pairs appeared to have made compacts to become partners. And they were determined to protect their nest-holes against all comers. On February 27th I watched one of these little barbets boldly and persistently dive-bombing a party of four Green Parakeets who had gathered nearer its nest-hole than it liked. Every one of its adversaries was three times its size.

Yet I saw no evidence of any pair of Crimsonbreasted Barbets actually mating until the beginning of March.

Common Mynahs were the only other characters whom I noticed positively preparing nests in the garden in February. More than once I saw these mynahs carrying building material into large cavities in tree trunks such as they sometimes favour as nurseries for their young. Whether any of them laid eggs before the month's end I do not know. As in the case of the parakeets and barbets, their homes were deep, dark, hidden galleries, and without tearing away a strip of wood—and so causing the birds to desert—I could not learn the exact state of their domestic affairs. But I doubt whether any of them produced eggs so early. According to various standard books on Indian birds, the Common Mynahs' nesting season is not supposed to open until April—but I do not think the mynahs' painstaking carriage of many scraps of building material into likely nest-holes in February was just a careless, irresponsible, premature expression of springtime joie de vivre. I incline to the opinion, instead, that the learned tomes set the date for the commencement of Common Mynahs' breeding too late.

III

In the garden a troupe of Fantail Pigeons lived in a dovecote on the lawn. They were a constant joy to behold: beautiful, gleaming white creatures with voluptuous figures and stately deportment worthy of being sculptured in sugar-icing and set as symbols of pure bliss on wedding cakes. I shall not record their customs and histories, for they were mere pets, docile and domesticated, living an artificial existence more or less apart from the flurry and vim of wild bird society.

Each morning and evening a sweeper threw handfuls of grain on the lawn as food for them, and with pretty flutterings of wings the birds descended from the dovecote to the feast. Strutting, pouting and pecking delicately, they appeased their appetites in a most genteel manner.

Some of their less well-bred, more natural brethren regarded this daily distribution of grain as an act of public charity, and they also flew down to the food in considerable numbers, like a crowd of clients at a government soup-kitchen. Green Parakeets in particular availed themselves of this free largesse. Always about a dozen and sometimes as many as forty of them breakfasted and supped at the feeding ground, jostling each other and squawking and sometimes quarrelling over the seeds. Others who joined the company were Ring Doves, Little Brown Doves and Red Turtle Doves, with Jungle Babblers, Common Mynahs, Brahminy Mynahs and House

Sparrows. Among them came a few animals, pretty, furry little Striped Squirrels, who foraged on all fours, selected the tastiest morsels by discriminating sniffs of their sensitively twitching nostrils, and then squatted on their haunches nibbling at corn held between their front paws.

The regular attenders at these assemblies got to know the times of the sweeper's morning and afternoon appearances, and would gather expectantly in surrounding trees ten minutes or so before he was due to arrive. To them he was a sort of St Francis of Assisi, a gentle, generous friend and benefactor. As soon as he had thrown his gifts on the grass they swooped down to claim their shares. It was pleasant to see those gatherings of various types of untamed creatures on the lawn, all united by a charming camaraderie with the decorous Fantail Pigeons. So long as the food lasted they seemed as tame, trustful and mutually tolerant as a throng of pigeons being fed in Trafalgar Square; but as soon as the meal ended they went their various ways again to their separate lives in the wild.

The gentlemen Fantail Pigeons often stuck out their swanky chests, bowed with solicitous courtesy, and crooned love songs to the ladies; and these advances were promptly followed by the further intimacies necessary for the ceaseless propagation of the fantail species. In due course each hen laid two eggs. That happened over and over again, and the number of pigeons should have multiplied at an embarrassing and indeed alarming rate. Yet somehow that never happened. Some eggs were addled, others were stolen by gourmet House Crows, numerous chicks who got born soon died of neglect by their astonishingly incompetent parents, and many of those who survived longer were murdered by stray cats or kidnapped by raiding birds of prey. Owing to these perpetual mishaps the effective birth-rate among the pigeons stayed nicely balanced with the natural death-rate, and the number of living birds remained around a dozen.

The pigeons developed a sharp sense of the approach of danger. They seemed to have some private radar system which warned them of the arrival of a greedy falcon before it actually appeared, though I think they must have depended on their quick, wary eyesight. Often I saw the whole party of fantails suddenly spread their wings, spring simultaneously into the air and flutter panic-stricken to a shelter on the house roof—and several moments later a Kestrel, a Shikra, or another pirate, would appear overhead, eyeing the dovecote covetously, and perhaps stooping to capture a chick left defenceless on its platform.

VIII

Delhi can boast a splendidly fierce galaxy of birds of prey, and I doubt whether their variety is fully appreciated. Some competent ornithologist should devote his talents to making a proper assessment of the numerous types of hawk, kite, buzzard and eagle which inhabit the neighbourhood, for it seems to me there are serious gaps in our local knowledge.

I have seen several hawks in my garden. The Shikra is a regular visitor, and Kestrels, Lugger Falcons, Redheaded Merlins and a Pale Harrier put in occasional appearances. Common Pariah Kites are of course a daily sight, and sometimes I have observed Brahminy Kites and Blackwinged Kites. White-eyed Buzzards perch now and then in my trees, Crested Honey Buzzards are not uncommon, and once in the middle of a hot, dry summer I saw a Longlegged Buzzard slaking its thirst at a hosepipe on the lawn.

Eagles are quite plentiful. One balmy afternoon in mid February I was sitting in the garden with a party of guests sipping coffee after lunch, when the shadow of a huge bird flitted across the grass at my feet. Looking up, I saw a large bird of prey travelling with leisurely, dignified wing-beats overhead not more than fifty feet from the ground. The white bars on its powerful pinions proclaimed it to be a Steppe Eagle. It was accompanied by two Common Pariah Kites, who were chasing it; and those usually sizeable-looking creatures appeared quite small beside it.

One of the kites had evidently taken a strong dislike to the eagle's presence, and harried it perpetually. The second kite followed at a more respectful distance; but it, too, occasionally joined in the skirmishing. Presumably the pair owned a nest with youngsters somewhere nearby. The more aggressive kite kept swooping at the eagle from above, like a fighter aircraft attacking a bomber plane. Usually the eagle flew onwards with majestic indifference; but now and then with a deft movement of its wings it turned a half somersault in the air and extended its claws towards the kite, as if to show its talons as a warning to the tormentor. Then it as swiftly righted itself again and journeyed nonchalantly forwards.

The Steppe Eagle is a winter tourist in the capital; but other eagles are regular residents in Delhi. A Tawny Eagle, for instance, drops into my garden now and then at any and every season of the year. Several times Bonelli's Eagles have soared overhead, and twice a Pallas's Fishing Eagle honoured me by stopping for a while in a tree-top. Its proud, light-coloured head—reminiscent of the American bald eagle—was unmistakable.

On a memorable day last winter an even more unexpected sight greeted me. High in the blue above the garden, not far from a party of soaring vultures, but slightly aloof from them, a strange eagle glided with easy, graceful, well-disciplined power. As it manoeuvred in wide, slow circles I had time to study its features. Its dark head seemed large in proportion to the rest of its body; its breast and under-wings were white finely flecked with brown, and its back looked almost black with a broadly barred dark-and-light brown tail.

I was astonished, for it was a Short-toed Eagle. The bird's appearances in Delhi were reported to be rare, and it is recorded in the most authoritative books as a doubtful resident in the neighbourhood, although some discerning ornithologists believed it to be a regular inhabitant. I felt elated at my good fortune at catching a leisurely glimpse of it.

A few months later, in June, there was a sequel to the incident. An acquaintance reported his discovery of a nest of a strange bird of prey containing a solitary chick in a tree in open country about twenty-five miles from Delhi. I went to inspect it, and found that the eyrie's owners were a pair of Short-toed Eagles.

February

FOUR

MARCH

I

The flower-beds in the garden—and in all Delhi's myriad gardens—were at their best in early March. Every one was a rich, billowing mosaic of countless individual blooms and many massed colours.

By the second half of the month this beauty began to fade, but it was succeeded by other lovely appearances. The plum trees wore their frail flowers like wraiths of white mist which gradually dissolved; the mango trees were covered with yellow-green blossoms sprouting among dark leaves; and the jacaranda trees put forth tiny shocks of fresh foliage with cascades of flower buds. By the month's end many of these buds had burst, and the jacaranda boughs were exquisitely laden with little carillons of blue-mauve bells. Other trees which had shed their leaves in the winter and stayed bare for several weeks—like the rusty shieldbearer, peepul and pagoda trees—now began to clothe their naked limbs with new greenery.

Before the end of the month, too, the water-lilies in a goldfish pond produced their first large, starry flowers, white-fleshed and golden-hearted.

II

On the first day of March the temperature rose to 86 °F in the shade; and thereafter, with periods of fluctuation down as well as up, it tended to amount to ever more sizzling heights. On March 10th it ascended above 89°, on March 21st it was over 93°, on the 23rd it touched 96°, and on the 24th it exceeded 99°. Then the hot spell was temporarily broken by wild wind-storms and fitful showers of rain, and in the next few days the mercury in the thermometer sank to the middle eighties. Nevertheless the oven that is Delhi in the summer was warming up—although it still had a long way to go before it really turned the heat on its occupants.

Most of the birds did not seem to mind, and indeed showed many signs of revelling in the warmth. But a few winter visitors did not relish the soaring temperature, and fled—like numerous of the city's human inhabitants—to the Himalaya Mountains or beyond. Until March 15th two or three sportive White Wagtails still tripped lightly across my lawn every day, but I never saw them after that. The Black Redstarts endured longer. A pretty hen bird and sometimes a handsome cock dallied in the garden until almost the close of the month; but I set eyes on them for the last time on March 29th.

The charming Hume's Leaf Warbler would also no doubt have departed before the end of March if it had read the expertly compiled *Reference List of the Birds of Delhi*, for that learned tome declares that the species does not appear in these parts after March 23rd. Admittedly the hot spell of weather in the middle of the month did seem to banish it for a while, since I saw no member of the species in the garden between the 12th and the 31st; but then perhaps the subsequent cooler days induced the birds to return more belatedly than usual, for one made a sudden brief appearance on April 1st. Possibly it was merely trying to make an April Fool of me.

A winter sojourner in Delhi that I had not seen in January or February, but which spent a while on my lawn and in my arbours one morning towards the end of March, was the Indian Tree Pipit. It flirted its tail up and down, as if in mild imitation of a wagtail, and then sped away.

The wild geese had migrated earlier, the Greylags probably flocking northwards first. I last saw a gaggle of them flying over the garden on February 26th. The Barheaded Geese loitered longer on our jheels, and at six o'clock on the morning of March 9th I heard the voice of one careering through the darkness above the house. Perhaps it was calling goodbye as it started on its long journey to central Asia, for I never saw or heard one again until the following November.

When the wild geese and most of the wild duck leave Delhi, the glorious, bracing winter is past.

III

These departures were compensated by the arrivals of spring migrants travelling in the opposite direction. Among the newcomers to my garden were some who are not entirely unknown in the Delhi neighbourhood in winter. A few of their kinds remain in the vicinity through the cold months; but most of them make local migrations to rather warmer regions, and then move back in February or March to reinforce their hardier kith and kin.

The first of these types had actually communicated its presence to my ears, though not to my eyes, in February. It was the Common Hawk-cuckoo, whose monotonously, maddeningly reiterated phrase—sometimes translated as 'brainfever, brainfever, brainfever ...'—gives it the nickname of Brainfever Bird. Several times in mid February it dinned this tedious utterance into my hearing from some hiding place in a next-door garden. It is a shy bird, but in March it revealed itself more than once as it hastened across the lawn from one thicket to another. Often during the rest of the year its wearisome chant was to echo and re-echo in the garden.

Other birds that appeared there for the first time in March—though small numbers of them had probably stayed in Delhi throughout the winter—were the audacious Black Drongo or King Crow, the slim, pretty Red Turtle Dove, and the plumper but even more beautiful Green Pigeon. Commoner residents in the city whom I had not happened to see in January or February, and who dropped in at King George's Avenue in March, included the flamboyant Blue Jay, the lively Whitebrowed Fantail Flycatcher, the long-shanked, peevish-voiced Redwattled Lapwing, and the cackling Whitebreasted Kingfisher.

The true migrants—really coming from afar—were two birds

of passage who stay in Delhi neither winter nor summer, but merely use it as a staging-post on their journeys to and from other climes. The first need receive no more than a passing mention; it was the unpretentiously pretty Common Rosefinch. The second must exact a greater homage, for it was one of the most fabulously gracious of winged creatures—the Paradise Flycatcher. With all due respect to the gentler sex, that description would not have been warranted if my visitor had been a female of the breed, for she is no more especially easy on the eye than numerous of her sisters of other species. As I have remarked before, the fair sex in bird society is often the male sex, and that is outstandingly true in the case of Paradise Flycatchers.

These flycatchers are uncommon in Delhi, for they are comparatively few in numbers there, and usually pay only fleeting calls. It is true that some have been known to build nests, lay eggs and attempt to rear families in New Delhi, but these were rare and mostly unsuccessful efforts. Almost all the birds only pass through the capital on their way to their customary breeding grounds in the Himalayas. Many of them resort for nesting to a beauty spot worthy of their own perfect loveliness, the Vale of Kashmir.

For three years I hoped to see a Paradise Flycatcher in my garden; but every spring when the moment for its brief appearance arrived, my hopes were dashed. Once in 1956 I experienced mixed feelings of delight at the sight and disappointment at its situation when I caught a transitory glimpse of a black-headed, white-bodied, ribbon-tailed bird skipping through the air from one tree to another along Akbar Road. Why, I wondered, should Akbar Road be vouchsafed the privilege of this marvellous visitation instead of King George's Avenue, a stone's throw away?

In 1957 the nearness to my home of the enchanting apparition was even more tantalizing, for a bird-watching neighbour two doors away reported one day that a male Paradise Flycatcher in all its glory had just lingered for two minutes on a shrub in his garden.

In 1958 there was not even a rumour of the bird anywhere in the district. So twelve months later I waited apprehensively

March

for a similar defeat. March had progressed to its last day, and it was high time for the flycatchers to put in an appearance. Or had they already (I speculated pessimistically) passed through Delhi on their way to lucky gardens clinging on mountain-sides in Kasauli, Simla, Mussouri and other pleasure grounds among the Himalayas? As I sat on my veranda oppressed by this gloomy thought and reconciling myself to a further disappointment, I noticed a bird flutter into a shrubbery at the far end of my lawn, trailing a long tail behind it. I seized my field-glasses, focused them—and saw a Paradise Flycatcher.

The obliging vision gave me ample opportunity to study it, for it dawdled for the next hour in the trees and bushes. It was a fully adult cock in most exquisite breeding plumage. Little more than the size of a bulbul—with the addition of that fantastic, fabulous, streaming tail—its jauntily crested head and neck were glossy blue-black, its body was snow-white with a few dark streaks, and its sixteen-inch-long tail behind its nine-inch-long body sported a mixture of white and black. It kept hawking for flies in the morning sunlight, and its movements as it gambolled, twisted and darted after the elusive prey, with its tail-feathers floating and rippling behind, had fairy-like grace.

IV

On March 1st the Magpie Robin found its voice. Hitherto it had expressed itself only in occasional tuneless, wheezing exclamations; but that morning I heard a cock bird break into song. The effort was soft, restrained and obviously tentative, a first rehearsal for later concerts; but the voice had delicious sweetness, promising that its owner would become an accomplished impresario.

The Magpie Robin is one of Delhi's finest songsters, and when the season is more advanced and its emotions are more aroused performs not only with confident power, but also with a surprising variety of musical phrases, which it tries one after another like an opera singer practising a series of different recitatives.

The pair of Green Parakeets in the jacaranda tree continued to enjoy the pleasures, and also to suffer the tribulations, of married life. Their admirable example in deciding to consummate their partnership by conceiving eggs was soon followed by several other species. Among the first were the Crimsonbreasted Barbets.

In the early days of March there was still some confusion about which cock barbet should pair with which hen, for occasionally I saw a bird pop into, and then immediately pop out of again, two nest-holes in quick succession, as if it were uncertain where its fiancee lived. Every now and then, too, sharp sparring matches still occurred between rival males. But many of the birds had definitely made their choice of a partner, and these couples now co-operated jointly in the protection of their homes. On March 8th I saw not one Crimsonbreasted Barbet alone but two together dive-bombing Green Parakeets who had perched too near their nest-hole. Each barbet in turn flew furiously at the large intruders, returning to the attack several times until the parakeets were discomfited and moved away. In the next few days I saw this combined operation between a hen and her mate employed several times in defence of various barbet nests.

Other signs that the birds were settling down in earnest to the business of producing families also appeared. Sometimes I saw a barbet fly into its nest-hole, stay inside invisible for a while, and then reappear at the entrance with its beak stuffed full of woodchips, which it hurled into the outer air before disappearing indoors again to continue the carpentry. It was chiselling the inner chamber to the right dimensions for holding a family.

The fact is that a considerable section of bird society in the garden was struck by the same idea at about the same time, and there was quite a sudden rush of nest building. Naturally, I was not aware of every act of every pair of every species on every occasion when it occurred, for I had other, more important if less congenial, things to do than stand on my lawn with field-glasses glued to my eyes surveying the carryings-on of the birds; and some nests undoubtedly escaped my notice. I can only record what I chanced to see.

On March 10th a pair of House Sparrows were gathering nesting material among rock-plants on a flagstone path, and carrying it into a rolled-up blind on a veranda. Not being sufficiently intrigued by the family affairs of sparrows, I paid no further heed to them.

On the following day I spied a Whitethroated Munia with a long wisp of grass held in its beak, clearly a strand to be woven into the wall of a nest. But the bird did not transport it at once to the building site, being distracted first by a more tempting occupation. On a near-by bough stood another munia. The first bird flew to the second's side, engaged in a bout of sexy skipping, and then the two mated.

Next day I saw a Common Mynah conveying building materials into a large cavity in a rotten tree trunk. On the following morning a pair of Little Brown Doves were busy plaiting a shallow saucer of twigs to support their eggs across the stems of a shrub. That afternoon two Indian Robins carried scraps of dried rootlet into a nest-box in a dovecote. A few days later I saw a Neophron fly over the garden with a large stick held in its beak, and watched it fitting the piece into its half-finished nest in a lofty tree next door. During the next ten days Redvented Bulbuls, Redwhiskered Bulbuls, Ring Doves and Ashy Wren-Warblers all added nests to the growing number of residences constructed on my precincts.

The method of work differed from species to species. For example, the cock and hen House Sparrows, Indian Robins, Ashy Wren-Warblers and Common Mynahs shared fully the labour of construction, both birds collecting building material, flying with it to the incomplete nest, and weaving it into place there with equal energy and skill. The Ring Doves and Little Brown Doves, however (like other doves and pigeons), employed a different system by which the labour was divided between the sexes. Only the male bird fetched and carried building material, and only the female fitted this into its correct position in the nest. So the hen sat all the time on the unfinished structure while the cock kept flying to and fro bringing bits and pieces which he gave to her at the nest-edge, and which she then wove into place.

The bulbuls had yet another arrangement. Neither the cock Redvented Bulbul nor the cock Redwhiskered Bulbul ever did a stroke of work finding, carrying, or weaving the grasses, horsehairs and other substances which composed their nests.

The hen alone performed all those tasks. Nevertheless, the male bird showed unflagging interest in her progress, and escorted her on all her journeys to and from the building site, flying a few wing-beats behind her wherever she went and standing guard over her when she was busy at the nest itself.

Other species adopted yet other systems for building. In all cases it was a laborious enterprise. Most birds worked ceaselessly for several hours a day on four or five consecutive days before their nest was completed; and some took much longer than that.

Nor was the effort always successful at the first attempt. For example, the pair of Ashy Wren-Warblers that I have mentioned made a mess of their initial trial at home-making. I found it on March 27th, a fragile cup of fine grasses sewn by strands of cotton and cobweb between two large leaves. It was abandoned in an incomplete state, either because its creators were dissatisfied with its situation or else because some other defect developed. Next day I watched the same couple start contriving a second nest, slung beneath a single leaf of a tobacco plant in a near-by flower-bed. That erection proved an entire success as a cradle for eggs and a nursery for chicks. But three days later I watched another pair of Ashy Wren-Warblers stitching a nest into a clump of dahlia leaves, and that effort also was abandoned soon afterwards—a failure. The structure seemed too insecure to be safe; the stresses on the foliage were not well balanced; and the nest went sadly awry. The birds' instinct in trying to build there was evidently at fault. This is not an uncommon experience with Ashy Wren-Warblers, who sometimes seem to be amateur rather than professional construction engineers.

Likewise, the first nest built by Redwhiskered Bulbuls in my garden was deserted before completion. These bulbuls are shy, nervous creatures when engaged in building, and presumably some disturbance frightened them away. They immediately started to fashion another nest elsewhere, using some of the material from the first to make the second.

Such failures, whatever their cause, rarely discourage birds from embarking on further attempts. The urge to reproduce their kind is so strong that they immediately renew their efforts in another, more promising, quarter.

By the end of March I knew of three Green Parakeets' nests, three Green Barbets' nests, six Crimson breasted Barbets' nests, one House Sparrows' nest, one Little Brown Doves' nest, one Ring Doves' nest, one Common Mynahs' nest, two Ashy Wren-Warblers' nests, two Indian Robins' nests, one Red whiskered Bulbuls' nest and three Redvented Bulbuls' nests in the garden. The breeding season was advancing at accelerated pace.

V

I saw two convincing bits of evidence—in addition to the Neophron carrying building material—of other nests not far beyond the garden wall. The first appeared on March 24th. Three Redwattled Lapwings were running about on the lawn, rather stately creatures with plover-like figures strikingly costumed in black, brown and white, supported on lanky yellow legs. The fleshy crimson wattle in front of each eye which gives the species its distinctive name was conspicuous.

That morning the trio seemed even more lively than usual, frequently sprinting a few steps forward and then abruptly halting and standing motionless, as children do when playing the game called 'Grandmother's Paces'. There was nothing childish, however, about the conduct of at least two of those lapwings, for their restless antics turned out to be a preliminary to copulation. Suddenly one of them, a male, started twittering loudly, and as he did so he chased after another, a female. She scuttled forward several paces as if to escape him, but then stopped, bent her legs and dipped her body in a sort of curtsy; and immediately he jumped on her back and waggled his tail. Then he hopped off her and she stood erect once more. Three times in as many minutes they repeated this succession of actions—the quick chase, the brief mounting, the apparently instantaneous mating, and the reversion to normal postures. Afterwards they tried to shoo the third lapwing away, apparently regarding it as an impertinent peeping Tom; but it refused to go. They then resumed their love game, regardless of its presence.

The couple must have owned a nest somewhere near, probably in the domain of my good neighbour, General Thimayya, the Chief of Staff of the Indian Army. Year after year I hoped a pair of lapwings would lay their eggs and rear their fluffy chicks in my garden. The birds were frequent visitors there; but they used the place only as a rendezvous, never as a home. I grew to suspect they felt a political prejudice against me, and that in their hearts they were rabid Indian nationalists who believed that squatting on my soil would be a reversion to oppressive, reactionary colonialism. Every year they nested joyfully on the private properties of my friends the Secretary-General of the Ministry of External Affairs and the Chief of Protocol in the same Department; but I never heard of them resorting to the equally suitable shrubberies of any member of the Diplomatic Corps. So no doubt a robust anti-British phobia was the explanation why the two lapwings who used my lawn as a place for their romantic encounters were careful to deposit the results of those meetings, with impeccable patriotism, next door in the hedges of the Indian Chief of Army Staff.

The second scrap of evidence of other neighbourly nests presented itself on March 31st when I saw a Hoopoe searching for worms on my lawn. Its zebra-striped body, gay speckled crest and long, down-curving beak dashed hither and thither impatiently, as if the bird were running a perpetual race against the clock. As soon as it detected a worm below ground, it halted, plunged its bill into the earth and made swift nibbling motions. Then it hauled the reluctant delicacy from its lair, hammered it into dutiful submission, gripped it between the tips of its mandibles, and flew with it out of sight—once more into General Thimayya's garden. Evidently a young family was waiting to be fed there.

VI

The residents in my own garden did not lag behind these zealous next-door neighbours. Indeed, five days earlier I had noticed two Crimsonbreasted Barbets carrying tiny grubs into their nest-hole. One or more chicks must have broken from egg-shells that morning. In one respect, however, barbets are unsatisfactory birds to watch: their offspring stay hidden from view at the bottom of deep, dark shafts in tree trunks, so no strange eyes can observe their growth.

Species who build their nests in the open are easier subjects for study, and among them no characters are more uninhibitedly bold than Redvented Bulbuls. Unlike their Redwhiskered relatives, they are not shy when constructing nests. On the contrary, they fly fearlessly to and fro with building materials and quickly reveal to any interested observer the precise whereabouts of their current creation. If a person had nothing better to do he could easily view the whole laborious process from start to finish.

Three pairs of Redvented Bulbuls built nests in my garden in the last week of March. They were all clearly apparent to me; but the most accessible was poised on a stout leaf of a gaily flowering hollyhock, four feet above the ground. The hen bird—invariably escorted by her otherwise unhelpful mate—came on the job at about 6.30 each morning, and stayed on it most of the day. She took five days to complete the work.

On the sixth morning she and her partner were conspicuous by their absence; and I wondered whether they had decided to desert the empty nest, for it seemed precariously balanced on the leaf. Indeed, it had slipped into a lop-sided position... At 6.20 on the seventh morning, however, a bulbul was sitting in the nest. A few minutes later it hopped out and sped away; and when I peered into the nest a pinky-white, red-spotted, new laid egg was there.

On the eighth day I looked at the nest at 6.30 a.m. It was unoccupied except by the solitary egg. But at 6.50 a bulbul was squatting there, and it remained in the nest for the next fifteen minutes. When it departed two eggs lay side by side in the grass cup.

At the same hour next morning there was again no bulbul in sight, and no change in the situation in the nest. I watched for some time, but a bird did not appear. I presumed the parents were going to be content with two eggs... but sometime later in the day the hen added a third egg to their collection. Then she stopped laying.

Most garden birds manage things in a similar manner. Each morning for several consecutive days the female of a pair lays an egg, until her clutch is complete. She does not stay long in the nest for the purpose, usually achieving her great act of creation in a session lasting anything between fifteen minutes and one hour. During those days the birds do not visit their nest very often, except for brief, inquisitive glances at its astonishing contents. Only when the full complement of eggs has been produced do they settle down to the tedious task of incubation.

FIVE

GREEN PARAKEETS

I

I have already mentioned that the first birds whom I observed mating in my garden this year were a pair of Green Parakeets. Like most of their kind, they were aristocratic-looking creatures with superlatively elegant figures. Measuring about sixteen inches from end to end, they were trimly streamlined, having well-rounded heads, smoothly tapering bodies and long sharp tails. Their colouring was radiant, the male being especially presentable. His prevailing hue was bright green with washes of bluish-grey on the head, a black band curling round his face, a rose collar circling his neck, and splashes of blue and yellow on his tail. The female was more uniformly green. To complete their charms, both birds had pale yellow eyes, cherry-red beaks, and the solemn, slightly supercilious demeanour of all parrots.

I had been watching the couple for more than six months, ever since they became regular inmates of the garden. The hen bird first flew into my life one morning in the previous July when I caught sight of her inspecting a hole in a jacaranda tree trunk which at the time was occupied by a family of Brahminy Mynahs. During the next two weeks she often visited the spot, gazing covetously at the hole; and when the parent mynahs were absent she occasionally flew to the opening, perched just below it and chiselled with her beak at the wood, trying to widen the entrance. Clearly she fancied it as a likely residence for herself.

When the mynahs finally departed she at once took vacant possession of the property and began in earnest to enlarge its inner chamber for her own use. For several days she occupied herself with the work of excavation, sitting inside the cavity, nibbling at its walls with her bill, and periodically hurling a mouthful of wood-chips through the doorway.

Often, as she worked, a cock Green Parakeet perched on a branch outside the hole and eyed her approvingly. Thus I became acquainted with her lord. He never lifted a feather to help her in her labour of home-making; but he lent her moral support by the hour. She seemed grateful for his admiration, and sometimes took time off to settle companionably beside him on his sentinel bough. Possibly these were not their first meetings; the pair may well have been a middle-aged married couple who had lived together in previous seasons. Male and female Green Parakeets seem to remain such constant comrades through the year that I should not be surprised to learn that they pair for life.

Before long the hole in the tree was sufficiently enlarged to suit their requirements; and after that the hen bird spent a lot of time in it. Often during the day I saw her peering like a jack-in-the-box from its entrance, and always at nights she slept there. The male did not share her bedroom, but flew at dusk to a lodging elsewhere in Delhi—I knew not where. Shortly before sunrise the next morning he would arrive in the jacaranda tree to bid her good day. She then issued from her sleeping apartment, and they flew away together for breakfast somewhere in the neighbourhood.

Often during those days I saw them standing side by side in the jacaranda tree near their nest-to-be. So their friendship remained, faithful but platonic, from the middle of July until the end of January.

II

Then came their initial intimacy on the first day of February. I have already described the brief encounter: her enticement of him, his initial indecisive response, her further encouragement, his mounting on her back, and then his gradual working up to a vigorous, passionate attempt at union with her. I write 'attempt' deliberately, though I am not sure that the word is justified. His experiment at love-making may have been successful; but I doubt it. The affair was too short—lasting only half a minute—compared with their later couplings, and her abrupt ending of it by pecking at his face showed too much displeasure for the incident to be convincing. However, whether they physically mated or not on that occasion, their partnership was emotionally consummated.

As it happened, later the same day I saw another pair of Green Parakeets go through similar motions of mating. They owned a nest-hole elsewhere in the same jacaranda tree, and had likewise established proprietary rights to it several months earlier. An odd circumstance characterized them; the hen had only one foot, her second leg being a broken stump. Perhaps by chance, their nest had also been occupied in the previous year by a pair of Green Parakeets of whom the female had a solitary leg; but I do not believe this was a coincidence. I think a hen often returns to the same cradle for her offspring each nesting season.

That hen's lameness sometimes led to a certain awkwardness in the pair's marital relations. If the male was too clumsy when he mounted her, she could not maintain her grip with only one foot on the bough where they embraced. So she lost her balance. Several times I saw that happen in the early days of their mating, before he had learned the correct gentleness towards her. Let me describe one such occasion. The two birds were perching side by side on a branch near the entrance to their nest-hole. The hen crouched invitingly with her head tilted upwards, as was usual when she wanted to be ravished. The male sidled up to her and rubbed his beak affectionately in the plumage at the nape of her neck; but after a few moments he stopped, raised his head and looked around nervously, as if he were fearful of being observed. At least ten times he tickled his consort's topknot, and then hesitated and gazed apprehensively round him, extremely undecided. But she did not change her seductive squat, continuing to solicit him.

At last he was sufficiently stirred, made his resolve, and climbed on her back. She crouched lower with anticipatory contentment, and he promptly thrust his beak into the back of her neck. He must have done it too suddenly or passionately, not working up gradually to his frenzy, for she was taken by surprise at the force of his jab, lost her balance and collapsed on their branch. He at once jumped off her, and she tumbled from their perch and hung in mid air by her solitary foot. With difficulty she struggled back to an upright position and recomposed herself. He remained at her side, and for the next ten minutes they stood so, both preening their feathers and performing other nonchalant, unemotional actions. Then she lowered her body into a suggestive posture once more and tilted her head in a fresh invitation to him to pleasure her—which he did with proper skill and apparent mutual satisfaction this time.

The males of both pairs betrayed various signs of inexperience in the earliest days of mating. Thus, a cock's clumsiness when mounting his partner sometimes so discomfited her that she pecked him protestingly, forcing him temporarily to dismount. That never happened when he became more experienced. Again, on several early occasions I saw a male climb on a female's back, attempt coition, and then hop off again three or four times in quick succession, obviously getting no results except frustration from the exercise. Moreover, in his first amorous approaches to his mate a male invariably engaged in protracted, indecisive preliminary gestures such as fondling her neck and head or gazing around to make sure no critical eyes were watching; whereas later he dispensed with these irrelevancies and proceeded with only the most cursory introductory motions to the serious business of coupling. Perhaps another indication of growing expertness was the fact that as the days passed a pair appeared to achieve successful coition more rapidly than in their initial essays, the male remaining on the female's back less than two minutes instead of the three or four minutes which they took before.

None of this was surprising, for the operation was somewhat complicated. It was difficult for a cock to keep his equilibrium on a hen's back while at one and the same time thrusting his beak vigorously up and down at her neck and jerking his posterior energetically to and fro at her rear. Nor was it easy for his lower quarters to make exactly the right contact with hers. To do this he had to twist and curl his body round her in a most awkward angular curve, and the trickiness of the contortion was increased by the existence of their long tails, which were apt to get in their way.

So I am inclined to think their first attempts to accomplish these sexual acrobatics were less than fully successful, and that they only gradually acquired the necessary skill. Certainly the spasmodic jerks of the male's rump in the beginning appeared ineffective compared with the obviously more regular, forceful and satisfying thrusts of his love-making in later days.

III

Every morning I watched the pair at the more accessible nest, hoping to detect a sign that they had reached the next stage in their family affairs by producing eggs. Thus I became quite familiar with their characters and customs. Sometimes the hen bird took the initiative in inviting him to pleasure her, by squatting seductively beside him; and at other times the cock made the first suggestion by sidling up to her and scratching tenderly at her head-feathers.

They were not in the least embarrassed if other parakeets showed keen curiosity about their love-making. Birds are, of course, all uninhibited children of Nature. Frequently half a dozen fellow members of their clan were perched nearby when the cock mounted the hen, and as their copulation proceeded one or two of these would move step by step closer to the pair, gazing inquisitively at their odd goings-on, until they were only a foot away. Completely unperturbed, the couple continued their passionate liaison until it reached a climax, when their ardour cooled and they separated. If the fascinated bystander were a male, he then sometimes tried to continue the sport. More than once I saw such a stranger lean towards the hen as soon as her lover left her and attempt to fondle her—only to receive from her a swift, vicious little peck of instant reproof.

The couple were more disturbed by the presence of other species of birds. In particular, if one of the Green Barbets who owned a neighbouring nest appeared while they happened to be mating, they at once desisted, assumed innocent stances and postponed their philandering until the intruder departed. This was common prudence, for they knew from experience that they must beware of physical assault by those short-tempered barbets.

After they started regular matings they themselves become more sensitive about strange birds approaching their nest. Their sense of landlordism seemed to grow, and they drove away Common Mynahs, Brahminy Mynahs and other trespassers who encroached too close. Another indication of their new preoccupation was that the hen parakeet became even more closely attached than before to their hole-in-a-tree. Each day during the previous months she had absented herself from the vicinity for considerable periods; but now she tended to become an almost permanent squatter either beside the nest-hole or actually inside it. She still left the jacaranda tree to fetch food, but otherwise was invariably there. Usually she sat invisible indoors, but frequently she poked her head through the entrance to survey with rather detached interest the world which she had temporarily renounced. There was something nun-like about her withdrawal from that green and pleasant prospect—except that she was engaged in a pastime in which no respectable nun would indulge.

The cock parakeet was very much in love with her. He spent a lot of time in slavish attendance on her, waiting as a sentinel just outside the nest when she was inside, and flying after her wherever she went as soon as she emerged. Impelled blindly by the strongest of all natural urges—the impulse to mate with her and so make his individual contribution to the preservation of their species—he sought at almost every opportunity to satisfy his craving for her. Nor did she object. Green Parakeets are ardent lovers in the breeding season. I watched carefully three pairs who nested in my garden, and they all enjoyed frequent sexual intercourse. It was invariably their first act on rising from bed each morning, and after that the couples mated about once every hour—and sometimes at shorter intervals—as long as daylight lasted. Possibly their ardour flagged a little in the sunniest, hottest noontide; but I doubt it, for sometimes I saw scraps of irrefutable evidence to the contrary.

For about a fortnight after they began to mate the hen continued to fly periodically from the tree, usually in the cock's company, to gather food at some favourite foraging spot. They were among the regular customers at the Fantail Pigeons' breakfast ground. However, the cock began to feed his partner also by regurgitation. I first noticed this extraordinary performance on the afternoon of February 4th, the third day following their initial mating. Whether it had occurred between them before I do not know; but apparently the male's feeding of the female started at about the time when their sexual relations began to prepare her for laying eggs, incubating them, hatching chicks and rearing a young family—in fact, for spending many weeks almost constantly occupied with domestic duties inside a nest-hole. Soon afterwards she completely stopped fetching food for herself, and became entirely dependent on her lord for nourishment. Thereafter for many weeks—until her chicks were growing quite large—she never left the immediate neighbourhood of the nest, and only emerged from the nest-hole itself for brief spells of fresh air, feather-preening, love-making and being fed.

That last operation was an astonishing spectacle. The hen bird would stand on a bough with an expectant air as the cock approached her. A pace away he would halt and stare at her with an inexplicable sort of curiosity, as if he had never seen her before. Then he seemed to take a decision, drew himself stiffly to his full height and bent his head towards her as he might do if he were about to exercise his husbandly right of possessing her. But instead of tickling her neck, he touched her beak with his beak, leaving their mouths in contact for a moment as if he were tenderly kissing her. Then he suddenly broke off the contact, jerking his head abruptly backwards as he raised his body again to its full height, and holding that pose for a while with an air of pompous dignity. All the time he kept his eyes on the hen, scrutinizing her appraisingly. Then he slowly raised one foot with its toes extended towards her as if he would like either to stroke or to scratch her; but suddenly he put the foot down again, shot his head towards her and once more touched her beak with his. This time his bill lingered for a while on hers and opened slightly to let her bill enter his. When they broke off contact again, the hen made small nibbling motions with her mandibles, chewing bits of food that he had passed her. Meanwhile the cock once more assumed a dignified, erect pose, holding himself with a stiff sedateness which was grotesque to the point of being comic. Occasionally he added to the ludicrous effect by puffing out his chest importantly—and that action revealed the real cause of all his odd gesticulations. Every time that he withdrew his beak from the female's he must regurgitate more food to give her at the next meeting of their mouths; and this process seemed rather difficult. To achieve it he had to contort his neck awkwardly and engage in other straining motions, including (apparently) raising one leg, to assist in the upward passage from his throat to his beak of a further titbit.

The meal always continued for some time, the male executing repeatedly the succession of strange antics which ended each time in his bending towards her, gripping her beak in his, and passing a morsel of food to her. To human eyes the operation looked like nothing so much as a protracted bout of passionate kissing between infatuated lovers.

Usually, though not invariably, this feeding of the hen by the cock was associated with mating. It followed immediately after the act of copulation. As soon as the male parakeet jumped off the female's back, he assumed the stance for feeding her, eyeing her to see whether she looked suitably hungry, and then drawing himself up stiffly for the first effort at regurgitation.

This combined act of mating and feeding was the birds' first preoccupation every morning when they woke. Often I watched the ceremony at the nest-hole in the jacaranda tree. As I have already written, the hen parakeet slept each night in the nest while the cock occupied some other dormitory at a distance. About half an hour before sunrise she would poke her head through her bedroom doorway for a preliminary glance at the reviving world.

Green Parakeets

Then she withdrew out of sight indoors again. A few minutes later the cock would fly across the lawn, shrieking joyfully as he came and making straight for the jacaranda tree. He would perch on a branch beside the nest-hole and at once call impetuously and impatiently. If he received no quick response, he changed his tone to one more gentle and persuasive.

No doubt he was venturing to remark to the occupant inside the hole: 'Good morning, my dear; have you slept well? A new day has dawned. Come out, you lazy bones! Oh, do come out.'

Sometimes she responded immediately, and at other times she kept him waiting for several minutes; but always before long she emerged. Flying straight past him, she made a short flight to exercise her wings, and then alighted in a neighbouring tree. When she appeared he instantly followed her, as close as a shadow and as eager as something much more substantial than a shadow. He landed near her, and after a barely decent interval he sidled up to her. She crouched compliantly, he climbed on her back, and they mated. Then he regurgitated her breakfast for her—after which she promptly took wing again and returned to the nest.

These rites were performed so regularly at almost precisely the same minute every morning that I could have set my watch by them. Nor—as I have already written—was the ritual a service celebrated only at matins every twenty-four hours. The love parts of it at least were repeated every hour throughout the day, day after day; and the feeding no doubt followed as often as the hen felt hungry.

At the beginning of February I assumed that these passionate exercises would not continue long. After several days, I thought, the hen would lay eggs and the parents would then switch their interest to the responsibilities of incubation. But I was wrong. The intimacies between the pair continued with unflagging zest for more than six weeks, until I thought the couple would never tire of their favourite pastime. For a period at the end of February she sometimes seemed reluctant to submit to his caresses; but that only provoked him to greater ardour, and he became so lecherous that several times he apparently tried to rape her. Later she recovered her amorous mood, and they maintained their matings several times each day until March 18th, when the practice suddenly ceased.

I could not discover when their honeymoon first yielded a material result in the form of an egg, because I could not peer into their nest. But I felt a strong intuition that the hen had borne her first youngster about the middle of February, on the day when she ceased to fly away to fetch food for herself, became entirely dependent on her partner for nourishment, and settled down to almost perpetual brooding indoors. However, I could not prove that.

Evidence mentioned in Hume's *Nests and Eggs of Indian Birds* suggests that an interval of several days can elapse between the successive laying of each of a Green Parakeet's three or four eggs, which no doubt accounts for the protracted continuation of a couple's mating after their first egg has been produced.

IV

The pair of parakeets in my garden stopped love-making on March 18th; so for nearly seven weeks they had mated every day, several times a day.

After that they continued to observe their customary ritual each morning, except for its solemn, complicated climax of copulation. The male bird arrived in the garden shortly before sunrise and flew to the nest to call his spouse. She promptly emerged, made a short sortie through the air to exercise her wings, and then alighted in some near-by tree. He followed and perched beside her. Occasionally in the next few days he tickled her head-feathers with his beak; but this opening gambit of their love-play was apparently only a reminiscent, fleeting, perhaps nostalgic, reversion to an earlier habit, and was never pursued further. Instead he fed her with all the absurd formal posturings required by regurgitation, and immediately afterwards she sped back to their home tree and disappeared into the nest. Evidently she was eager to return quickly to her clutch of eggs. Most of the rest of the day she stayed indoors, no longer reappearing at hourly intervals for romantic dallyings with her mate.

From time to time he visited her, flying to the nest-entrance, perching just below it, and peering solicitously within. Periodically she fluttered out to receive refreshments from him, but always as soon as she had fed she hurried back into the nest. Her whole being seemed concentrated on the business of hatching eggs, which seemed to be almost a full-time job. Some writers on Indian birds have declared that both Green Parakeets share in the labour of incubation, and no doubt their statements are based on careful observations; but I did not myself often see male birds enter their nest-holes at that period. Certainly their share of the work was very much lighter than that of the hen.

On March 28th I noticed an incident at the main nest which might indicate that one or more youngsters had hatched that morning. The female parakeet seemed a trifle agitated because a number of other parakeets showed an inordinate interest in her home. They kept fluttering inquisitively around its doorway, trying to alight there and peer inside. Several times she dashed at them and drove them away; but for some mysterious reason they were always attracted back again. I had not observed any such episode before. Did it mean that the mother bird was sensitive about strangers approaching her residence because it housed newly-born chicks, and that the group of other parakeets were aware of the birth and anxious to inspect the babies? I do not think this is too human an explanation; but I cannot be sure. I could no more tell when the eggs hatched than I had been able to learn when they were laid, for the whole early life of the youngsters was hidden from view deep in the jacaranda tree trunk.

That situation continued with no apparent change for several weeks. The hen bird spent most of her time in the nest, her departures from it being rare and her absences short. At some moment towards the end of March or early in April her progeny must have hatched, and her maternal duties changed from incubating eggs to coddling chicks. After that the cock bird's task as the bread-winner for the family became more exacting, for now he had more than his wife's mouth to feed. The authors whom I have already quoted state in their books that, just as both birds help in incubating eggs, so also they partake in the work of feeding nestlings. I do not know whether these writers intended to convey that the cock bird feeds the youngsters directly. For myself, I can only record that my observations rarely yielded evidence of that. It seemed to me that the male parakeets continued to feed their mates by regurgitation, that they gave them enough rations to appease not only their own hunger but also that of their chicks, and that the hens then promptly flew into the nest to pass the extra provisions to their offspring. Only occasionally did a male fly into the nest-hole to feed the family himself.

As the weeks passed the mother birds began to absent themselves more frequently from their nurseries. Presumably the nestlings needed less constant attention as they grew up, and the parents were freer to divert themselves elsewhere. So they took more protracted flights out of doors to exercise wings and bodies which must have become out of practice for such physical vigour during long weeks of cramped incubation. Until towards the end of April, however, the hen at the nest which I watched most closely did not (so far as I could see) interrupt her vigils at home to the extent of resuming the fetching of her own food. For nourishment she remained entirely dependent on her mate. The first occasion when it looked as if she might have gone on a foraging expedition on her own was on April 23rd; but if that was the case, she also continued to be partly fed by him for a few weeks afterwards. Throughout the occupation of the nest-hole by her youngsters she slept in the tunnel every night with them.

V

One morning, as she sat taking the air alone on a bough in a nearby tree, a strange bird darted at her. With a startled cry she leaped from her perch and flew towards the nest; but the attacker gave swift, wicked chase, and to avoid being struck she had to swerve away. Weaving a skilful zigzagging course in and out among the branches of a row of trees, she fled in panic with the aggressor almost on her tail all the way. Then I saw that the stranger was a Shikra, a hawk so sporting that falconers train it to capture various birds on the wing. The chase was very exciting; several times the bird of prey seemed on the point of catching up with its intended victim; and my heart was in my mouth, for I feared it would deliver a mortal blow and bring an end to my tale of family life among parakeets. But the parakeet showed remarkable resource in evading its pursuer, and the Shikra soon wearied of the hunt. After a tense couple of minutes it suddenly veered away in another direction. The parakeet sped back helter-skelter to its nest-hole, and hastened inside.

Five minutes later the hawk returned to frighten and scatter a group of half a dozen other Green Parakeets clustered in a neighbouring tree. They screamed as they fled in all directions, and the Shikra whimsically settled on the very spot where they had perched. It was evidently in sportive, playful mood.

On a later morning another kind of intruder disturbed the peace surrounding the parakeet's nest. A Brahminy Mynah arrived on the scene with a strip of lavatory-paper gripped in its beak. Brahminy Mynahs and Common Mynahs are fond of stuffing odd bits of rubbish like the Cellophane wrapper off a cigar, silver paper torn from chocolate boxes, or scraps of coloured rags, into their nests as decorations; and this Brahminy Mynah was apparently intent on adorning its home with toilet-paper. Moreover, it seemed resolved to make that home in the very nest-hole already occupied by the Green Parakeets, for it alighted at the entrance and peered hopefully indoors. The hen promptly flew out of the nest in protest and shoo'd the vulgar visitor away. But the mynah was not to be easily discouraged. Often it returned to the tunnel and tried to carry its booty inside; and every time the parakeet intercepted it and drove it off.

Eventually the mynah gave up, retreated to a bough, and let the paper drop from its beak. As it fluttered towards the ground a

Common Mynah caught sight of it, felt attracted by its decorative quality, dashed at it, retrieved it and carried it to another nest-hole elsewhere in the same tree. As the bird alighted on the bark, however, something made it open its beak to emit a squawk—and the slip of paper once more descended earthwards. At that the Brahminy Mynah could not resist the temptation to make another attempt at incorporating the flimsy sheet in a nest. Leaping from its perch, it caught the trophy in mid air and carried it again to the doorway of the Green Parakeets' home. But again the parakeet confronted the trespasser and chased it away. Disconsolately, the mynah let the toilet-paper drop.

Then the Common Mynah returned to the charge, dashing at the scrap as it settled on the ground, picking it up and flying with it triumphantly to its own nest-hole. But the triumph was short-lived. A Jungle Babbler apparently questioned its good taste in wishing to adorn a nest with such an article, for it flew so viciously at the mynah that the bird took fright, released the paper and took refuge, empty-beaked, in a clump of foliage.

The game of catch-as-catch-can with the sheet of paper was over. Like a forgotten shuttlecock, it fluttered to the ground, and the various players dispersed. The Common Mynah hopped into its nest-hole, the Brahminy Mynah hastened away, the Green Parakeet returned to its nursery, and only the Jungle Babbler stayed on a bough, eyeing the bit of paper with seeming disapproval... But I cannot help thinking that one of the mynahs returned surreptitiously to the spot later, reclaimed the prize lying on the grass and carried it at last safely into a nest. If that was so, the repository was not the Green Parakeets' home. Several times in the next few weeks I saw a Brahminy Mynah trying to effect an entry into that desirable residence; but always in vain. The parakeet landlady invariably appeared and made effective landladyish protests, driving the would-be gate-crasher away.

VI

Not until May 7th did a young Green Parakeet reveal itself in the

Green Parakeets

nest-tunnel. That morning I saw a nestling eyeing me dubiously from inside the shaft. After long hesitation it plucked up courage to poke its head through the entrance to catch a glimpse of the outside world; but something must have frightened it, for at once it withdrew indoors again and disappeared from view. I did not see it again for several hours.

In the succeeding days it grew steadily bolder, craning its head ever further out of the nest-entrance to enjoy some sightseeing in the strange, fascinating out-of-doors. It was a charming-looking youngster with a sleek, softly plumaged head, large, innocent dark eyes, and an unblemished pale red beak. Always it displayed curiosity, and sometimes astonishment, at what it saw in the landscape. Silently and cautiously it would stare for hours from its window, no doubt having been warned by its mother that the world is a dangerous place to be regarded with all due prudence.

I never saw a second youngster in that nest, and I suppose this chick was the solitary fruit of all those long months of passionate mating, patient incubation and devoted care by its parents. They continued to nourish and tend it there for another three weeks; and then, on May 27th, it ventured from the nest, flying away gaily with them.

That night the tunnel in the jacaranda tree was empty for the first time for many months. More than ten moons had waxed and waned since I first saw the hen parakeet chipping at its entrance as a signal that she intended to rear a family there. Hers had been a remarkably protracted occupation.

VII

On the day that the parakeets departed I watched a Common Mynah and a Brahminy Mynah both enter the nest-hole several times on inspection visits; and for the next few days they quarrelled over possession of the place. Their contest was vicious; but in the end the Common Mynah and its mate won a decisive victory—and not long afterwards the hen of the pair was sitting on a clutch of attractive blue Common Mynahs' eggs.

VIII

Two other pairs of Green Parakeets nested in the garden. The first was the couple with the one-legged female. Her deformity was no bar to the production of a lusty family, for she bore, hatched and reared three chicks. I first noticed them peering shyly from their residence on April 25th, nearly two weeks before the youngster in the other nest made its similar debut. They left their birthplace on May 15th, also almost a fortnight before it followed suit.

The tale of the third pair of nesting Green Parakeets had a different beginning, a different middle and a different end from the stories of the other couples. As for the beginning, whereas each hen bird of those pairs occupied her nest-to-be as sleeping quarters for several months before she began laying eggs—and so established unchallengeable proprietary rights there—the female in this third case took no such precaution. On the contrary, she and her male partner made their first reconnaissance of the hole-in-a-tree which they favoured only on February 22nd, a considerable time after the breeding season of the others had already begun. They then disappeared for many days, and I did not notice them at the site again until March 8th. In the meantime a pair of Common Mynahs had taken a fancy to the place and made elaborate preparations to occupy it. These mynahs therefore resented the reappearance of the parakeets as potential residents, and a violent scuffle occurred then and there between the rival claimants. The Green Parakeets won this first round, presumably because they were heavier-weight contestants; but what the mynahs lacked in power they made up for in obstinacy. Again and again that day they returned to challenge the parakeets' right to ownership. In fact, they kept renewing the fight every day for the next several weeks.

At the middle of the story, therefore, the parakeets occupancy of their home was never peaceful. That they established their tenancy was beyond doubt, for each day the pair mated frequently on boughs near the nest, the hen bird spent hours at a stretch squatting within, and she and her mate shoo'd away all intruders, exactly as other members of their tribe did on their respective private properties. Yet the two Common Mynahs never became reconciled to defeat; every morning they bitterly challenged their rivals by standing outside the nest and shrieking at the hen inside, dashing hostilely at the cock whenever he appeared, and making themselves a public nuisance in other ways.

As for the end of the story, either the relentless opposition of the mynahs or else some other circumstance caused the parakeets to desert the nest before their eggs can have hatched. Both birds were there (the cock outside and the hen inside the nest-hole) on April 15th—and both were absent all day on the 16th. In their places that morning the Common Mynahs kept flying in and out of the doorway, carrying bits and pieces of all the bric-a-brac which goes to make a mynahs' nest. They lived there happily ever after—or, to be exact, until their youngsters flew from the apartment many weeks later.

I never saw that pair of Green Parakeets again.

IX

During the nesting season Green Parakeets disperse in separate family parties, although I believe some families choose to breed in considerable colonies. Afterwards all the birds revert to their more customary sociability, gathering, travelling, feeding and for ever chattering in large flocks.

These flocks began to assemble in the tree-tops in the latter half of April. Among them were perhaps the most precocious of the new generation of youngsters just emerged from nests. Certainly by the early days of May these adolescents accompanied their elders. More than once I saw small squadrons of parakeets flying overhead at a much slower pace than is usual with those fast-travelling birds. Their wing-beats were leisurely, their movements seemed halting and their whole progress was hesitant, as if they were troops performing a slow march. I presumed they were family groups including fledglings fresh from nurseries, now venturing into the outer world and having their first lessons in flying.

Gradually the flocks grew larger, until companies of fifty, sixty, or more parakeets were a common sight. They were especially active in the early mornings, when they flew from their beds to breakfast off crops in the fields outside Delhi, and again in the evenings when they returned to their roosting places. Every night multitudes of them congregated in various suitable spots in the city, such as Lodi Gardens, where many trees became noisy parakeets' dormitories.

At dawn and dusk, therefore, countless flocks of parakeets sped across the sky. Every few minutes a fresh party of anything between a dozen and a hundred birds would appear, all hastening in the same direction like a ceaseless fly-past of squadrons of aircraft in an air pageant. A flight of Green Parakeets is a beautiful sight. The birds move swiftly and usually in a direct, unswerving line, like arrows shot from bows; but every now and then some whim makes them abruptly change their line of advance, and they turn sharply this way or that, rising and tumbling, twisting and veering in a nervous series of quick, zigzagging, acrobatic manoeuvres. They seem to ricochet from point to point in the air with carefree abandon. Their speed never alters; always it is swift and purposeful. An acquaintance of mine who made a habit of pacing squadrons of Green Parakeets in his motor-car as they sped along the edges of India's straight roads told me that the birds overtook him when he was driving at forty miles an hour, and that he overtook them when he accelerated to forty-five miles an hour. So their normal cruising speed must be about forty-three miles an hour. No doubt if pressed they can distinctly increase this haste. Their speed and capacity for sudden alterations in their line of flight explains why my Green Parakeet was able to evade the hot pursuit of a Shikra.

The number of Green Parakeets who inhabit Delhi must be legion. On several evenings in July and August I have counted the birds flying above my garden in the last hour before darkness, when they were travelling to their nightly lodgings. Each time between 1,200 and 1,500 of them passed overhead. That is an astonishing throng to journey in sight of one confined lawn. If every other citizen of Delhi were to take a similar census, the grand total of parakeets must amount to tens of thousands.

No doubt the birds are pests to farmers, for they guzzle ripening corn and fruit. Nevertheless, such beauty in such masses is one of Delhi's loveliest natural treasures.

SIX

APRIL

I

The tale of the Green Parakeets has reached forward into May; and I must now return a few weeks to the beginning of April. The garden then appeared somewhat dishevelled, for most of its flowers had faded, and if aesthetic horticultural appearances had been my chief concern, I would have uprooted all the vegetation and turned the beds into smooth, neat surfaces of flat earth. But some birds—like Ashy Wren-Warblers, Yelloweyed Babblers and Redwhiskered Bulbuls—favour the tangles of withered herbage as places for concealing nests; so I asked my gardeners to leave the ruined chaos undisturbed. Each bed appeared a miniature unkempt jungle of rotting plants, but in them were secreted the homes of various small birds, just as the real jungle is a haunt of larger and wilder beasts.

Not all the flowers had given up the ghost. Here and there a clump of stalks still bloomed amid the surrounding cemetery of foliage. In the cool mornings and evenings the tobacco plants, for example, opened their many bright blossoms, which only wilted and shrivelled in the oppressive, intolerable heat of full daytime.

The death of many lovely colourings along the flower-beds was partially compensated by the birth of new brilliance in shrubberies and trees. April is one of the months when bougainvillaeas flaunt themselves most riotously, and their various tints of pink, brick red, crimson and purple gleamed in numerous corners of the garden. Yellow elders displayed posies of bright trumpets, bignonias were drenched in showers of golden, honeysuckle-like blooms, coral hibiscus produced its flaring orange-red petals, and other shrubs were also gorgeously adorned.

Some trees likewise donned their spring dresses. The tall Australian silver oaks were garlanded with flame-coloured flowers, and delicately scented white blossoms sprinkled enchanting pagoda trees. But most beautiful of all were the jacarandas. Their boughs were laden near every twig tip with clusters of mauve-blue bells so dense in quantity that the trees seemed cloaked in them, and yet so light in quality that they wore a misty, unearthly, ethereal air, as if they did not quite belong to this world. Nor was that gracious manifestation confined to the branches overhead; it was repeated also on the ground, where countless flowers had fallen beneath each tree and lay like pools reflecting the splendour above.

The temperature during the month was erratic, sometimes plunging whimsically down to the lower eighties, and at other times soaring to even greater heights than earlier in the year. Its loftiest summit reached above 104 °F. But worse—or better, according to your taste in such roastings—was to come later in the summer.

II

The rising heat drove the last of the winter visitors away from Delhi. Thus, the engaging little Chiffchaffs and Lesser Whitethroats disappeared before the end of the month. In other years, when the onset of summer was perhaps not so fierce so early, the Whitethroats lingered longer, staying into the first few days of May.

Other warblers who are mere birds of passage in Delhi flitted through the garden in April. Among them I recognized Blyth's Reed Warbler, but others I failed to identify. Many warblers are difficult to distinguish with certainty unless you are either an expert on the tribe in general or familiar with particular species, for their greeny-brown costumes are often confusingly similar.

Another bird of passage was the Redheaded Bunting, and a resident who made a solitary visit in April was a Brown Rock Chat. In addition three notable characters put in appearances: the Bluethroat, the Rufous Turtle Dove and the Rosy Pastor.

The Bluethroat is a regular winter tourist in Delhi, frequenting damp areas beside rivers and jheels. It dropped into my garden only twice to my knowledge, in successive Aprils. In 1958 one tarried for six days towards the end of the month. During that time it never left the same confined corner of the garden, where it hopped around on a small stretch of lawn between a shrubbery and some flower-beds. Very shy, it usually retreated into one of these patches of cover as soon as I appeared. An immature bird, its blue bib was only faintly developed.

In the following year a fully plumaged adult of the breed stayed in the garden for a day. The Bluethroat's name well describes its appearance. Brown on its upper body and buffish-white on its lower parts, there is little to distinguish it from other similarly unpretentious, six-inch-long pygmies except a sudden surprising splash of blue on its throat. The daub is of a very bright hue, covers the bird's entire chin and fore-neck, and is accentuated by a chestnut blob in its centre and black and chestnut borders along its edge. Characteristically, this striking decoration is present in the male but lacking in the female.

In the same week in 1958 when the immature Bluethroat dallied in the garden an even more unusual visitor lent distinction to my lawn. It was a Rufous Turtle Dove, a rather rare bird of passage in Delhi. One of the largest of the doves, it has beautiful, scale-like markings of mixed shades of brown, grey and black. The specimen which visited me stayed two days in my compound, sometimes strolling over the ground, occasionally sipping drinks of water from the fishpond, and at other times fluttering into the trees. Then it continued its northward journey.

Rosy Pastors are regular and multitudinous birds of passage in the capital. They are glorified starlings—and glorified pastors, too, for that matter. Similar to a Common Starling in size, build and habits, the bird is more gaudily attired than its notorious cousin, boasting a bushy crest on its topknot and wearing glossy black plumage on its head, chest, wings and tail, and rose-pink feathering over the rest of its body. Both sexes look alike. Countless flocks of Rosy Pastors travel northwards in the spring and southwards again in the late summer, beginning to arrive in Delhi in March, though

I never noticed them over my garden before the first few days of April. For the next three weeks parties of them would often scurry overhead, and at dusk they sometimes settled in a large peepul tree where they made the deafening, chattering shindy typical of any assembly of starlings just before they drop off to sleep. By the end of the month they had all disappeared on their further migrations.

III

The place of the departing winter trippers was taken by fresh waves of summer tourists to the capital. Most welcome among them was the Golden Oriole. According to the *Reference List of the Birds of Delhi* it is not supposed to reach the city before April 2nd, and I was therefore delightfully astonished when in 1957 its gorgeous presence appeared in my garden on April 1st. In 1958 I migrated myself elsewhere in early April, and so could not check the bird's punctuality; but this year it behaved more according to the book by not arriving until April 4th.

As I have hinted before, an earnest student of natural history in Delhi will often feel disconcerted by the ignorance which numerous birds display of what is written about them in local ornithological literature. Constantly they break the rules laid down for them by Hume, Stuart Baker, Whistler, Dewar and other pundits. For example, Hugh Whistler's *Popular Handbook of Indian Birds* is an invaluable reference work, clearly written and packed with accurate, illuminating information on various aspects of bird life; yet its estimates of the breeding seasons of many species are misleading. That is not surprising, for when the volume was first published more than thirty years ago the number of bird-watchers in India was small, and their knowledge of such matters as nesting habits was therefore scrappy. Even now, in spite of the devoted work of India's great ornithologist Salim Ali and his disciples, our knowledge is lamentably incomplete. I am sure that some species will take no notice of what I have written about them in this book and will behave differently. Birds are not uniform, regimented creatures; even members of the same families betray diverse temperaments and habits.

So Indian birds will continue for a long time to spring surprises on their devotees; but no surprise will ever be more pleasing than the arrival of a Golden Oriole twenty-four hours ahead of schedule. Even among the world's many beautiful orioles this individual is pre-eminent. It has a right-royal appearance. The female has lovely grace; and she seems to be aware of this, for she carries herself with self-confident dignity, appearing to flaunt her fine figure as she flies with slightly undulating movements through the sunlight. Her upper parts are yellowish-green, her wings are brown tinged with green, her tail is brownish-black tipped with yellow, and her whitish breast is washed with yellow and streaked with dark brown.

But if the hen is striking, the cock is dazzling. No Emperor was ever more regally robed. From head to tail he is golden-yellow except for a black stripe through each eye, black central tail-feathers and almost completely black wings. Here is masculine beauty at its boldest!

Nor is his radiance confined to his physical appearance. His voice, too, has bewitching quality. Its clear, liquid whistle is one of the pleasantest sounds issuing from the thick summer foliage where, shyly and modestly, he is apt to hide his grandeur.

IV

The pair of Redvented Bulbuls with a nest among the hollyhocks hatched two chicks on April 10th and a third on the following morning—ten and eleven days respectively after the last of their trio of eggs was laid. The youngsters grew rapidly, survived all the hazards of life in a nursery which sagged ever more perilously on its large leaf as they grew in weight, and leaped safely into the outer world soon after sunrise on April 22nd.

Three other Redvented Bulbuls' nests were built in the garden this April, all rather charmingly situated. My front door is sheltered from the assaults of monsoon rains by a large porch, and its pillars on either side of the entry are covered with thick-growing coral creeper. Every year Redvented Bulbuls built nests in the creeper,

April

one against each pillar. This year, again, in the last week of March a pair of birds started making their home among the leaves on one side of the door, and on the very same morning another pair began work on a nest in the foliage on the other side. By early April a hen bulbul was sitting on three eggs in each nest. They were situated like military guards posted in sentry boxes on either flank of my door. But the bulbuls were less concerned with guarding me than with being guarded by me. They instinctively knew that by laying their eggs on my driveway, where the traffic of human beings and vehicles was very heavy, they would be safer from raids by animal enemies, who would think twice before approaching all this diplomatic bustle. Certainly the nest-owners seemed to enjoy a serene sense of security, for they continued to sit on their eggs unperturbed while people gossiped, motor-cars hooted and lorries trundled backwards and forwards within a foot or two of their faces.

On April 22nd three fledglings flew safely from one nest; but in the meantime the second clutch of eggs had suffered a disaster. They were stolen by some thief, and the parent birds deserted. However, either the same couple of bulbuls or another promptly built a third nest a few inches away in the same creeper; and less than a month later their family of chicks made a successful getaway.

By contrast, three pairs of Redwhiskered Bulbuls started nests in different parts of the garden in April, but each was abandoned by its timid owners before they laid eggs.

A third type of bulbul paid short visits to the garden at various times of the year; but it never built a nest there. It was the Whitecheeked Bulbul, which prefers thick, wild bushes to light garden shrubs for the purpose of breeding. The three species of bulbul are similar in size and form, but different in plumage. They all sport head-crests, but whereas those of the Redvented and the Whitecheeked varieties are not very prominent, that of the Redwhiskered is a well-developed, jaunty cockade. This head-dress and the bird's crimson moustachios, spotless white shirt-front, broken black necklace and bright red tail-base make it the dandiest of the trinity. The black cheeks, white rump and crimson vent of the Redvented Bulbul, and the white cheeks and sulphur-yellow vent of the Whitecheeked Bulbul are the most distinguishing features of its two relatives.

V

Indian Robins were other early nesters on my property. Usually they plaited their neat, cup-shaped repositories for eggs inside holes in rotten tree trunks or in crevices along brick walls; but one pair experimented with a different environment. On the lawn stood a brand new, 'highfalutin' dovecote designed by a Ministry of Works architect especially for my flock of tame Fantail Pigeons. The pigeons scorned the place. Its design was too fanciful, its accommodation too roomy, and its amenities too hygienic for their old-fashioned, squalid taste. They preferred an ancient, tumble-down, overcrowded, dirty dovecote nearby—as a community of slum-dwellers might refuse to budge from a ramshackle tenement to which they were accustomed into a clean modern housing estate. So the pigeons continued to puff out their chests, spread their tails and coo love-ditties to each other in their old sordid lodgings—and the new dovecote was 'To Let'.

Some Common Mynahs became its tenants. Those exuberant creatures are not at all pernickety about where they should build their unsightly nests—in a pauper's shack or a king's palace. Their taste is catholic, and so they felt no objection to the fabulous dovecote. With customary gusto two pairs made homes, laid eggs and reared chicks in its boxes. So the genius in the Ministry of Works had not laboured in vain.

Indeed, his handiwork attracted double patronage, for others besides the mynahs became ambitious to occupy one of the nest-boxes. In 1958 a pair of Indian Robins began carrying building material into it. But Common Mynahs are not tolerant characters; they resent other types intruding on their private pleasance; and they do not believe in peaceful coexistence. So they harried and bullied the robins until those smaller birds, after two days of courageous

April

perseverance, admitted defeat and abandoned the attempt.

The inspired official who designed the dovecote had provided shutters for each nest-box which could be closed at nights to let the hoped-for Fantail Pigeons sleep in peace; so this year I half shut one of these so as to make the entrance to its cubicle too small for a Common Mynah but large enough for an Indian Robin to enter. I hoped a pair of the latter birds would again be tempted to use the place for nesting, and would achieve their heart's desire undeterred. That is exactly what happened. On April 6th a pair of robins began carrying building material into the box, and for many days the cock and hen both laboured energetically at the task. They took much longer than usual to construct their nest, because they first had to cover the spacious floor of the apartment with a deep-pile carpet of fine twigs, and then to fashion a depression in its farthest corner to hold their eggs. Mynahs often protested as the robins flew in and out of the sanctuary, but in vain, for they could not force an entry and destroy its new furnishings. Just over a month after the robins commenced to build, they led their youngsters safely from the dovecote into the outer world.

VI

Birds' nests exhibit many different styles of architecture. One of the simplest and yet most ingenious is that adopted by Tailor Birds. Those pretty, cheerful, clever creatures construct a nest by sewing the edges of two or more large leaves together with bits of cotton, cobweb, cocoon silk, or other similar fine fibres, thus forming a sort of purse with an open entry at its top. To make the stitches the tailors—for that is what the birds literally are—use their sharp beaks as needles. They then upholster the interior with horsehair, thin grasses, cotton wool and down, forming soft cushions for eggs. Usually the nest dangles a few feet from the ground, but sometimes it is skied twenty feet or more up in the air.

An even more impressive architectural achievement is the nest of the Purple Sunbird. Whereas Tailor Birds are aided in their construction by ready-made materials in the form of leaves, these sunbirds contrive their creations where nothing existed before except thin air.

On April 13th I noticed the first sign that two sunbirds were inclined to produce a family, when a hen bird displayed her charms to a cock. She tilted her tail in the air, flirted her wings suggestively and gazed at him with dumb, sexy appeal. He appeared to take no notice on that occasion, but must have responded later; for on April 21st I saw her building a nest. She had begun it either that morning or else on the previous day, for the construction was still a shapeless collection of fine grasses suspended from a bougainvillaea stem.

Unfortunately the shrub stood close beside a path along which a thousand guests passed to and fro that afternoon to a garden party held in honour of the Queen's Birthday. Either the constant movements of the throng, or their ceaseless noisy chatter, or the boisterous music played by the band proved too much for the Purple Sunbird. Disturbed and frightened, she abandoned her labour.

Next morning she started to build a second nest in another bougainvillaea bush at the opposite end of the garden. As is almost invariably the case with these sunbirds, she received no help whatever from her mate. At rare intervals he would suddenly appear from nowhere, give a cursory glance at the progress of her work, sing a brief song of felicitations to her, and then disappear as quickly as he had come.

She, on the other hand, toiled ceaselessly hour after hour and day after day on a charming little creation. First she selected the most suitable tip of a drooping bougainvillaea stem on which to attach a chamber for her accouchement, and then she flew away to fetch the original strand of building material. As soon as she had stuck this near the end of the bough, she hurried away to find a second piece, and when she had added this to the first she promptly went in search of a third. In quick succession she brought dozens and dozens of fine grasses, bits of hair, twigs, silky fibres, strands of cobweb, small leaves and other substances with which to establish first a firm link on the slender bougainvillaea stem, then a sort of

April

loose string-bag suspended from this link, and afterwards a thick-walled nest woven on the foundation of that network.

I appeared on the scene when she was still engaged on the initial stage of the task. She worked with extraordinary energy and dedication, flying constantly to and from the site without allowing herself any interval for rest. I timed the periods between each of her visits, and the successive statistics written into my diary read as follows: 50 seconds, 60 seconds, 30 seconds, 50 seconds, 30 seconds, 70 seconds, 60 seconds, and so on, in a continuous series of arrivals and departures. Later her pace slackened somewhat, and my statistical notes record the intervals between her departures and next arrivals as 100 seconds, 60 seconds, 110 seconds...

I could not stay watching more than a quarter of an hour, so I did not observe how long she maintained this intensity of labour; but I returned to the bougainvillaea several times later that morning, afternoon and early evening, and whenever I went she was still travelling to and fro fetching building material, carrying it to the gradually forming nest, fitting it with deft movements of her beak into the right place, and then flying away again to fetch another load of stuff.

Some months afterwards I read Mr E. H. N. Lowther's account in his book *A Bird Photographer in India* of how he watched more protractedly the toil of a hen Purple Sunbird similarly employed, and how he timed her visits to her uncompleted nest. He reckoned that she came to it forty times in the first 40 ½ minutes, and fifty times in the first 60 ½ minutes. Later she slowed her pace, rested completely for 2 ½ hours in the midday heat, and then resumed again.

On the first day that I watched my bird she was already building before 6 a.m., was slaving hard whenever I looked later in the morning and afternoon, and was still on the job when I paid a final visit at 5.55 that evening; so she worked more than a twelve-hour day, no doubt with periods of rest now and then. For the next two days she continued at more or less this pace, and on the fourth morning had reached the stage of importing soft upholstery into the nest's interior. Then disaster befell. When I visited the bougainvillaea that noon I found the nest broken. Its link with the supporting branch had been severed, and its torn bag hung limp against a lower stem. Some animal must have despoiled it, either an egg-eater hunting for eggs or a nest-builder coveting its material.

Probably the tragedy had only just occurred, for, as I watched, the hen Purple Sunbird flew into the bush, went to the nest and examined it curiously. She uttered soft, anxious noises, and the cock bird promptly came and perched on a stalk overhead. He stared down from aloft, but did not approach nearer. The hen paid two perplexed visits to the nest in quick succession, alighting each time on its ruined wall and inspecting its interior. Then she flew to a near-by bough of the bougainvillaea, where she gazed nonplussed for a few more moments at her shattered handiwork—and then started unconcernedly preening her feathers. The cock stayed on his perch and likewise began to clean his plumage.

It was a notable example of the matter-of-fact manner in which birds take such disasters. There was no avian equivalent to human wringings of hands, sheddings of tears or gnashings of teeth. An awful thing had happened; but that was how Nature conducted her affairs; and there was nothing the little sunbirds could do about it, so they turned automatically and immediately to the next thing of importance to them—preening their feathers. Later the hen would start to build another nest.

She actually began it four mornings later in a shrub next to the bougainvillaea where she had made her first attempt.

A Purple Sunbird takes anything between five and, in unusual cases, fifteen days to complete a nest, and the finished article is a work of skill and beauty. Dangling from its branch-hold, responsive to every breeze, it is an oval bag shaped rather like a small mango, with an entrance near the top of one side (where a dip occurs in a mango's profile), a cornice projecting above this doorway to keep out rain, and a tassel hanging from the nest-bottom which seems to serve no purpose except decoration. Inside is a snug, well-cushioned apartment where the hen lays her two or three eggs.

Everything considered, I give the prize for the finest architectural achievement in my garden to the Purple Sunbird, though some samples of the nest are more artistic than others. Different individual birds of the same species—like different members of the human race—seem to be endowed with somewhat varied temperaments and talents. I have seen sunbirds' nests that appear untidy and formless compared with the neat, shapely ovals of others. The hen of whom I have written was a truly accomplished artist.

VII

Eighteen different species of birds built nests in my garden this April. They included Tailor Birds, Purple Sunbirds, White-eyes, Ashy Wren-Warblers, Indian Robins, Whitethroated Munias, House Sparrows, Redvented Bulbuls, Redwhiskered Bulbuls, Yelloweyed Babblers, Jungle Babblers, Common Mynahs, Brahminy Mynahs, Crimsonbreasted Barbets, Green Barbets, Little Brown Doves, Ring Doves and Green Parakeets. In earlier years Green Pigeons and Hoopoes also nested on the property in April—making a list of twenty different types.

The most surprising of these nests was that of Yelloweyed Babblers. A pair of the birds often flitted through the flower-beds and shrubberies, travelling, feeding and consorting together almost as inseparably as if they were Siamese twins. Though I hoped their companionship would in due course yield fruit in the form of a nest, I did not suppose that product would be in season until the rains came, for authoritative books declared that these babblers do not breed except in the monsoon. I was astonished therefore when on April 21st, almost three months before the time was ripe, I found a nest belonging to the yelloweyed ones concealed in a herbaceous border. Moreover, it was already near completion. Bound tightly between four supporting stalks of tobacco plants, it was a deep, thickly woven cup of grasses, much more painstakingly and substantially formed than most nests, which must already have taken ten days or more to build. One bird, if not both, continued with devoted industry and skill for another three or four days to put finishing touches to the structure.

Two days later a babbler was sitting tight in the nest from early morning until mid afternoon. The nest's cup was so deep that only the bird's eyes and forehead were visible peering cautiously above its edge, with its tail sticking upright behind. Not wishing to frighten it, I refrained from looking into the nest until the babbler left of its own accord. Then I saw one glossy, red-mottled egg lying within.

For three days a bird sat deep-sunk in the nest most of the time, but whenever I looked inside only one egg lay there. This seemed a very small mouse to be produced by the babblers' mountain of labour; and I felt an indefinable concern, for Yelloweyed Babblers are supposed to lay a clutch of three or four eggs. My worry increased when I observed that throughout the third afternoon no bird at all occupied the nest. When I watched again that evening there was still no babbler on view, so I went to see whether the egg also had disappeared. As I approached the flower-bed I heard a heavy rustling among the tobacco plants containing the nest, and a moment later a jackal slunk away from their clump and trotted across the lawn with its tail tucked cravenly between its legs. A solitary egg still lay in the nest, but on the ground below was a crushed mass of vegetation where the jackal must have crouched hidden for several hours.

The egg remained in the nest for another three days; but I never saw the babblers near the place again. After that the egg also disappeared.

I supposed the birds had been scared away by the jackal. Or was their apparent unorthodoxy in building a nest two or three months ahead of schedule punished by their laying only one egg, and an addled egg at that—a misfortune which they instinctively realized after a few days' incubation?

VIII

It is an exciting moment when eggs come to the point of hatching.

The first clutches laid by Tailor Birds reach that crisis by the beginning of April. One morning I saw four eggs lying neatly in the little bower of a nest; but when I looked again that afternoon only two remained—and beside them sprawled a couple of minute chicks. One youngster was still in process of emerging from incarceration, for its hindquarters were enclosed in half an egg. The egg-shell had been trimly chipped round its middle, and the other half lay in fragments on the nest floor. The second chick, also, could not have been emancipated more than an hour or so; yet at once it craned its neck and opened its beak towards one, already making the instinctive motions for being fed.

When I inspected the family twenty-four hours later a third chick was semi-hatched. It was free of its egg except for a wide collar of shell encircling its neck like a halter round a donkey. Bits of broken shell lay on the floor. The fourth chick did not hatch until the following day, when the nest was completely clean of egg-shell. As soon as each youngster freed itself from this encumbrance, a parent carried the broken shell away and dumped it at a distance. Like most species, Tailor Birds are very house-proud.

IX

Sometimes in early April a pair of Hoopoes indulged in flirtations, their antics looking like an exhibition of trick flying above the lawn. The birds climbed and tumbled prettily in the air, advancing towards each other and then retreating again in movements reminiscent of the stately pirouettings and curtsyings of two partners in a minuet. But the Hoopoes were more impassioned than those dancers, their crests being alternately raised and lowered, their wings fluttering rather excitedly, and their mutual gazes betraying a touch of infatuation.

At the same time these handsome birds were making nests, resorting for that to holes in trees and similar crevices. In two Aprils a pair laid eggs on a ledge beneath the corrugated-iron roof of a shed in the garden. I used to see the parents inserting themselves with beakfuls of food through one of the apertures under the roof, but could not see the chicks hidden within. I caught my first glimpse of them when they emerged in early May. For several days after that they and their parents stayed together as a party in the neighbourhood.

One year I watched the family on its first day out of the nest. An adult Hoopoe and four youngsters scurried about on the lawn, feeding. The fledglings had the same elegant, cockatoo-ish figures as their parent, with similar theatrically striped markings; but they were slightly smaller in build and their beaks were much shorter. Those delicately down-curving implements had not yet developed a strength which enabled the youngsters to dig effectively into the ground and fetch up worms; so the quartet were dependent on their elder for getting food. Wherever it hastened over the grass they followed, their bills held expectantly, like four little Oliver Twists always asking for more. The adult bird had a full-time job keeping them satisfied. It ran hither and thither, twisting and turning this way and that in search of signs of subterranean treasure in the form of bugs and worms. The whole garden was a colossal larder stuffed with these delights; but they took a little finding, and then a lot of unearthing. Every few moments the bird jabbed its beak into the ground with pecking, nibbling and grabbing movements; but usually with no result. Now and then, however, it felt a delicacy, seized it and lugged it into the light of day. Immediately the young Hoopoes ran to it, opening their beaks in pleasant anticipation; and one or another of them received the prize. The adult fed each in turn. Once when a youngster tried to get two helpings in succession the parent reprimanded it with a sharp peck, and then deliberately gave the catch to another. But none of them ever seemed replete.

Occasionally one fledgling strolled away to try an experiment in foraging on its own, simulating the prospecting, digging and delving of its elder's long beak with its own shorter one. The effort was praiseworthy, but fruitless; and soon the youngster gave up and ran back for more rations from its tutor.

Once when the parent caught a fat worm and was about to

feed a youngster, a Black Drongo pounced at it viciously, trying to steal the food from the captor's very mouth. It was a characteristic piece of audacity by a drongo. The aggressor did not actually strike the Hoopoe, but hovered in the air within an inch of its head, seeking by forceful persuasion to induce it to drop the booty. At that the Hoopoe jumped into the air and fluttered defiantly in the drongo's face; and these martial courtesies were exchanged several times between the two protagonists. It was a pretty duel. All the time the Hoopoe stubbornly kept the worm dangling in its beak, refusing either to drop or to swallow the morsel. The food was for a youngster, and none but a youngster should enjoy it.

After a while the Hoopoe wearied of the contest—for the drongo was very persistent—and turned and flew thirty yards away. A young Hoopoe who had been a spectator of the combat flew after it. But the drongo also followed, and the fight began again. Suddenly the fledgling joined in. Opening its wings and pecking towards its parent's assailant, it made as if to shoo the bully away. That settled the matter. The drongo apparently judged its opponents now had a decisive superiority of numbers, for it turned tail and fled. At once the old Hoopoe gave the worm to its youngster—a well-deserved reward for its courageous help.

During the next few days the young Hoopoes' beaks grew quite rapidly, and the birds became steadily more proficient at feeding themselves. Soon they became independent of their parents, and the family broke up.

X

Many other animals besides birds lived in the garden. Among the most engaging of them were small Striped Squirrels, with sleek brown-and-white striped backs and long fluffy tails. They seemed to be at home in all places and all circumstances, whether they were gambolling across the lawn, playing touch-last in a flower-bed, sprinting up and down tree trunks, or leaping from bough to bough high in the air. No situation disconcerted them. Usually they ate their food squatting on their haunches on the ground and munching titbits clasped between their forepaws; but one day I saw one hanging upside-down by its hindlegs in a tree—in the posture of a bat asleep—nibbling nonchalantly at a nut clasped between its hands. As soon as it finished the fare it coolly righted itself and scampered away.

These squirrels usually had a pleasantly relaxed, mutually tolerant, civilized relationship with the birds. Always two or three of them, and sometimes more, joined the mixed party of Fantail Pigeons, Green Parakeets, Ring Doves, Jungle Babblers and other characters who breakfasted together when grain was thrown on the pigeons' feeding ground. Sometimes a bad-tempered parakeet swore at a squirrel and tried to nip it, if it thought the squirrel was grabbing more than its proper share of food; but the furry little beast calmly side-stepped the assault and went on eating.

Invariably the squirrels were calm and pleasant-mannered. Once a House Crow and a squirrel were guzzling near each other. The crow—a giant compared with the pigmy animal—became irritated and pecked at its neighbour. The four-footed diner jumped agilely sideways, landed three inches away and continued its meal as if nothing had happened. Thrice the crow repeated its attack, and thrice the squirrel took the same evading action. It did not protest or attempt to retaliate; it was neither angry nor frightened; it remained serene. When the crow then lost its temper and made as if to exterminate the squirrel, the little beast turned tail and cantered, as if casually, to a bird-bath five yards away, where it helped itself to a drink. Clearly one of the qualities of these animals is not only physical but also emotional self-control.

One April morning a squirrel scampered across the lawn and started to climb the trunk of a mango tree. A Common Mynah flew at it to baulk its ascent. The squirrel immediately went into reverse, scurried down the tree and ran halfway round its foot, intending to scale the trunk on the other side. Thereupon the mynah also alighted on the grass, walked round the tree in the opposite direction, and confronted the squirrel again. The little creature turned and retraced its steps to its original position; the bird did likewise; and once more they came face to face where they had first met. Both stared at each other for a startled moment, then promptly turned and repeated the performance. They did this three or four times, each clearly inspired by a contrary purpose—the squirrel wishing to avoid the mynah and climb the tree, and the mynah determined to prevent this. The conflict was conducted by both parties in a most gentlemanly way, as if they were engaged in an innocent game of hide-and-seek.

Soon a second mynah appeared and assumed a policeman-like stance on the opposite side of the tree from the first bird. There the squirrel on its next journey unexpectedly ran into it. The animal betrayed momentary astonishment, collected its wits, realized that it was now effectively checked by two opponents working in collaboration—and turned, retreated across the lawn and climbed another tree trunk instead.

The pair of Common Mynahs had a nest in the mango tree! It was built in an empty petrol tin tied on a rope which I had placed among the branches to frighten parakeets away from eating the ripening fruit.

XI

Some Green Pigeons stay in Delhi all winter, but the species is commoner in summer. In 1957 and 1958 pairs nested in my garden.

Throughout the last week of April 1957, I watched a Green Pigeon sitting tight on a nest high in a tree, evidently incubating eggs. Sometimes its mate stood on a near-by branch. They were a handsome couple, stout and prosperous looking, with identical glorious plumage in which green, yellow, yellowish-green and grey were the predominant colours, offset by touches of lilac, chestnut and black. When the sunlight shone upon them they were a perfect picture.

While I was gazing at the nest and its occupant on the morning of April 30th—trying to discover whether, as I suspected, two chicks had hatched that day—another winged creature darted through the surrounding foliage and settled on the tree trunk just below the nest. It was a trim-figured, long-tailed, gaily-coloured, swashbuckling member of the crow clan called a Tree Pie. At once the Green Pigeon betrayed alarm, rose to its feet and peered anxiously over the nest-edge. And well it might! The Tree Pie began stabbing viciously with its beak through the thin twig floor of the nest, seeking to punch a hole there.

The pigeon grew more agitated, shifting its position nervously from place to place in attempts to get a better view of its half-concealed enemy. Fortunately help was near at hand. The pigeon's mate flew into the tree, dashed angrily beneath the nest and drove the trespasser away.

The hen bird settled calmly in its couch again, and the cock remained on guard close by. All seemed well.

That afternoon, however, as I sat drinking tea on a veranda a hundred yards away, I heard a sudden agitated chattering of babblers, bulbuls and other birds in the vicinity of the pigeons' nest. With an instinctive foreboding, I ran to see what was afoot. Sure enough, a skirmish was being fought there. Once more a Tree Pie (no doubt the same as in the morning) had perched just below the nest and was trying to tear a hole through its floor. A furiously embattled Green Pigeon stood on the nest with its neck-feathers fluffed out in anger, its tail widespread and its wings held akimbo like the arms of a boxer poised to deliver blows. At each stab by the Tree Pie the pigeon leaned over the edge of its platform and tried to peck the aggressor; but the pie crouched close to the trunk, keeping just out of reach and refusing to be deterred by mere threats. The combat was spirited and vicious, and the attacker's beak jabs at the nest-floor had murderous force. It was indeed bent on murder, for all crows dearly love to sup on the eggs and chicks of other birds.

I wanted to throw a stone at it to drive it away, but realized that such intervention on my part would be futile, for the Tree Pie would merely withdraw, wait until I departed, and then return to the fray. Moreover, what right had I to interfere? The ways of Nature may be mysterious, but presumably there is a motive behind her acts; she knew better than I did how to order properly the affairs of birds and beasts. I was not much good at my own job, so why should I presume to try to teach her how to do hers? Therefore I left her to settle this dispute between two of her attractive creatures in whatever way she decreed.

I hoped that the pigeon's mate would fly once more to the rescue, decisively reinforce the defence, and relieve the siege of the family. But it did not put in an appearance. So the grim duel between the pigeon and the pie continued without interruption, except for an excited running commentary by a small audience of babblers and other birds, who mobbed the Tree Pie much as some species mob an owl. Alas, they expressed their hostility only in bold words, not in effective deeds.

The two protagonists stabbed and counter-stabbed, the Tree Pie successfully dodging every blow from above and continuing to drive its own thrusts home from below. Every now and then it shifted its stance, either to increase the force of its attack or else to evade better the ripostes. Thus the battle continued for about five minutes, neither side yet gaining a decisive advantage.

The Tree Pie's brutal persistence was sickening to behold, and the pigeon's defence grew more and more desperate as it leaned ever further over the nest-edge in attempts to strike the foe. Perhaps the Tree Pie deliberately moved further out of reach so as to tempt the pigeon to crane its neck too far and overbalance; or perhaps the enraged pigeon purposely jumped off the nest in a final attempt to come to grips with its enemy. Whatever the cause, suddenly the pigeon fell through the air, the pie dashed at it, and the two birds tumbled towards the ground, locked in mortal combat.

They passed out of the vision of my field-glasses, and I did not see what happened in the next few moments; but they must have disengaged quickly, for some seconds later I saw the Tree Pie fly triumphantly, alone, to the nest. Alighting on the edge, it started pecking cruelly at some object there; and through the scanty, now partly transparent nest-floor I could see a flapping of tiny wings. So a chick had recently been born. The killer struck again and again, and then appeared to tug and wrench at something—perhaps dismembering its victim. A moment later I saw another spasm of tiny wing-beats, probably the protests of a second chick. Then the crow hopped off the nest, perched for a brief while on a near-by branch, and afterwards flew away. Two Jungle Babblers chased it, hurling shocking curses at its head.

Against the now darkening sky I saw the silhouette of a small corpse dangling from the Tree Pie's beak. I tried to follow the bird, but it disappeared into a thickly foliaged tree, no doubt to enjoy an undisturbed meal.

Returning to the ravaged nest, I found a disconsolate Green Pigeon standing there. Though its beautiful plumage was unruffled, the bird was obviously agitated, looking around sharply in all directions, constantly shifting its stance, troubled by some sad, unaccustomed absence. Finally it squatted in the nest with a sort of automatic, instinctive, unreasoning gesture. Was this the vanquished bird revisiting the awful scene of its defeat, or was it the partner of that bird arriving unwarned at the site of the tragedy? I searched, but saw no sign of a wounded pigeon on the ground below.

Next morning the nest was empty, a deserted ruin; but two Green Pigeons were flying around in the garden, evidently very much interested in each other. The male constantly chased the female and made naughty advances to her whenever they settled in a tree. He thrust out his chest at her and kept raising and then depressing and immediately afterwards raising again his tail, as if to display to her its attractive chestnut-hued, buff-tipped feathers. She seemed quite impressed, but not disposed to surrender herself then and there.

No doubt she changed her mind later.

XII

The cold-blooded killing of two young pigeons by a Tree Pie was nothing unusual in the garden. Pillage, robbery and murder were normal, and frequent, occurrences in bird society there, for the avian population included several characters who were professional thugs. In human society they would have been branded as thieves,

April

kidnappers, assassins, sadists or some other criminal types, but in bird society they were accepted as perfectly respectable members of the community. Of course they were feared by the species on whom they preyed, and those victims often expressed strong disapproval by mobbing them. But no moral code condemned them as less law-abiding citizens than the others.

Among the pirates who operated regularly in the garden—in addition to the hawks, kites and eagles, who came less often—were House Crows, Tree Pies and Koels. They often stole their neighbours' eggs or nestlings. Certain four-footed animals also hankered after fresh-laid eggs or day-old chicks, such as mongooses, lizards and an occasional monkey. There was nothing extraordinary in the spectacle of a mongoose climbing a tree in pursuit of a scent leading it by the nose to a well-stocked birds' nest. To prevent this I had broad tin collars fitted round the trunks of the trees most popular for nesting, since the mongooses' clawed feet could not grip and cross the metal. That was my sole interference with the normal functionings of nature.

As a result of the presence of this criminal class, the casualty rate among eggs and chicks was enormous. In some cases it seemed excessive and shocking. It was highest among species who built exposed, ill-protected nests. The countless flimsy-looking, easily accessible stick platforms constructed by Ring Doves, Little Brown Doves and Red Turtle Doves were all despoiled. Not one pair of doves ever managed to rear even a single fledgling. The same applied to several pairs of Green Pigeons. The experience of Redvented and Redwhiskered Bulbuls was little better. In 1957 ten Redvented Bulbuls' nests, were built in the garden, and in only one did a family of youngsters safely survive. In 1958 eleven Redvented Bulbuls' nests were built, and again from only one did fledglings eventually escape into the outer world. In 1959 these bulbuls had better luck. Of six nests that I observed, three had their eggs or chicks stolen, while the families in the other tree lived to become adult birds.

Every one of the Redwhiskered Bulbuls' nests constructed in

the garden was robbed. In some cases their eggs and in others their chicks were kidnapped by voracious marauders. The same was true of all the nests completed by Purple Sunbirds. Some, though not all, of the Tailor Birds' nests suffered a similar fate, as did a few homes of other species. Many families nevertheless survived; but almost the only nests that completely escaped murderous assaults were those of parakeets, barbets and other types who laid their eggs in tunnels deep in tree trunks. Those holes were veritable fortresses against attack—though mongooses would have raided them if I had permitted those nimble beasts that liberty. Several times in the breeding season I watched Green Barbets—in addition to half a dozen other species of birds—vehemently dive-bombing a mongoose as it trotted across the lawn, sure evidence that the barbet recognized the animal as an enemy. So violently was the bird's hostility aroused that it repeated its attacks over and over again, stooping each time so close above its target's back that it almost struck a physical blow. Usually the mongoose remained completely indifferent, continuing its progress with admirable nonchalance; but once the assault became so dangerous that it flinched, broke into a sudden gallop and raced to cover in the nearest shrubbery.

April

SEVEN

THE COPPERSMITH

I

That attractive creature, the Crimsonbreasted Barbet, is more familiarly known as the Coppersmith Barbet. The first name it owes to its colourful appearance and the second to its drab voice. It is indeed a rather gorgeous sight emitting a very dull sound. Not that its figure is perfect, for like all barbets it is short-tailed, squat and perhaps a trifle top-heavy by the strictest standards of avian beauty; but if its vital statistics leave something to be desired, its plumage—which is identical in both sexes—displays a delicious pattern of greens, yellows, reds and black.

I shall refer to it in future as the Coppersmith for simplicity, and because this small, six-inch-long barbet is generally recognized by that bucolic title. The nickname was originally suggested by the bird's love song, which is a single note frequently and insistently reiterated, like the oft-repeated knock of a hammer on metal in a village coppersmith's workshop.

Coppersmith Barbets are all-the-year-round residents in my garden. At any season they can be seen, usually perched idly in a tree-top, but sometimes searching energetically for food in a woodpecker-ish manner. Crouching upright against a trunk, the bird taps and explores the bark with its beak to extract a grub or insect; for although Coppersmiths are mostly fruit-eaters, they also occasionally like these meatier delicacies. In winter they relapse into silence, but when warm weather returns their monosyllabic but repetitive call is one of the most persistent of Nature's small bugles heralding a new spring. As the barbet utters each phrase its whole body jerks with the effort, as if it were suffering from a bad attack of hiccoughs.

Most species start to build nests only about a week before the necessity arises to accomplish that task, but Coppersmiths anticipate the need months earlier. Nest-building is for them a formidable labour. Whereas bulbuls, babblers, mynahs and most other garden birds take only a few days to throw a nest together, a Coppersmith devotes at least as many weeks to the work. That is because it lays its eggs at the bottom of a tunnel bored deep into a tree trunk. Usually it chooses a trunk which is already beginning to decay, so that its excavations are assisted by the timber being softer than would otherwise be the case; but even so the process of hammering, chipping and chiselling a gallery far into the wood with the solitary implement of the barbet's tough little beak is protracted. When the nest is complete its entrance is a neat round hole through the bark no wider than is required to admit the bird's body, and from that doorway a tunnel leads two or three inches horizontally into the tree and then plunges perpendicularly many more inches down into the trunk. A few wood-chips on its floor provide a rough mattress on which the hen barbet in due course deposits three or four plain white eggs.

In my garden the Coppersmiths' breeding season lasts from February until September. In preparation for its opening I have seen birds tapping at the beginnings of holes in likely trees as early as the previous September. I am not sure how regularly or frequently the little barbet works on the job, for I never enjoyed leisure to make a thorough study of its habits. This is one of the many matters touching Indian birds which needs further research. My observations seem to indicate that barbets' nest-building practice varies to some extent from individual to individual. Most of them (I think) work daily for several weeks in the autumn until their tree-tunnel has developed to a point where they can use it as a bedroom throughout the winter. A bird which I watched carefully in 1958 started hammering at the smooth surface of a tree trunk on October 2nd, toiled very hard for several hours every day for the next three weeks, had driven a neat, round shaft three inches horizontally and another seven inches perpendicularly down into the trunk by October 23rd, and then stopped work. Well it might take a rest! In twenty-one days it had punched into tough timber a hole ten inches long and two inches in diameter. In the following February it found a mate and then resumed work on the tunnel, deepening it another inch and enlarging the chamber at its bottom so that there would be room to house a young family.

Most Coppersmiths in the garden seemed to follow this pattern of completing the nest-shaft in two stages, the first in the autumn for sleeping purposes and the second in the following spring for breeding purposes. But every pair of Coppersmiths did not excavate a new nest every year. Some hens used the same shaft in successive years, merely deepening it each twelve months, until some plunged more than two feet down into a tree trunk.

II

One November 10th I watched a Coppersmith beginning its task. It had just chipped a small patch of bark off a tree and was starting to hammer at the surface of the wood beneath. Three weeks later the hole had penetrated three inches into the trunk. Possibly its timber was tougher than in the case of the barbet I have cited above, or perhaps this second bird was a lazier worker than that model of industry. Anyway, to force this bore through the obstinate, resistant trunk the barbet turned itself into a veritable battering-ram. With its feet gripping the tree just below the entry, and its short tail pressed like a woodpecker's against the bark to act as a purchase, it swung its body vigorously backwards and forwards in and out of the hole, striking repeated, determined beak-blows at the tunnel's interior. It was working at the inside walls, loosening and stripping them to enlarge the cavity—and every now and then it would turn its head and fling a billful of sawdust out of doors. Its sole implement was its short, thick beak, which it used sometimes as a hammer to bash the timber, sometimes as a chisel to cut away chips of wood, and at other times as a shovel to gather up heaps of those chips and hurl them into outer space.

Two months later the tunnel had advanced not only inwards

but also downwards into the tree trunk. One morning then I watched the Coppersmith at work. First it chipped at the entrance to the hole, either slightly enlarging the opening or else smoothing its edges; and then it thrust its head further into the shaft and struck repeatedly at the back wall where it turned to descend towards the prospective nest. Later the bird penetrated deeper still, more than half its body disappearing from view. Only its hind-quarters protruded from the trunk, and they jerked every time its fore-quarters stabbed at the interior. Sometimes the jerks were so many and swift that the barbet's posterior seemed to shake like a jelly. Each spasm of this carpentry was short, lasting only between five and ten seconds; but it was remarkably vigorous. After every sustained spell the bird withdrew itself backwards from the tunnel, its entire figure reappearing, with a mouthful of sawdust gripped in its beak which it cast away with a sharp twist of its head. The toiler would then immediately thrust itself into the gallery again for another bout of excavation. It continued to labour thus, ceaselessly, for half an hour.

Previously the bird had worked alone, but now a second Coppersmith—no doubt its prospective mate—sat on a branch close by. Sometimes this barbet faced the nest-hole and watched its partner's progress, and at other times it turned its back and gazed around the garden; but it did not stir from the bough. Probably it was there partly for companionship, but mostly to act as a sentinel against unfriendly or unduly inquisitive intruders. The building bird also kept a sharp look-out for uninvited visitors, for whenever it withdrew its head from the tree trunk it glanced round to make sure it was unobserved by any creature except its betrothed. Eventually the guardian barbet grew restless and flew away; and the other at once ceased working, cast itself from the tree, and followed.

A few days later the pair of Coppersmiths were still industriously on the job; but now the nest-shaft had been sunk deeper into the tree. I observed the progress one morning in late February. When a bird was at work it disappeared completely inside the tree trunk. With feet gripping the inner instead of the outer wall of the tunnel, it stood upside down, and only the extremity of its tail was visible within the entrance. The vibration of its hind-quarters revealed how rapidly and powerfully its beak was operating as a pickaxe stabbing at the wood; and its spells of carpentry often lasted for two minutes at a stretch. At the end of each effort the barbet would emerge, fly to a neighbouring branch and scatter a beakful of sawdust in the air. Then at once it returned to its labours.

While it slogged at the timber its mate flew to the tree and perched on the trunk beside the nest-entrance. This was the cock bird, the hen being usually, if not invariably, the worker. She must have heard his arrival, for she promptly extracted herself from the hole. For half a minute the two stayed motionless side by side, gazing at each other intently, with their beaks almost meeting in a kiss, like a pair of fond lovers. Then they flew together to a bough where the male fluttered his wings eagerly at the female and fed her with a plump berry which he had brought for her. She accepted the gift, but would not pay for it (as he had hoped she might) by satisfying his masculine ardour; for when he made the next suggestive movement she flew away. He chased her in and out among the branches of the tree, but she always withdrew before him; and, realizing that she was not in a mood for intimacy, he turned tail and disappeared. She instantly returned to the nest-hole, popped inside and continued her house-building.

She worked feverishly hard in those days, for—as that incident revealed—a new stage had arrived in her and her mate's domestic life. Deep instinct told her the nest must be finished quickly—just as deep instinct also told him he should woo her with gifts of food and proposals of marriage—for it was almost time she laid eggs at the bottom of the tunnel which she had spent so many months in boring.

A few days later the nest was completed. Whenever one of the Coppersmiths flew to it after that, the bird immediately disappeared inside. Probably it was making small, final arrangements for comfort in the inner chamber; for it soon came out again with no sawdust in its beak, and settled elsewhere in the tree. Neither barbet visited the nest often, both spending more time squatting idly on some near-by bough—and every now and then they engaged in a flirtation. Having finished the long labour of making their cradle, they proceeded deliberately to the next task of making youngsters to lie in it.

III

The courtship of Coppersmiths is a lively, playful, passionate episode. Mild preliminary gestures of love-making begin to be exchanged towards the end of February, and soon afterwards shameless (of course) public exhibitions of Coppersmith copulation are frequent. The female bird sits stodgily—rather cowlike—on a branch near her nest-to-be. The male then arrives, always with a tempting berry gripped in his beak. In Coppersmith life this is the equivalent of the bouquet of flowers or the box of chocolates which a human wooer brings to the lady of his choice. Often the cock bird does no more than present the fruit to the hen, and she accepts it (taking it in her beak from his) and swallows it. He flies away, and she stays in the tree. Soon afterwards he returns with another similar gift; and thus he comes again and again, each time with an offering.

Every now and then, however, his demeanour when he alights near her indicates that he thinks the moment has come when he may claim a favour in return for his generosity. On those occasions he eyes her sentimentally and wriggles his posterior several times from side to side in a lascivious manner. It is his preliminary expression of sexual desire. Then he flies closer, perches right beside her, half opens his wings, and flutters them vigorously in a shivering sort of motion. He makes no attempt to offer her the food in his beak, though he holds it there for her to see as a prospective reward for compliance with his wishes. Either she is willing, in which case she crouches and he hops on her back; or else she is unwilling, in which case she shows utter indifference to his advances. Sometimes in the latter case he presses his suit with renewed ardour until she makes her rejection more emphatic by shuffling a few paces away from him. I have even seen two or three rude females express their coolness towards a suitor by lifting their tail in his face and letting a splash of excrement drop. At that he accepts the repulse, ceases his passionate gestures, gives her the berry without more ado, and flies away—no doubt hoping for a friendlier reception next time.

When she accepts his proposal and he mounts her, he stays sometimes only briefly but at other times for a longer while on her back, perching there and flapping his wings excitedly as their mating occurs. Sometimes he mounts her two to three times in quick succession, presumably when the operation is not successful at the earlier attempts. She does not stir, crouching with her head sensuously tilted until she tires of his weight on top of her, when she indicates discomfort by shifting so that his balance is upset and he is compelled to dismount. All the time he clasps in his beak the fruit which is a bribe for her, and only when their love-making has concluded does he present it to her. She accepts it then as a matter of course—and he flies away.

Frequently copulation takes place three or four times within a few minutes in the course of separate food-bearing visits paid by him to her; and these potent flirtations continue for several days. The order of procedure is precisely set by (presumably) centuries-old custom, and it never varies. For example, on the occasions when mating takes place I have never seen a cock present the berry to a hen before coition occurs; the bribe always follows the granting of the favour. Not many days later she produces the results of their embraces in a clutch of eggs laid in their apartment.

One morning I watched an intriguing incident. The male of the pair of whom I am writing had just visited the nest-tree, and the two had been deliciously, rapturously amorous together. He flew away, and she stayed contentedly on the branch which served as her bridal bed. Then another cock bird arrived in the tree and approached her purposefully in a succession of short flights from perch to perch. He seemed distinctly interested in her—but suddenly her spouse reappeared, flew briskly to her side, and then darted angrily at the intruder and drove him away. It seemed a charming instance of a husband defending his wife's virtue.

IV

As soon as the clutch of eggs is complete the birds begin to incubate them. Both share in the labour, taking turns to squat for long spells in the inner darkness of the tree trunk. To a watcher outside they are invisible, but periodically he sees one of them fly to the tree and perch near the entrance; after a few moments the sitting bird emerges through the door and speeds away; and the new-comer promptly disappears into the hole to take its place. The barbet inside the nest must hear the whirring of its partner's wings as it alights, or by some other means become at once aware of its arrival, for usually no call or other audible signal is exchanged between them. Sometimes, however, the new-comer does call two or three times to the hidden bird, announcing its readiness to take a turn at keeping their eggs warm.

Coppersmiths are jealous guardians of their home, resenting the intrusion of any other creature near its doorway. I first noticed this when a Common Mynah happened to perch beside the nest-hole and start extracting grubs from a branch of rotten wood there. The barbets who owned the property were sitting not far away, and evidently decided the mynah was too near their nursery. Each in turn rose in the air and swooped angrily down at the visitor, exactly like small aeroplanes dive-bombing a target. They passed so close over the mynah's back that they almost touched it; and then they swerved up again to a higher bough. Shortly afterwards they both returned to the charge, once more following each other in rapid succession. Every time a Coppersmith hurtled past it the mynah flinched, but then it nonchalantly resumed its search for grubs. Again and again the barbets launched their attacks, but to no avail. Eventually the mynah hopped away of its own volition.

At various times I saw the Coppersmiths dive-bombing not only Common Mynahs but also Brahminy Mynahs, Jungle Babblers, Magpie Robins, other Coppersmiths and even their much larger cousins, Green Barbets, all of whom for one reason or another ventured near the nest. Once a Green Barbet actually flew to its entrance, alighted below its threshold and began hammering with its beak at the wood in an evident attempt to enlarge the opening. No doubt the bird fancied the place as a possible nesting site for itself. But the tunnel was already occupied by my friends the Coppersmiths, and I suspected that at that very moment one of them was sitting on the eggs within. So I waited to see what would happen.

A Coppersmith squatting higher in the tree became alarmed and flew agitatedly from bough to bough round the Green Barbet. Then it plucked up courage to dive-bomb its large relation, hurling itself several times on rushing wings towards the interloper. The Green Barbet turned its head on each occasion and made a swift stab with its formidable, broad-sword beak at the attacker—who evaded the thrust. But after a while the Green Barbet became disturbed by this constantly repeated interference with its work, cast itself from the tree trunk and perched on a neighbouring bough. Soon afterwards, however, it fluttered back to the nest-site and again began chiselling frantically at the entrance. Three times the Coppersmith's attacks drove it away, and three times it returned to continue its hammering at the nest. The smaller barbet's assaults became more vicious, the bird passing closer and closer over its adversary's head, and as it passed it emitted an irate buzz of protest. It had all the fury and dash of a Spitfire—though it never actually struck the Green Barbet a physical blow.

At its third visit the Green Barbet stayed a long time at the nest, becoming increasingly indifferent to the ineffective swoops of the Coppersmith outside. It now poked its head frequently into the entrance to batter at the inner walls. I was not sure whether the second Coppersmith was indoors; but began to hope this was the case when, suddenly, the Green Barbet withdrew its head hastily from the cavity as if it had been struck an unexpected blow. Four times that happened, and then the bird abandoned its attempt to requisition the nest. It flew away. Sure enough, shortly afterwards a Coppersmith's head emerged from inside, peering out cautiously. It had been there all the time, and whenever opportunity offered made its effective contribution to the defence of the family.

On another occasion—later in the year, when the first brood of fledgling Coppersmiths from numerous nests had left their nurseries and ventured into the garden—a few of those youngsters alighted in the tree. They showed an inordinate interest in the nest-hole, which disconcerted an owner keeping guard nearby. The adult barbet kept darting at them and shooing them away. But their curiosity always got the better of them, and they soon returned to the site. Older Coppersmiths would have taken the proprietor's strong hints that they were inviting trouble if they persisted in their inspections, and would have flown away; but these youthful birds were ignorant, inexperienced and inquisitive. They were so obstinate that the adult Coppersmith grew tired and less zealous in his attempts to drive them off, perhaps recognizing that they were only innocent children of his own tribe who could do no harm.

Taking advantage of this lull in his attacks, the youngsters flocked to the tree trunk. It happened to display not only the true nest-hole, but also two 'false' holes where Coppersmiths had begun to excavate tunnels and then abandoned them unfinished. Nature had planted in the fledglings an instinctive interest in little round holes bored into rotten tree trunks. They were fascinated by the sight of three of them all together on one stump, and they could not resist the temptation to crouch beside them, gaze closely at them and test them with their bills.

One went to the actual nest-hole several times, attracted to it like an iron filing drawn to a magnet. It examined the entry carefully, and then rashly poked its head inside. Gradually it grew even bolder, pecking first a few times at the opening in a childish effort to improve it, then thrusting its head confidently within and taking a few stabs at the back wall, and finally heaving half its body into the tunnel. At once it was in trouble. Its wings began to flap wildly, its body shook with convulsions as if it were suffering an apoplectic fit, and for a few moments it struggled in vain to extract its head from the noose into which it had placed it. At last it succeeded, reappeared, and hurled itself panic-stricken from the tree. Presumably the parent bird indoors had struck at it and for a while gripped its feathers in an infuriated beak-hold.

The youngster had learned its lesson, and did not take such liberties again. Nevertheless, it and its companions stayed in the tree and continued to alight from time to time beside the false nest-holes—though they now gave the true nest a wide berth. They kept making reconnaissance inspections of those others, in spite of the older Coppersmiths' renewed fluttering concern and occasional protesting plunges at them. Nothing would deter them. They behaved like a gang of juvenile delinquents indifferent to all attempts by staid grown-ups to discipline them.

The incubation of the eggs began early in March. Many times every day a bird would fly from the nest-hole after a period of sitting, and its mate would immediately go inside to relieve it. I often saw this changing of the guard. The chamber with the eggs is very confined, measuring only a few inches across at the bottom of a deep shaft. Squatting in its darkness must be a tedious pastime, and sometimes the barbet on duty got bored. It climbed up the tunnel and poked its head and shoulders out of the entrance for some breaths of fresh air and glimpses of the garden, protruding from the tree trunk like a jack-in-the-box.

My observations of several nests incline me to believe that incubation lasts rather more than a fortnight, which is longer than earlier writers reckoned. I cannot be certain, for it was impossible to view through the tree trunk the precise timings of developments in a nest, and even in the interests of exact scientific knowledge I could never bring myself to cut a tree open and so upset its occupants. I therefore had to judge the progress of events by the behaviour of the parents, trying to determine the date when incubation began by the commencement of their long vigils indoors, and the date of the hatching of the eggs by their first arrival at the tree with food.

When the chicks emerge from their egg-shells both adults share the happy duty of feeding them. As the youngsters grow, this becomes an increasingly taxing task, and the parents start it at sunrise in the morning and continue all day until sundown, perhaps with a respite during the hottest hours. At first they bring tiny morsels, but these gradually get larger as the infant barbets wax in size and their appetites become more voracious, until the elders carry to them veritable banquets of successive courses of berries.

They fetch these provisions from afar, at intensive feeding periods coming to the nest-tree every few minutes with fresh rations. On arrival a bird perches first on a branch at a distance and looks round cautiously to make sure it is not observed by unfriendly eyes. Sometimes it then flies direct to the nest, and at other times it approaches in a series of short stages, glancing round carefully again at each staging-post to assure itself that no enemy is watching. Finally it alights just below the entrance to the nest, with the fruit bulging from its beak; and then it pops inside. A minute later it re-emerges, its beak now empty, and dashes away to seek another portion of food.

Periodically when a bird leaves the nest after a visit its beak is empty of food but stuffed with another substance—a small package of a chick's excrement. Like all parent birds, the Coppersmith is very particular that the youngsters' nursery shall not be fouled. It carries the stuff to a distance, and then drops it.

For many days the adult birds disappear right into the nest-shaft to feed their family sprawling helpless inside; but as time goes on and the youngsters grow bigger and can stretch their hungry mouths higher towards its entrance, the parents do not need to reach so far. Then they disappear first three-quarters and later half and later still only a quarter indoors. Eventually the head of a youngster itself appears at the window, poking out eagerly whenever an elder arrives with food and greedily snatching the delicacy.

V

Often in the following days a Coppersmith nestling's face gazes from the hole in the tree, staring with wonder on the strange, sunlit, colourful earth out of doors. At first it is shy and nervous, and withdraws quickly into the tunnel at the appearance of any unknown monster like a strange species of bird, a squirrel, or an ornithologist; but later it gains confidence and shows a perpetual, insatiable interest in goings-on in the outer world. Its face turns constantly in various directions, sometimes peering upwards towards the sky, sometimes downwards to the ground and at other times twisting quickly from side to side to follow events. No child at a Christmas pantomime watches the antics on a stage with more fascinated curiosity than does an infant barbet making its first observations of Creation.

Its juvenile plumage is less colourful than the costume of its elders, lacking, for example, the scarlet cap and the yellow-and-scarlet bib of a mature bird. As there is room only for one barbet to look from the nest's doorway at a time, sometimes one member of the young family and sometimes another appears there. Each can be recognized by slight differences in their facial markings.

They spend several days peeping inquiringly from the doorway before the firstborn finally takes its courage in both wings and leaps into outer space. During that period it becomes increasingly restless in its nursery; its countenance assumes an ever more self-assured look, its glances in this and that direction grow more alert, and it cranes its head and shoulders further and further from the nest-hole in efforts to glimpse more—until it seems on the point of tumbling headlong out of the tree. Obviously it is sorely tempted to end its long childhood confinement, and to escape into the beckoning landscape and claim the privileges of adolescence; but it is restrained by some inner instinct whispering that the time is not ripe for that grand adventure. It is also counselled by its parents to remain prudent a little longer. More than once as I watched a youngster leaning far out of a nest-hole—apparently on the verge of deciding to make a jump—an adult bird flew from a near-by bough, darted close past the nestling's head and buzzed an alarm-call as it went by. The fledgling at once withdrew inside, disappearing altogether from view. Its parent had no doubt uttered a warning that it was getting too rash and should stay closer indoors.

But at last the great day of emancipation dawns. One morning I witnessed a young Coppersmith make its breakaway from home. At 5.20 a.m. its face first appeared at the entrance, and for the next hour and a half it seemed to dither between making a dash for freedom that morning, and staying another day confined in the tree trunk. Sometimes it appeared enterprising and ready to depart, but at other times it seemed passively content to stop where it was. I began to think the exciting moment of action had been postponed for twenty-four hours. Yet one circumstance made me doubtful. During that long, uncertain interval neither parent came to the nest with food. On the contrary, both adults occasionally appeared in the tree, settled on a bough and gazed at the nest-hole as if waiting for something significant to happen. Once or twice they flew to the entrance and popped for a few moments inside, without food. They seemed to go from curiosity, to see what was afoot indoors; and when they emerged again they did not fly away as usual, but perched once more near the nest, waiting there to observe. I suppose they knew the days of their youngsters' dependence on them were over; and probably they understood intuitively that they should not bring berries any more, so that the harsh stimulus of hunger would prompt the fledglings to go and forage for themselves.

At 6.50 a chick was staring from the nest-hole. Suddenly it fell out of the doorway, as if accidentally—though it must have ejected itself deliberately. Clinging frantically upside-down on the bark below the threshold, it flapped its wings wildly and cocked its stump-like tail awkwardly in the air. A parent barbet flew immediately to a bough close by, ready to offer help in case of need. The fledgling manoeuvred cautiously to correct its stance, and finally perched upright on the trunk in the comfortable pose of an adult arriving to feed the inmates. But it looked around anxiously, peering for a place whither it could make its next move. For nearly a minute it hesitated nervously; and then it cast itself from the trunk and fluttered to a near-by branch. It landed clumsily but safely. At once the older Coppersmith flew to its side; and a moment later the second parent joined them. For a while the three stayed together; and then both elders darted away while the youngster stayed prudently where it was.

Soon one adult returned with food and fed it. Afterwards that bird flew to another branch, and the young barbet promptly followed. The second parent reappeared, bringing its offspring another ration of fruit; and for a brief spell the trio perched together once more. Then an adult flew out of the tree and the youngster dashed after it, speeding through the air with the apparently effortless skill of a professional aviator.

The second mature Coppersmith returned to the nest, disappeared inside, and after a while re-emerged carrying a package of excrement in its bill. At a distance it threw this away, and then went back to the nest. One or more chicks were still at home and would no doubt fly later.

I think the three or four youngsters leave the nest on two or more consecutive days. From the time when they hatch to the moment they fly, about five weeks elapse.

It is a long stay in the nursery, much longer than that of the chicks of most small species. One reason for this may be that when a fledgling Coppersmith leaves its birthplace it must be able to look after itself entirely. In the case of numerous species the parent birds remain with their progeny for many days and even weeks after they take to their wings, continuing to bring them food, teaching them gradually how to forage for themselves, finding roosting places for them at nights, and in other ways protecting and guiding them through the transition period of adolescence. But that does not happen in the case of young Coppersmiths. When they leap from their nests they jump at once into independence. They and their parents bid each other farewell for ever. Neither mother nor father accompanies them on their next series of journeys and adventures; they must take complete care of themselves. That is possibly an explanation why they stay so long in their nests, building up their strength and self-reliance for this supreme undertaking.

Why do their parents not accompany them? Because the pair turns at once to the business of producing a new clutch of eggs, a fresh brood of chicks, a second family. They hardly lose a minute before starting that effort. I saw this at the nest which I have been describing. On the morning of the first chick's flight, when one or two youngsters were still in the tree-trunk home—but also about to leave—a sudden change occurred in the parents' behaviour. One of them was perching at the nest-entrance, about to go inside to visit the family, when its mate arrived on a neighbouring bough. The new-comer immediately shook its rump from side to side in the abandoned gesture associated with courtship—the preliminary expression of sexual desire. For nearly two months no flirtation had occurred between them; they had given no thought to making love; their energies were absorbed by other interests. But now those interests were fading; their young family was graduating from tutelage—and automatically, instinctively, abruptly they switched back to another set of concerns. Nature revived in them reflexes and mechanisms which would lead without delay to the accomplishment of their next function in the continuous cycle of Coppersmith survival and existence.

That afternoon I saw the hen Coppersmith sitting passively in the tree, waiting for something to happen. Before long it occurred. Her lord arrived with a berry as a gift for her. Eyeing her with fond approval, he gave the naughty wiggle-waggle to his posterior which is the customary inquiry whether he might seduce her. She consented, and crouched obligingly as he hopped on her back. So the whole series of processes by which a new Coppersmith family is born and bred began all over again.

It is remarkable—that insatiable, compelling urge of Nature to promote the reproduction of her species, which makes a pair of Coppersmiths within a few minutes of bidding goodbye to one set of offspring begin the actions necessary to create the next set. The instance I have described was no freak; I often saw it repeated in the cases of other Coppersmiths at other nests.

Exactly two months later, to the day, I watched the fledglings of that second brood leave home. It was the end of June. When their second family departed the parents felt they had done their duty; they did not contemplate creating a third. The hen bird continued to sleep in the nest-shaft every night; and later she would deepen it for next year's activities.

Afterwards, for many more weeks, other young Coppersmith families were being fed by other parents in other nurseries; and I have seen nestlings still in their nest-holes as late as mid September. Before that, industrious, unattached adult birds are already giving preliminary taps to tree trunks in search of suitable sites for their next year's nests, and soon afterwards they start to carpenter these in earnest.

Being a Coppersmith is a full-time, all-the-year-round job.

EIGHT

TWO MYNAHS

I

The Common Mynah is as typical an Indian figure as a fakir, a maharajah or a babu. In character it is nearer a babu than a maharajah or a fakir, for it struts around self-importantly, talks ceaselessly, and does not always display impeccably refined taste. Indeed, a hypersensitive critic might assert that this bird is a trifle vulgar. Presumably the adjective 'common' got attached to its name because the species is so numerous and widespread that its members appear everywhere, and are one of the commonest sights in the Indian landscape; but the word might equally well be interpreted as suggesting that the mynah is common in quality as well as in quantity, that its personality is not quite so cultured as it might be, that its manners leave something to be desired—that, in fact, Common Mynahs are not entirely comme il faut.

The bird's black and brown plumage is unenterprising, though the white flashes on its wings and tail-tips in flight are rather decorative. Nor does the yellow wattle on its cheeks behind the yellow beak really add to its pulchritude; the feature is a rather ugly birthmark. A mynah's figure is trim enough, but there is a hint of swagger in the way it throws its chest out as it walks, of clownishness in its ludicrously pompous air, and of quarrelsomeness in its attitude to other breeds. But it is blessed with some engaging talents.

Its skill as a mimic is, for example, remarkable. An incorrigible talker, its chattering rarely ceasing, its voice is customarily rather harsh and raucous, not wholly agreeable to the ear; but at other times it is melodious, and occasionally a listener, enchanted by a sentimental carolling issuing from a tree-top, wonders what new sweet songster has arrived—and is astonished to discover that it is a Common Mynah pretending to be a prima donna. Its repertoire is extensive. I have heard one uttering a softly agitated, repetitive murmur in seeming imitation of an Ashy Wren-Warbler whispering its alarm notes, or shrieking loudly like a bird of prey proclaiming its fierce presence, or gabbling with inconsequential, nonsensical insistence in perfect imitation of a group of Jungle Babblers squabbling close by. I have even seen a Common Mynah perched on a tree trunk in the posture of a woodpecker or a barbet and hammering at a hole in the bark in apparent emulation of one of those birds. On that occasion the performance was a failure. The mynah was apparently trying to enlarge the hole with its beak, as those other species do when they are nest-building; but a dozen vicious pecks made no impression whatever on the obstinate timber. The bird grew mightily irritated, and at every successive beak-stab got more furious—but still to no avail. At last it gave up in frustration and flew away.

Had it actually watched one of the numerous barbets in the garden chiselling its nest? Or had it heard the loud rat-a-tat-tat which resounds as a woodpecker batters on a tree trunk? And was this an extraordinary example of the mynah's love of mimicry?

Its cleverness in copying sounds enables it under proper tuition to become quite an accomplished linguist. These mynahs are favourites with people who like to keep pet birds in cages. They are probably popular because they so readily pick up a few phrases in English, Hindi, Mandarin or any other human tongue, and are therefore an unfailing source of entertainment. I remember entering a friend's house one day and seeing a type of mynah perched on a chair-back in the sitting-room.

No one else was there, and the bird apparently felt it should do duty as host.

'How are you?' it inquired in English with a suspicion of a Bengali accent.

'Very well,' I answered.

It cocked its head curiously and observed, 'Damn your eyes!'

I felt truly welcome.

Sometimes the birds' comments on affairs are more unprintable than that. Like parrots, Common Mynahs seem particularly fond of English swear-words, which they utter with fruity gusto; but in that, of course, they merely reflect the taste of their masters.

They seem to have a keen appreciation of life. Endowed with even more energy than most species, they are among the first to start gossiping in the early mornings, are perpetually bustling hither and thither, and show an insatiable curiosity about anything and everything around them. No matter how foul the weather they never appear depressed. They can adapt themselves to any circumstances, and their dispositions are cheerful. Often they seem to be enjoying a joke, for their demeanour frequently has a suggestion of the comical.

When the nesting season arrives they are catholic in their choice of sites. Their skill as builders is nothing to boast about; indeed, it is deplorably elementary, for they merely collect a lot of miscellaneous twigs and other materials and dump them rather shapelessly together in any convenient hole or corner. On my property they amass these unsightly piles in rotten cavities in tree trunks, drain-pipes on the house wall, nest-boxes in dovecotes, footholds above sun blinds on verandas, empty petrol tins strung in mango trees to scare away greedy parakeets, and other likely vantage points. If I allowed them indoors they would similarly defile ledges supporting curtain pelmets, recesses on bookshelves behind serried ranks of volumes, brackets holding electric fans, and other convenient nooks. There is no skilled workmanship about their structures; the builders do not patiently and cunningly weave or plait or sew into attractive shapes the repositories for their eggs. When the nest is finished it looks like an untidy heap of rubbish accidentally blown together by gusts of wind.

Yet, if there is no distinguished craftsmanship about it, there is often a touch of artistry. Common Mynahs have an aesthetic instinct—but unfortunately it is an instinct akin to the gaudy, tinselly taste of a suburban boarding-house landlady. Their notions of interior decoration are decidedly vulgar. Thus they delight in tucking into the walls of their home a piece of silver paper from a discarded chocolate-box, or a strip of glistening Cellophane wrapper torn off a cigar, or a bit of tattered, dirty rag picked out of a gutter. When they spot one of these objects lying on the ground they rush at it enthusiastically, seize it in their beaks as ardently as gourmets sampling an especially succulent morsel, and fly with it to their nests with a look of beatific joy on their faces.

One morning I saw a mynah which had carried a piece of shiny toffee-paper to its nest-hole drop it by mistake at the entrance. The look of disappointment on the bird's face as the scrap fluttered to the lawn twenty feet below was pathetic. However, its mate appeared, noticed the glittering fragment on the grass, was likewise irresistibly attracted by it, and hopped down to recover it. The first bird gave a mighty chirrup of gladness as the second arrived at the nest and carried the booty safely indoors.

One of the Common Mynah's virtues is its courage. It sometimes displays daredevil recklessness. I have seen it giving chase to monsters much bigger than itself, like kites; repeatedly dive-bombing a mongoose who ventured too near its nest; disputing violently with a pair of Spotted Owlets about a building site; and in the vanguard of a troupe of birds mobbing an eagle. The species certainly has the bravado of its impertinence.

A pair produces a clutch of between three and six eggs, and out of the eggs emerge in due course a group of frowzy-looking chicks. For a few days they are respectfully silent; then they start to emit a low buzzing whenever they feel hungry; and before long they squawk lustily at the slightest provocation. So the population of bumptious, garrulous, cheeky Common Mynahs is reinforced. But if some of their qualities have dubious merit, others are more endearing. These mynahs add lively touches of cheerfulness, humour and gaiety to society in the garden. They are the clowns in the circus there.

II

Only once did I see a Pied Mynah in the garden, but another cousin of the Common Mynah is also a permanent, all-the-year-round resident there. This is the Brahminy Mynah. It, too, is an indubitably Indian character, but with a somewhat different nature from its relative. As its name proudly declares, it is a Brahmin, whereas the Common Mynah betrays signs of belonging to a lower caste. Possibly for this reason the Brahminy Mynah appears a dandy, whereas the Common species looks a buffoon; it usually (though not invariably) maintains a quiet reserve, whereas the other is a chattering extrovert; and it wears a certain solemn air in contrast to its cousin's boisterous cheerfulness.

The Brahminy Mynah is a creature of real beauty, with a slim figure, silky sleek plumage, and lovely, subtle colourings. Both sexes look alike. The crown of its head is sable with a crest jutting out behind; the face, neck and underparts are rich buff; the back and wings are grey edged with black; the tail is brown tipped with white; and the thighs and vent are pure white. A green tinge lights the sparkling eyes; the bill is blue at the base, greenish in the middle and yellow at the point; and the legs are bright yellow.

Yet occasionally the birds reveal traits of lesser breeding reminiscent of their commoner cousins. Sometimes a suggestion of cheekiness infects their strut; they, too, are inclined to decorate their nests with cheap bric-a-brac; and they can suddenly become irate and hurl loud curses at uninvited intruders near their eggs or youngsters.

They usually nest in holes in tree trunks; but, unlike barbets, they do not excavate these caverns for themselves. Their fine beaks are too feeble for such heavy work. Not for a Brahmin the weeks of menial labour which barbets put into tunnelling a home! Brahminy Mynahs wait until other, slavish creatures have completed the task, and then appropriate the result for their own use. They favour particularly the handiwork of Green Barbets, no doubt because the size of its accommodation exactly suits a mynah's needs. A Coppersmiths' nest-hole would be too cramped.

This arrangement is not unduly inconvenient to either party, since Nature (with her usual competence in such matters) provides that in many cases a pair of Green Barbets finishes breeding about the time when a couple of Brahminy Mynahs wish to begin. Nevertheless, there are occasional clashes between individuals of the two species who become rival claimants to the same desirable piece of property.

One June I saw an encounter of that sort. For several weeks a family of Green Barbets had occupied a tunnel bored deep into a jacaranda tree. The eggs had hatched, the chicks were grown up, and it was time for the youngsters to leave home.

As I approached the tree one morning I heard a commotion and saw two barbets perched on a bough on one side of the nest-entrance, while a pair of Brahminy Mynahs stood on a branch on the other side. One barbet crouched stock-still, but the other was agitated; and suddenly it darted viciously at the mynahs. They promptly shifted their positions, fluttered to the nest-hole, poked their heads inquisitively through its doorway, and then returned to the bough from which they had just been rudely driven. At once the barbet uttered a war-cry and hurled itself at them again, jabbing its beak towards them as it passed close above their heads. They retorted with angry screams and retreated prudently to a perch slightly further away. But not for long. Soon afterwards they went back to their first stance, only to be targets for another furious assault by the barbet. At that they flew once more to the nest-entrance, alighted beside it and inspected its threshold. Clearly they were extremely interested in it with a view to occupation.

I looked at the second barbet. It still crouched motionless, as if it were a casual, unconcerned spectator of the brawl. Then I saw that it was a youngster, slightly smaller than the adult bird, with paler juvenile plumage and a shorter beak. I realized it must be a fledgling which had made its first exit from the nest only a few minutes earlier. So naturally it lacked the experience, equipment and emotion to join in the battle being fought by its parent.

The mature bird had all those attributes, and exerted them

with splendid vim whenever the mynahs came near the youngster. Yet for all its forceful fury it could not drive them away. If they retreated a few paces now and then, it was only a tactical withdrawal. Soon afterwards they would leap back to a bough close by the fledgling, with what I thought foolish stubbornness, for the old barbet looked capable of murder.

I wondered whether the barbet was more obsessed with defending its nest than with protecting its youngster, and concluded that the latter was the case; for it seemed comparatively unconcerned when the mynahs perched at the nest-hole and poked their faces within, permitting that liberty with impunity. Only when they settled near the juvenile bird did its agitation rise to fever pitch and cause it to hurl itself with fearsome velocity at them. From this circumstance I gathered that the rest of the family of young barbets had already left home, that the fledgling in the tree was the last of them to go, and that its parent was shielding it as it made its getaway.

Probably the mynahs had watched the nest for several days, understanding instinctively that the barbets would soon depart, that this ready-made residence would then be empty, and that they might take vacant possession of it. They wished to produce a family themselves and were compelled by such a strong, elemental urge to acquire a secure lodging for their eggs that not all the frightening attacks of the barbet could deter them from their purpose.

So the noisy, lively conflict continued. For a long while the younger barbet looked on with strange indifference; then it grew bored and decided to go exploring in the tempting new world around it. Quietly it stretched its wings and sped into another tree ten yards away, where it hopped cautiously from one branch to another, nibbling now and then at foliage as if it were rather intrigued at the novelty of using its bill. After a few minutes it became even more adventurous, spread its wings again and flew unfalteringly across the lawn to a shrubbery at the far end of the garden.

Its parent was so preoccupied with waging war against the mynahs that it did not notice this momentous event; and the birds' quarrelling continued long after the fledgling departed. Indeed, before the combatants stopped to draw breath the youngster had taken yet another step away from its birthplace, disappearing across the shrubbery into the next-door garden.

Suddenly the older barbet glanced round to make sure that its offspring was safe—and to its obvious astonishment saw only an empty bough where the fledgling had crouched before. Immediately it broke off the engagement with the enemy and hastened to the branch to investigate this situation further. It gazed around in all directions, first intently, then with anxiety and finally with consternation. Shouting phrases which I had never heard uttered by a Green Barbet before—and which clearly meant, 'Hi son, where are you? Where have you gone? Please answer me'—its manner and speech indicated sharp alarm. Entirely forgetting the mynahs (who promptly dashed back to the nest-entrance), it started leaping from branch to branch in the tree, halting on each for a few moments to stare earnestly about it. It performed the oddest antics, often pirouetting on its own axis so that its head was where its tail had been an instant before, and twisting and turning and peering in quick succession in every direction, like a frenzied player of hide-and-seek searching for someone who had suddenly, unaccountably disappeared into thin air. The youngster did not materialize; nor did it answer its parent's insistent cries. The old barbet grew visibly more upset, retracing its steps many times from branch to branch, twisting, twirling, hunting, staring everywhere.

At last it felt convinced that the fledgling was nowhere in that tree, and (either by accidental chance or by unerring intuition) flew into the next tree to the precise spot where the youngster had stopped on the first stage of its journey. There it repeated its frantic movements and calls, once more in vain; and then it sped (again by the exact route taken by its chick) to the shrubbery at the far end of the garden.

Within a few seconds of its departure both mynahs had entered its deserted nest-hole. After a brief inspection they emerged, apparently satisfied with what they had found, for they flew to the ground, picked up some twigs in their beaks and carried them back to the hole. For the next twenty minutes they worked industriously, constantly fetching and carrying bits of building material into the jacaranda tree trunk. It was extraordinary; they did not lose a moment after the ex-owner's departure in starting to construct their own nest. The barbets had laid eggs on bare wood-chips at the bottom of their tunnel; but the mynahs were more fastidious. They wanted to cushion their chicks on soft grasses and twigs.

A few minutes later I heard the parent barbet's normal call uttered many times in quick succession from the next-door garden. Its tones were ringing and joyful, no doubt proclaiming its reunion with its youngster. I felt very pleased, for now everybody was happy again.

III

On another occasion I watched a contest between Green Barbets and Brahminy Mynahs for a nest-hole which did not proceed so smoothly. For a long time a tunnel in a tree had been the residence of two barbets who were the proud parents of a family of chicks. The youngsters had grown to weeks of discretion and had just left home. A couple of mynahs had been eyeing the place hopefully for several days, and now assumed that the adult barbets would move out so that they could move in.

But the barbets seemed to have different ideas, for after their young family had flown away they continued to frequent their old abode. Wondering whether they proposed to produce a second brood, I watched the situation with interest.

Early one morning I saw the two Brahminy Mynahs blithely carrying bits of grass and feathers into the nest. They were energetic in this pleasant duty, both frequently flying from the ground to the hole in the tree with beaks stuffed with building material, and then returning to the ground empty-billed to fetch more. Sometimes a twig was too long to be carried easily through the nest-entrance; it overlapped both sides, and the birds had to make several attempts before succeeding in thrusting it indoors. That seemed to be their only difficulty; no other obstacle presented itself. There was no sign, for example, of the Green Barbets who had lately occupied the place. Apparently they had lost interest and flown away, leaving the mynahs in undisputed possession.

But when I looked again half an hour later the scene had changed. The two mynahs were perched defensively side by side on a bough near the nest-hole, and on another branch equally near sat a Green Barbet. It looked cross and forbidding. Evidently the mynahs had taken too much for granted and were now found out in their plot to acquire the nest. They looked crestfallen in the face of their accuser, like two mischievous schoolboys summoned before a headmaster.

All three birds were quiet, but watchful of each other. Then, in a flash, the peace was broken. The barbet flew to the nest-hole intending to assert its right of entry; but immediately both mynahs launched themselves like a couple of shrieking thunderbolts at it, determined to prevent the attempt. They succeeded. The barbet perched at the threshold to the nest, but in self-defence had to twist its head and make fierce jabs at the attackers as they passed; and, in turning, it lost its foothold and fell from the tree trunk. Recovering its balance in mid air, it dashed furiously at the mynahs to shoo them away; but they refused to go. Both returned coolly to their base near the nest-entrance, and the barbet retreated to its bough close by.

For a few moments a silent, uneasy truce prevailed; and then the barbet made another attempt to visit the nest—with exactly the same result. The angry mynahs dashed at it in swift succession and would have struck it if it had not turned its head to stab at them. But the barbet could not at one and the same time face the nest-entrance to go indoors, and face its assailants to protect itself. Self-defence demanded the latter action; so it was forced to abandon its plan to disappear into the tree-trunk. After three or four vain efforts to jerk itself quickly through the entrance—each in turn foiled by an onslaught from the mynahs—it gave up the attempt, cast itself from the trunk and withdrew again to its bough. From there it launched several fresh offensives, hurling itself time and time again in a rage at its opponents, and trying to frighten them away; but they refused to leave the battlefield, merely moving a sufficient few inches each time to avoid the barbet's vicious beak-strokes, and then returning to their vantage point for guarding the nest.

The contest continued for about ten minutes and was packed with martial incidents. Almost every half-minute either the barbet darted at the mynahs to drive them away, and they took evading action; or else it flew to the nest-hole to effect an entry, only to be thwarted by an aggressive assault by the mynahs. It was a thrilling engagement, with constant attack and counter-attack between the rivals. All three were extremely angry, and the mynahs often yelled furiously. They had an advantage, for they were two swordsmen against one.

The barbet decided to summon help. It sought reinforcements. Settling on its bough, it began a string of barbetish yodels. 'Ko-ko-ko, Kotur-kotur-kotur' it called over and over again.

At first there was no response—but after a minute another Green Barbet appeared. Purposefully it flew into the tree. Now the teams were even—two against two—with the advantage perhaps tipped in favour of the barbets, since they were heavy-weight combatants compared with their middle-weight opponents.

The first barbet flew to the nest-entrance. Both mynahs at once attacked it; but they in turn were promptly assaulted by the second barbet. They had to scatter to avoid its lunging beak—and as they did so the first barbet successfully disappeared into the nest! The mynahs and the second barbet returned to their respective perches, to wait and see what would happen next. The brahminys looked very dejected.

Soon the barbet's face appeared in the tunnel doorway, its beak stuffed with a bunch of grasses which half an hour earlier the mynahs had laboriously carried into the tree trunk. It leaped from the hole, sped across the lawn, alighted in a distant tree, and with a contemptuous toss of its head cast the grasses into the air. The mynahs were helpless to stop this desecration of their would-be home, for the second barbet sat watching them two feet away, as alert as a policeman eyeing suspiciously a couple of well-known malefactors.

Before long the first barbet returned and perched at the nest's doorstep prior to re-entering the tree. Both mynahs at once flew desperately towards it; the second barbet immediately intercepted their flight; and the first barbet popped into the nest. Its audience of two hostile mynahs and one allied barbet resumed their seats in the front row of the stalls, to observe the next act in the drama.

After a minute it was performed. The first barbet reappeared in the nest-entrance with its beak filled again with a load of grassy rubble from the mynahs' now ruined building. It flew purposefully across the lawn to the same distant perch, and with a shake of its head hurled the stuff into space. The toss of its beak had an impatient, irritated, intolerant air. Then the bird returned once more to its home tree, to receive precisely the same reception as before—an attempted assault by the mynahs foiled by a successful defence by its mate. Within the next few minutes this all happened four times, every incident in the act occurring in exactly the same sequence each time.

On its next return to the tree the barbet disappeared as before into the trunk—but it did not re-emerge. Evidently it had completed the demolition of the mynahs' nest-to-be, and decided to relax and put its feet up at home. The mynahs waited ruefully outside, while the second barbet kept an eye on them.

Early the next morning the conflict was resumed. Apparently the barbets flew away at that time for breakfast, and the Brahminy Mynahs took advantage of their absence to stake out a fresh claim to the property. So long as neither barbet was in sight they busied themselves light-heartedly, carrying fresh building material into the nest-hole; but as soon as a barbet appeared their whole manner changed. Then they loafed around idly on nearby branches as if they were accidental, casual, harmless visitors. However, they observed the barbet closely, determined to prevent it from entering the nest.

That morning only one barbet appeared. Occasionally a scuffle occurred between the rivals, but of a milder nature than on the previous day. Periodically the barbet left the vicinity for a while, and at once the mynahs resumed their carriage of grasses, twigs, dead leaves and other material into the tree trunk. Afterwards the barbet would return, and promptly they assumed again an innocent demeanour. The barbet gave them dirty looks, but it made no attempt to go to the nest, seeming less zealous, less interested than twenty-four hours earlier—although still irresistibly, nostalgically attracted to the place.

On the following morning the mynahs appeared to be definitely winning this endurance test. Several times I saw them carrying building straws into the nest-hole without any qualms. Nevertheless, whenever a Green Barbet appeared they forthwith stopped their labour and perched quietly on their usual sentinel bough. And at the sight of them a reminiscent antipathy filled the barbet's breast, for it flew at them, harried them, and tried to 'shoo' them off—but with less vim than on the previous day, and with nothing like the sustained, bitter, triumphant dash of two mornings earlier. Its interest soon flagged, and it flew away. At once, as if automatically, the mynahs recommenced their fetching and carrying of nesting substances.

During the next two mornings they continued their work of construction with only an occasional interruption from a barbet. Yet that bird could still exert a restraining influence on them, for as soon as it appeared they ceased working, and the three birds would then perch in their customary stances, regarding each other with frigid hostility. They did not come to blows, however. Once the barbet yodelled mournfully for a minute or two, but no response came; its mate did not fly to its aid. Its call seemed like the vain bugling of King Charlemagne when Roland failed to appear.

Yet on the next morning—the sixth day of the contest—both barbets together mustered their energies to make a desperate attempt to recapture their lost fortress-home. As I approached the tree I saw a Brahminy Mynah and a Green Barbet sitting opposite each other, exchanging glances of mutual dislike. Suddenly the barbet flew to the nest-entrance, and at once the mynah launched its counter-attack. Gripping the tree trunk with its claws, the barbet turned its head to strike back; but at the same instant a second mynah appeared from inside the nest and stabbed the barbet in the face. The barbet lost its foothold and fell; and as it did so both mynahs closed with it. It gave a wild cry of pain as the birds descended together to the ground, where a scuffle took place. Then all three disengaged and flew separately to their various perches near the nest-entrance.

A second barbet now appeared, in response no doubt to its mate's agonized cry. It joined its partner, and after a moment's hesitation flew angrily at the mynahs. For the next several minutes a bitter pitched battle was fought. At the end of it the barbets must have been worsted, for they flew away, leaving their rivals in possession of the field.

Several times that day I saw repetitions of these vicious skirmishes. More than once the mynahs struck physical blows at an opponent, causing it bodily harm; and at the conclusion of one duel I saw a mynah carrying two white-speckled barbet's feathers jubilantly in its beak—flags captured from the enemy!

On the following day the barbets' protests against the mynahs' occupation of their nest-hole were milder, and on the next morning they ceased. By now the hen mynah had laid her first egg; and afterwards the pair were left unmolested. About twelve days later their chicks hatched, and the parents began bringing food to them. Just over a fortnight afterwards the faces of fledglings appeared for the first time in the nest-window; and six days later still these adolescent Brahminy Mynahs flew from home.

IV

That was not the end of the story of this nest-hole in a jacaranda tree which had produced first a brood of young Green Barbets and then a brood of young Brahminy Mynahs. When I visited it two mornings later I saw an adult mynah perched on a bough beside it—and a hen Green Parakeet sitting on its opposite side looking at the mynah with the same disapproving glances as had characterized the barbets. June was drawing to a close, and parakeets were beginning to look for likely cavities in tree trunks in which to lay eggs some months later. Parakeets seldom find lodgings naturally shaped to their requirements; so they have to improve them with their beaks. As it may take several weeks for the accommodation to be made comfortable, they start house-hunting early.

This parakeet was attracted by the dwelling which was presumably now for disposal in the jacaranda tree. But its inclination was premature; some Brahminy Mynahs had other ideas. In fact, they still frequented the place themselves. Whether they were the same pair as before, intending to produce a second brood, or a new couple contemplating rearing their first family rather late in the season, I do not know. All I know is that in the upshot they occupied the nest-hole for the next few weeks, that their youngsters were successfully born and bred.

Throughout those weeks the hen parakeet never lost her interest in the place. Indeed, on several occasions she perched on the tree trunk, nibbling at the outer edges of the doorway and gradually enlarging its size, even while the mynahs were feeding their chicks indoors! Sometimes the mynahs were displeased at this bland assumption that the apartment was already partly the parakeet's property, and drove her away; but at other times they philosophically tolerated the situation. Discreetly, the parakeet never interfered with their domestic family life.

At the end of July the young mynahs flew, and their parents also deserted the nest; and early in August the Green Parakeet began in real earnest to widen the nest-tunnel. She was, in fact, the parakeet whose tale I have already told; so the reader knows not only that she successfully reared a chick several months later, but also that as soon as those parakeets left, a pair of Common Mynahs produced offspring in the same spot. Thus, within a comparatively short period the same cavity in a jacaranda tree was the birthplace of a family of Green Barbets, two families of Brahminy Mynahs, a family of Green Parakeets and a family of Common Mynahs—a record of which any hole in a tree might justly feel proud.

NINE

MAY AND JUNE

I

Summer reaches its scorching climax in Delhi in May and June. Quite often the thermometer records a temperature of 110 °F in the shade, and sometimes it rises a few degrees higher. All day, day after day, the sun burns fiercely in a clear blue sky. Many people object to such unapologetic heat and flee for refuge from it to the Himalaya Mountains in the north or to the Deccan Plateau further south. In earlier years the whole Government of India joined in this annual exodus, transporting itself ponderously to the lofty summer capital at Simla; but now it remains in the plains. One reason for this is that the introduction of air-conditioning into houses and offices in New Delhi has made existence there quite tolerable throughout the hot months. However exuberant the temperature may be out of doors, one can work and sleep indoors in pleasantly cool rooms.

Nor are conditions outside too disconcerting for those who prefer unashamed sunshine, however hot, to the overcast skies, chilling rain-storms, sniffling mists and pea-soup fogs which are apt to afflict some of the Earth's other great cities. Customarily no recognizable drop of rain falls on Delhi in May, June and the first week or two of July; so the atmosphere is dry. The season's chief defect is an occasional dust-storm blowing clouds of sand from the neighbouring Rajasthan desert into the capital. Otherwise the climate is healthy for those who can stand it. One feels distinctly warm out of doors, but fresh and energetic; not moistly slack as one does in the humid though somewhat cooler tropics.

Nevertheless, the oven-like heat of Delhi then is a physical shock for those accustomed to live in temperate zones; and so, just as many of the city's local residents escape to the comparative cool of the nearest hills, prudent visitors from abroad also avoid the place during the sizzling hot months. That is one of the advantages of remaining in Delhi at that period. We are left alone there. May and June are a pleasant, peaceful interlude after the busy social winter season which has just ended, and before the next one begins. Delhi has two monsoons every year: first, the monsoon of rains which descends from mid July until the end of September; and second, the monsoon of V.I.P.s who pour into India's capital from October until the following March or April.

Delhi's lovely winter has become irresistibly attractive to distinguished tourists. In fact, many very fine birds fly into the city then—Kings, Presidents, Prime Ministers, Dictators, Foreign Secretaries, Field Marshals, Finance Ministers and other dignitaries galore come to bask in perpetually perfect sunlight, and incidentally to woo non-aligned India. It is almost impossible to keep pace with their comings and goings; they follow in one another's footsteps in a constant, continuous torrent; and they cause as much distraction, if not devastation, as any other flood. To do them proper honour Delhi's Cabinet Ministers, high Government officials, Ambassadors, Chiefs of Staff and other busiest inhabitants are summoned to attend non-stop programmes of airport welcomes, luncheon parties, civic receptions, public meetings, cocktail parties, banquets and airport farewells for each and all of them in turn. While the deluge lasts it is difficult to find time for coherent work, relaxed leisure, refreshing recreation, adequate sleep or any other normal activity. Of course, that is a trifling price to pay for the honour of assisting at the grand additions to international understanding and amity which (we must all hope) these entertainments stimulate.

But, naturally, many good citizens of Delhi heave sighs of relief when May arrives, the thermometer rises above 100 °F, and the V.I.P.s go home.

II

We are free then to do a lot of consistent official work. I for one write all my most longwinded, pompous and boring dispatches to London during the summer. We also have leisure after office hours to appreciate the amenities of Delhi, enjoy glimpses of personal friends, catch up on sleep lost in the hectic winter, and pursue a few chosen hobbies. For a bird-watcher the timing is fortunate, since the most active nesting period in Delhi lasts from April until August.

Unfortunately, some handsome species which I always hoped would nest in the garden then, never did. One of these was the Blue Jay or Indian Roller. In May this year a pair seemed on the verge of deciding to set up their establishment in a jacaranda tree overlooking the lawn, but for some reason they were discouraged. One morning both birds perched and stayed there for a while, eyeing covetously two or three likely cavities in its trunk, for Blue Jays favour spacious natural holes in trees. Next day one of them returned to make another reconnaissance of the available properties. First it gazed through the doorway of a cavern which some Common Mynahs had already commandeered. Uncertain, it hopped away, but returned a few minutes later for a second view. Presumably signs of occupation by the mynahs deterred it, for it left again and went to glance in two other holes in the vicinity. The jacaranda was in fact well furnished with these conveniences, but the best of them were already tenanted by Green Parakeets, Green Barbets and Common Mynahs. Some Jungle Babblers, too, owned a nest in a shrub below the tree, and all these local residents seemed to resent the Blue Jay's visit. Throughout its stay they perched round it wherever it alighted, swearing lustily at it. For a while the jay appeared indifferent to their rude reception, but eventually it abandoned its search for a home and departed.

Nevertheless, on each of the next few mornings it returned for quite protracted visits, hanging around in different trees, obviously attracted by the neighbourhood. Sometimes it uttered the ugly, grating—but presumably jubilant—ejaculation which is the courting song of this very beautiful creature; and I hoped that it and a mate would select my garden as a suitable paradise in which to spend their wedded life. No flirtation between lovers in bird society is more romantically dramatic than that of Blue Jays. In each other's company a pair work themselves up to a state of high excitement, soaring into the air and climbing, fluttering and somersaulting there in a paroxysm of emotion, uttering hoarse cries of passion all the while. The performance continues for many minutes with an intoxicated abandon that is astonishing. No tumbling acrobats of genius in a circus could cast themselves around more recklessly. The birds are literally head over heels in love, flashing their brilliant Oxford-and-Cambridge-blues wings as they flip hither and thither, ascending, hesitating, capsizing, falling and rising again in a breathtaking exhibition of the craziest trick flying. Often they plunge downwards like aeroplanes out of control, apparently intent on dashing their brains out on the ground, only to recover their equilibrium within a few inches of the grass and shoot up again like rockets towards the sky. Eventually their crescendo of emotion reaches its climax, and they alight on the earth to consummate their love.

It is these antics that earn the species their alternative name of Rollers. I hoped a pair would choose to spend their honeymoon in my garden, and for a while this seemed possible. For six consecutive mornings one of the birds perched in a tree and stayed unmoving for nearly an hour, for all the world like an established resident. The parakeets, mynahs, barbets and babblers had apparently become reconciled to its presence and left it undisturbed. Then a Shikra flew aggressively into the tree, and the jay left with a protesting cry. Some time later it returned to the same spot and dallied there for another long wait; but after that I never saw it again.

III

Another species whom it would have been fun to count among the inhabitants of 2 King George's Avenue was the Grey Hornbill. Numerous pairs nest every year in the early summer in Delhi. Their marital arrangements are very odd. When a hen bird is about to lay eggs she enters a large, naturally decayed chamber in a tree trunk and proceeds to seal up the entrance with a screen made mostly from her own dung, imprisoning herself within. She leaves only a narrow slit in the screen through which her mate can pass her food during the next few weeks. There she stays while she lays, incubates and hatches eggs, and until her chicks are about a week old. Throughout that period the cock bird pays regular visits to her, pushing berries and other titbits through the narrow slit for her and, later, for their brood of youngsters. Afterwards she breaks out and joins him in the labour of foraging for their fast-growing family.

These hornbills are large birds, measuring two feet long. Their huge, casque-topped beaks lend them a certain ugly charm, like gentle-mannered clowns. It always seemed to me that the hornbill's figure was ungainly to the point of appearing unnatural, for its oversized head-cum-bill did not seem to belong properly to its comparatively undersized body, and the diamond-shaped tail again looked out of trim with the curves of the hind-quarters—as if these three parts had been made for three different creatures, and then got stuck on the same animal by mistake.

A group of hornbills needs a spacious home, and unfortunately no tree trunk in my garden contained accommodation roomy enough for this strange household. But for several years a family was reared on the property of a friend a few streets away, and in May 1957 and June 1958 a party of two adults and four juveniles used to come sometimes to perch in a tree-top above my shrubbery. This was presumably shortly after the mother and youngsters had burst out of the chicks' birthplace.

Throughout the year Grey Hornbills used to visit the garden. Sometimes a single bird appeared and at other times a pair arrived together. They stayed for a while, expressing themselves occasionally with high-pitched, plaintive cries, and then becoming airborne again on ponderously flapping wings, like heavy planes taking off. Once a pair became romantic in the garden. A hen bird flew into a tree, and a cock alighted not far away. Hop by hop he approached her with a tiny berry held with exquisite delicacy between the utmost tips of his hefty mandibles. She waited coyly. On arrival beside her he offered her the fruit, and she accepted it gracefully. In the hornbill world that was the equivalent of Adam giving Eve the apple.

IV

The two Spotted Owlets lived in their retreat in the house wall above my bathroom window all the year round. Every evening at dusk they left home to spend the night in the garden. If I went on the lawn around midnight and stayed there quietly for a while, I was almost certain sooner or later to hear them utter squeals of pleasure or annoyance as they hunted; and on moonlit nights I caught occasional fleeting, shadowy glimpses of them fluttering from tree to tree. Always at dawn, when I looked out of my window, they were perched together on a branch of the Australian silver oak, on their way back to bed.

On the morning of May 29th, 1957, there was a change. Three Spotted Owlets sat in the tree. As soon as I poked my face out of the window two of them became agitated, shifting uneasily from bough to bough, facing me with unaccustomed concern, swearing at me, and bobbing up and down like children trying to frighten someone by pretending to be bogies. The third owlet did not stir. Slightly smaller than the others, its plumage was downier in texture and lighter in colour, and its tail was less developed. Evidently it was a youngster, an offspring of my two acquaintances, taking its first airing out of doors. Very sleepy, it kept blinking its eyes, and eventually it fell asleep.

Every day for the next three weeks I saw it in the tree with its parents. No second youngster appeared, and I presume this was a solitary chick, although Spotted Owlets sometimes hatch successfully as many as six nestlings.

It was amusing to see the young owlet gradually acquire adult habits. For the first three days it took little notice of me, although it was aware of my presence and stood stock-still at my approach, hoping to avoid observation. But on the fourth day it stared at

May and June

me more intently, as if suddenly recognizing me as a possible enemy; and it bobbed at me slightly three or four times in absurd, amateurish imitation of its elders. Yet it still did not stir from its position when I came close, for it could scarcely fly. Instead it waited until I withdrew a few paces and then, when it thought I was not looking, shuffled several steps along the branch to a spot where it could hide behind the tree trunk.

It was livelier at nights than in the daytime, already more at ease in darkness than in light. On the fifth evening I saw its silhouette on a branch against a starry sky. Much wider awake than at dawn, it literally ran along the bough when it spotted me; and later I caught sight of it on another branch, showing that it had fluttered a foot or two through space.

For several more days its plumage remained much fluffier than that of its parents, and when it scowled at me its eyes were less fierce than theirs. As time passed, however, its gaze became more suspicious, and the little creature bobbed its body up and down at me with ever increasing energy. Nevertheless, its genuflexions were less abrupt, less threatening, more like curtsies, than those of its elders. On the tenth day I heard its voice for the first time, and its screech was a tolerably good, though feebler, echo of theirs. It demonstrated forcefully to me that it had already learned an impressive vocabulary of oaths. That morning, too, it flew quite confidently from branch to branch in attempts to escape my notice.

A few days earlier a pair of Common Mynahs had conceived the idea of usurping the owlets' nest-hole. It is remarkable, that instinct of one species for knowing when another has finished with a desirable residence, and for seeking at once to become its next tenants. But in this case the mynahs had misjudged the situation, for the owlets' hole in the wall was not just a temporary lodging used for the purpose of breeding, but a permanent habitation. So the parent birds resented the mynahs' notion, and a furious battle began between the two species. Day after day it was fought with remarkable obstinacy on both sides. The mynahs would perch on the roof just above the nest-hole, or on a bough just opposite it, or beside its very threshold, and shout challenges to the owlets to come out and joust. The owlets would retaliate by charging at the intruders from inside the hole, or by dive-bombing them from outside. Sometimes the rivals closed in actual wing-to-wing duels and a few feathers would fly, owlets' and mynahs' plumes alike floating to the ground below. The mynahs used to give broad hints that it was time the owlets vacated their nest by plucking twigs of building material and trying to carry them into the hole in the wall; but the owners of the establishment never gave way. They fought back with unrestrained vigour, swearing like sergeant-majors whenever the enemy opened a new offensive. Always in the end the mynahs conceded victory to their opponents and flew away with vain shouts of defiance.

The battle became a war which continued for many weeks, the mynahs seeming unable to understand why the owlets wished to retain possession of their nest-site after their chick had graduated into the outer world.

During some of the skirmishes the young owlet observed the fight from a perch on the tree. Usually it appeared indifferent to the altercations between its parents and their tormentors, staring in some other direction or dozing off to sleep. But sometimes it gazed with uncomprehending interest at the fray, and once it became directly involved when the two mynahs alighted for a breather on a branch close beside it. Drawing itself up to its full height with a look of defensive dignity on its face, it stared hostilely at them and bobbed three or four times. It seemed prepared to protect itself to the death—but that resolution was never put to the test, for a few moments later the mynahs launched another assault on its elders and betters.

After that the young owlet grew up fast, though its agile movements were still for many days and nights confined to the small playground of its home tree, since it lacked confidence for longer flights. In the mornings it sat there sleepily, yawning and dozing much of the time. At dusk I sometimes caught sight of its silhouette, and more often I heard it calling in a low squeak, demanding food from its parents. They passed to and fro like shadows, bringing a frog, a lizard or some other delicacy each time in response to its requests.

I think three weeks passed before the youngster ventured from the tree. Soon after dark on the evening of June 18th I met the whole family at the further end of the garden. Both parents were very active, winging noiselessly from perch to perch as they hunted, calling gently now and then to each other or to their junior, and sometimes cursing me when I came in their line of flight. The youngster was more stationary.

That was the little owlets' coming-out party. Like a debutante, it was launched on the world.

V

I cannot get at all excited about House Sparrows. Usually when I see them gathering nesting material and carrying it to some favourite nook, I do not even trouble to record this event in my diary. Yet these sparrows are permanent, perpetual, unavoidable features of the landscape in the house and garden, and no sketch of bird life there would be complete without a passing glance in their direction. So let me mention a pair who brought up their youngsters in a learned environment which should have endowed them with considerable literary gifts.

Early on the morning of May 11th this year I noticed a cock and hen sparrow both paying frequent visits to my library. The day was still young and fresh, the air-conditioning plant had therefore not yet been turned on, and the French windows from the room into the garden were open. The birds inspected two or three bookcases and finally selected one filled with tomes about Malaya and Borneo. The cock perched on H. M. Tomlinson's *Tidemarks* while the hen sat on Frank Swettenham's *Malay Sketches*, and there they had a brief confabulation together. Afterwards the female hopped on to a first edition of George Maxwell's *In Malay Forests*, gave an inquiring glance at me to see whether I would disapprove, and then disappeared into the shelf behind some of

Joseph Conrad's works. When she reappeared she evidently gave an encouraging report to her mate, for he too went to examine the rear-quarters of *Almayer's Folly, An Outcast of the Islands, The Mirror of the Sea* and their companion volumes. Both birds then flew into the garden, and soon afterwards they returned with the first wisps of grass for a nest.

They worked hard for the next ten days, bringing enough building material to make a miniature haystack, for they judged it necessary to fill the whole space on the shelf behind the books with an untidy heap of dried grasses. On top of this the hen eventually laid eggs. Having permitted them to begin the task, I had not the heart to interrupt them later, although this caused my house guests and me considerable inconvenience. For a month we could not close the windows of the library, in order to let the birds have free access to their lodgings; and therefore we could never use the air-conditioning, and sat instead under inadequately whirring fans in a sweltering room.

On May 30th I saw a House Sparrow carry a bite of food into the shadowy recess behind the serried ranks of Malayan classics, an indication that chicks had hatched that morning. The space between the top of the books and the shelf above was too narrow for me to peer into the nest; even the birds had to crouch to squeeze themselves through it; and so I never knew how many eggs and youngsters there were. But the family must have been numerous, hale and hearty, for both parents were kept busy throughout the next fortnight carrying rations of food into the bookcase.

As they grew up the nestlings chattered ever more volubly in their nursery, following the opposite maxim from that laid down for human infants. They could be heard, but not seen. As my friends and I sat conversing in the library we were frequently interrupted by their chirruping comments. We could not tell what the young sparrows were saying, though it might have been worth understanding, for they had excellent opportunities to improve their minds and imbibe knowledge. Around them in their earliest, most impressionable days was a collection of historical, political, literary and pictorial works about the mixed races of Malaya and the wild men of Borneo which was the envy of many scholars. I hoped that my young proteges were becoming erudite bookworms, but I feared that the only worms in which they were interested were those which their parents imported by scores from the garden every day.

On June 17th the young sparrows left the nest. When I passed through the library before breakfast I could hear them gossiping excitedly but after breakfast the bookcase was silent. They had gone. No doubt they were with their parents somewhere out of doors. So they graduated from their school on the bookshelf into the great university of the wider world.

With relief I closed the French windows and turned on the air-conditioning.

VI

There were few months in the year when Ring Doves and Little Brown Doves did not flirt, mate, build nests and lay eggs in the garden. Most days one could hear the males murmuring their invitations to the females to romance. The Ring Doves cooed three syllables, with the emphasis on the second, which sounded very like 'I lo-ove you', and the Little Brown Doves added two further syllables which made their sentence, 'Darling, I love you.'

In many ways birds behave like human beings in their love affairs. Some species pair faithfully for life; others change their husbands and wives every year like certain Hollywood film stars; and the males of yet other species are polygamous, supporting two or more official wives in two or more establishments at the same time. Ring Doves seem to be philanderers. One day I saw a cock bird carrying building materials to his mate sitting on an unfinished nest. Every few minutes he flew to a bare flower-bed from which plants had been uprooted, selected a suitable bit of broken rootlet and bore it to her. Once when he had chosen a sample of the right size and weight, and was about to take it to her, another hen bird alighted a few feet from him. He promptly dropped the gift for his wife, skipped jauntily to the new-comer's side, puffed out his chest, bowed and murmured 'I lo-ve you'. She indicated that she was not that kind of girl by turning her back and flying away. He then returned to his rootlet, seized it again, and carried it to his true partner.

Red Turtle Doves also built nests in the garden in May and June; but they invariably shared the experiences of their cousins in having their eggs or chicks stolen. I saw House Crows, Koels and Tree Pies all stealing these treasures from various doves' nests. Like the Green Pigeons of whom I have written, the parents always fought vicious battles in defence of their young, striking back furiously at their attackers. Far from behaving like Doves of Peace on those occasions, they seemed more like Angels of War.

A rare sight in Delhi is the Spotted Dove; but twice in midsummer one paid fleeting visits to the garden. Once its presence seemed to be resented by a pair of Little Brown Doves, for they tried to chase it away.

For all I know, Blue Rock Pigeons may have successfully produced fresh generations of themselves on the house-top. All the year round members of the species frequented the roof in considerable numbers, as if it were a pigeons' club; and many stone ledges existed there such as the species favour for the lodgment of eggs. But I did not often bother to go in search of them.

VII

One June a pair of Black Drongos or King Crows built a nest which, as always with that species, was a work of considerable engineering skill. Slung like a hammock from branch to branch in the fork of a tree about fifteen feet from the ground, it was a thinly woven, transparent mesh of slim grasses secured to each bough by cobwebs, horsehairs and other fine cables and encircled by thick, buttressing walls. Both drongos toiled energetically at the construction, working more than a thirteen-hour day. Even so they took twelve days to complete the structure, perhaps a more protracted period than usual because in its early stages three wild wind-storms in succession damaged the work and compelled the builders to make repairs.

Black Drongos are famous for their audacious courage, and it is said that other species of birds often choose to build their nests in the vicinity of their homes because those sturdy fighters keep all marauders at a respectful distance. My pair of drongos certainly gave many demonstrations of fearlessness. The first duel I watched one fight was against a Common Mynah, on whom it made a vicious bodily assault which drove the mynah helter-skelter away. On another occasion one shoo'd a Green Barbet from the neighbourhood with screams of rage as well as pugnacious physical attack. When a Green Pigeon alighted near the nest one morning a drongo standing guard flew on to the visitor's back and pecked wickedly at its head and neck. Taken by surprise, the pigeon seemed too astonished to move at first; but then it collected its wits and made a hurried escape. Several times a drongo chased House Crows away from the nest, and twice I watched one hurl itself at a passing Shikra regardless of that bird's hooked beak and sharp talons. On one of those occasions it sang a wild battle song as it advanced on the enemy. Even more convincing proof of the drongo's bravery was its readiness to fight a Common Pariah Kite, beside which it appeared much as David must have appeared before Goliath. Several times I have watched Black Drongos attacking various types of eagles, when the small, audacious bird did not merely give chase to the giant but actually alighted on its back and rode there for a while, as if it were a jockey whipping a steed away from the vicinity of a nest.

As the pair of drongos in my garden neared the end of their building labours they prepared for the next stage of domestic life. One morning the cock bird was working busily in the nest when the hen arrived and perched on a bough beside it. She flirted her tail energetically, and he promptly ceased his toil, leaped on her back and mated with her. Then he flew away, and she took his place in the nest, where she started weaving bits and pieces of building material into place. Sometimes she squatted low in the nest-cup and squirmed her body so as to shape it comfortably to her figure, preparing it for the long days of incubation which would soon begin.

Several times during the next three days I saw the pair make love on a bough near by. The floor of the cradle-to-be was so thin that it was transparent, and I kept a watch through it to see when eggs would be laid. At six o'clock on the third morning the nest was empty; but soon afterwards the hen settled in it. She seemed in a concentrated, preoccupied mood. Every now and then as she sat she flicked her wings with a nervous gesture, and occasionally she bowed her head and touched the nest-wall with her beak. After three-quarters of an hour she suddenly rose, sped gaily across the lawn, dipped gracefully like a swallow to the surface of the goldfish pool to take a sip of water as she passed, and disappeared over the garden wall.

Through the translucent floor of the nest I saw an egg.

A moment later the cock bird arrived in the tree and settled paternally on it, staying there as long as I continued to watch. Indeed, whenever I looked at the nest throughout that day the male was doing duty, sometimes sitting on the egg and at other times standing over it with wings slightly spread to protect it from the terrific heat of the sun. The temperature was 112 °F.

When I looked at the nest at 5.30 the next morning the cock bird was still in occupation of it. He left at six o'clock, and I saw that there was still one egg. Soon afterwards the hen arrived and perched on the next branch. She kept fluttering half-opened wings and calling a throaty series of phrases, as if she were anxious for sexual play; but her mate must have gone out of earshot, for he did not reappear. After a while she hopped into the nest and squatted on the egg. She was restless, however, and left after five minutes. Twice in the next ten minutes she returned, but stayed each time only briefly in the nest before flying off again. Always there was still one egg in it.

At 7.30 she arrived with what appeared a more purposeful air, and settled in the nest for twenty minutes. During that time a

Green Pigeon perched close by, but she did not leave the nest to shoo it away, as she would normally have done. Instead she merely fluttered both wings agitatedly, and at once her mate swooped into the tree, made straight for the pigeon, and drove it off. The cock then stayed on guard beside her, and she calmed down.

I wandered away for a few minutes, but when I looked again at 7.55 the male still stood beside the nest, the female had disappeared—and two eggs lay in the slender hammock.

Again, the cock bird stayed on the nest most of the morning. After her great effort in producing an egg the female seemed to tire, and to leave her partner to shoulder their family cares. That afternoon, however, she relieved him for a while.

When I inspected the situation early the next morning the nest was unoccupied, and only one egg lay in it! What had happened to the second? I could only guess that for once the daredevil gallantry of the drongos had not been sufficient to keep all enemies at bay, and that at some careless moment when both were absent an egg-thief raided their home. While I was speculating on this, the cock bird arrived and settled in the nest. Soon afterwards the hen perched nearby, he flew on to her back, and they mated.

I was absent from Delhi for the next thirty-six hours; but when I returned I went to see the drongos' nest, hoping to find three eggs in it. No bird was in the nest, but the male stood on guard on a bough nearby. Yet there was nothing to guard! No eggs lay there. The nest was neat and intact, but empty. So the cunning thief had followed its first raid by a second, and perhaps by a third, and made a clean sweep of the drongos' clutch.

Two days later there was an odd sequel to the episode. That morning no Black Drongo was in sight, and instead a Redvented Bulbul sat in the nest. After a moment it flew off, but soon returned with a strand of building material which it wove into the nest-floor. I thought this a very dubious experiment, for the drongos' precariously suspended hammock seemed too fine to sustain the weight of extra nesting material and the clumsier movements of a bulbul. The bulbul judged otherwise, and for the next two days kept flying to and fro with wisps of grass, always closely attended by its consort. The structure began to look like a muddled mixture between two different types of nest.

On the third morning the nest hung broken in its tree-fork, with a large hole punched in its middle. The bulbul must have collapsed through the floor. That was the end of the tale of the Black Drongos' effort to raise a family in my garden.

VIII

In May the fruit of the mango trees begins to swell towards ripeness, and by the end of June many thousands of mangoes should have been ready for eating in the garden. To me the mango is the king of fruits, endowed with a sweet succulence unequalled in the products of any other tree. Unfortunately this opinion is shared by Green and Blossomheaded Parakeets. Moreover, whereas I like the fruit only when it is entirely ripe, they are partial to it from almost the first moment when its young flesh starts to form round its nut; so from early May each year the birds began to raid my trees, and by the first half of June formidable parties of them feasted there every day. One evening I counted more than seventy nuts lying on the grass beneath one tree, all chewed bare of their flesh that day.

There was little I could do about it. The birds quickly got used to any form of scarecrow, treating it with the contempt which it deserved; and if I had hired a boy to stay around the trees all day, shooing the parakeets away, he would have frightened other birds as well, and bird life in the garden would have been disrupted. So I resigned myself once more to leaving Nature to pursue her own interrupted course. I did, however, preserve two hundred mangoes for my household and myself by tying light satin bags round them to prevent their violation.

All the countless hundreds of other mangoes were demolished by parakeets. I do not think any other kinds of birds ate them. If they did, their depredations were insignificant compared with the gigantic hauls made by the Green and Blossomheaded guzzlers. In a way it was delightful to see the enthusiastic satisfaction which their gargantuan repasts afforded them. The Blossomheaded Parakeets in particular gave frequent high-pitched squeaks of pleasure as they fluttered from bough to bough selecting the choicest morsels at the banquet. Among them were numerous youngsters fairly fresh from their nests, proving that the species is not just a bird of passage but a regular resident in Delhi.

Parakeets' tastes are catholic, and they fell with equal zest on various other fruits. However greedy they may be, parakeets are elegant eaters. There was a touch of fastidious artistry about the way in which a Green Parakeet attacked the prizes to be gained on a plum tree. Picking its steps carefully, it would strut along a well-laden bough, select a plum, bend its head with a chivalrous air (as if it were paying the fruit a compliment), nip the morsel off neatly with its beak, and then perch on one foot while it held the fare in the other with the genteel, crooked-finger manner of a lady holding a cup of tea in a drawing-room. A swift series of nibbles and gulps soon demolished the plum.

Occasionally in spring or early summer I saw a rather bigger parakeet fly over the lawn, the Large Indian Parakeet, which seems to be only a bird of passage through the capital.

IX

Various birds came to the garden in the hot, dry midsummers for much-needed, hard-to-come-by liquid refreshment. Sometimes one or two hose-pipes played on the lawn, watering the parched grass and leaving shallow pools lying over the hard ground. I saw numerous species slaking their thirst at the little fountains, some drinking water as it gushed from a pipe, others catching drops in their beaks while they hovered before a sparkling spray, and yet others sipping from the miniature pools. Several of these bibbers were quite hefty creatures. Often Common Pariah Kites stood beside a leaking hose and kept dipping their bills in it as they drank their fill; and occasionally a Longlegged Buzzard, a Bonelli's Eagle or a Pallas's Fishing Eagle alighted on the grass, strolled to a splash, and quaffed deeply. The exceeding heat must have given them inordinate thirsts.

Quite frequently a Tawny Eagle would thus refresh itself, sometimes in the company of two or three kites. House Crows with a nest in the neighbourhood objected to these visitations, and always swooped boldly at the formidable bird in efforts to frighten it away. The Tawny Eagle was never much impressed, merely lifting its head with open beak and jabbing mildly at each impertinent crow, half in boredom and half in warning, it seemed, and then bending down again for another drink. Once, however, two crows became braver. Landing on the lawn beside the eagle, they kept circling round it in attempts to catch it in the rear. Whenever they succeeded for a few moments they stretched forward their necks and tweaked its tail-feathers with their beaks. After a while the eagle grew irritated and flew away.

The most imposing assembly that ever gathered at one time for refreshments at a hose-pipe was a Tawny Eagle, a Bonelli's Eagle and a Crested Honey Buzzard. They stood within a few feet of each other, all plunging their beaks into the water and imbibing with obvious content. No party of aristocratic carousers celebrating together in an English public house could look more distinguished.

One May day I saw a Crested Honey Buzzard enjoy more than a drink in the garden. A multitude of wild bees treated a large hole in a jacaranda tree as a hive, and at most hours they could be seen flying in and out of its entrance. That morning I was attracted to the spot by a loud, agitated chattering of many birds; and I saw that this chorus was mobbing a Crested Honey Buzzard which had landed in the tree. I counted eighteen House Crows, seventeen Green Parakeets and a dozen Brahminy Mynahs, Common Mynahs and Jungle Babblers all yelling excitedly at the intruder. For a long time the buzzard kept shifting its position from perch to perch in the tree, and sometimes it flew into a neighbouring tree and then quickly returned again. Obviously it was attracted by something in the jacaranda; and it more or less ignored its crowd of critics.

Eventually the bird settled near the bees' home and kept peering towards its entry; and then it jumped deliberately to a branch beside the cavity. Leaning its body across the intervening space, it poked its head through the entrance. Immediately a swarm of bees flew out of their fortress and buzzed around the bird of prey, darting at it, alighting on its body and no doubt attempting to sting it. The buzzard extracted its head and shook its wings in annoyance, trying to get rid of the pests; but it was not unduly disturbed by them, for its plumage was trusty armour against their slings and arrows. Soon it stuck its face into the tree trunk again, and evidently liked what it found inside, for it edged closer, and thrust its head and neck further into the hole. The bees swarmed round it and buzzed in ever greater protest, but the bird showed less and less concern for them, merely wriggling its shoulders occasionally to dismiss them. A regular jolting of its body started, showing that the thief was now pecking vigorously at something inside the tree. Then it withdrew its head and began tearing with its beak at the bark below the hole, trying to rip the wood away so as to give it easier access to the interior; but its bill was too weak to make any substantial impression on the timber, so it thrust its head into the cavity once more. It stayed in this position for some time, no doubt helping itself to the bees' appetizing handiworks within. The bees grew even more distressed, whirling and murmuring round it furiously in a constantly shifting cloud of misty wings.

As the buzzard tried to poke its head progressively further into the hole, biting more greedily into the delicacies indoors, its position—leaning across from a near-by branch—became increasingly uncomfortable. After a while it tired of this awkward posture, withdrew its head from the hole, spread its wings and fluttered ten yards into the next tree. Its appetite was now whetted, however, and its glances towards the distracted bees betrayed that it itched to make another raid on their property. A few moments later it fell to temptation, hastened back to the attack, and this time took up a position of much greater advantage for the assault. Gripping the bark below the cavity with its claws, it spread its body against the tree, with its tail fanned out, its rear-quarters pressed against the wood, its wings stretched across neighbouring branches to give it firmer purchase, and its crested head held erect as it faced the trunk—like a gigantic woodpecker poised to enter a nest-hole. Its upright figure and outstretched wings gave it the powerful, majestic appearance of an heraldic eagle; but it did not hold that pose for long. Bending towards the tree and hunching its shoulders, it plunged its head once more avidly into the trunk's interior. The bees swarmed again from their stronghold, like squadrons of Lilliputian aeroplanes; but with less avail than ever. Utterly indifferent to them, the buzzard threw all caution to the winds, neither looking around to see whether enemies were watching it from the rear nor taking any other precaution to protect itself from hostile attack in its exposed position. Intent solely on its delicious meal, it shoved its head further and further into the hole, pressing its body ever closer to the tree, and every now and then flapping its outstretched wings to help itself forwards. It seemed to be tugging at something inside. Suddenly, with a final wrench, it pulled its head backwards out of the hole—and in its beak was gripped a large chunk of waxy, honey-soaked bees' cake. Casting itself from the jacaranda, it flew with the prize to another tree.

There it settled on a broad bough, where it transferred the honeycomb from its beak to one foot, pinned the food firmly by its claws to the branch, and started ripping at it with its sharp bill. Deliberately it sipped and gulped the contents from each of scores of cells in the cake, one after the other. The bough became wet with liquid flowing from the comb, and the voracious bird tried to drink this escaping sweetness as well as to consume it at its source. I timed the feast; it took twenty minutes for the buzzard to demolish the whole slice of cake. I never saw any animal—human or otherwise—enjoy food more.

X

Green Bee-eaters were frequent visitors in the garden during much of the year. They absented themselves in March, April and May, when they nested in tunnels bored deep into rustic sandbanks outside the city; but in June they returned in considerable numbers.

Parties of them would sit side by side on high, slim branches where they could catch quick sight of dragonflies and other winged insects that hove into view. Whenever one of these tempting morsels appeared, a bee-eater would sally into the air, swoop as gracefully as a ballet dancer after its prey, capture it deftly in its fine beak, and return to a perch to enjoy the delicacy. No bird is more fairylike than a bee-eater, with its sharp-winged, slender-bodied, long-tailed figure dressed all over in bright green tinged with blue, rufous and black.

These Green Bee-eaters are regular residents in Delhi. The larger and equally beautiful Bluetailed Bee-eaters are summer visitors, and in successive Junes groups of them also sported in the garden.

Other distinguished species of birds appeared there in midsummer. Goldenbacked Woodpeckers seemed to come more frequently then than at other times of the year, uttering wild cackles as they arrived, alighting on tree trunks and moving up them in a jerky series of hops as they searched the bark for insects. I always hoped a pair would adopt a hole in one of my trees as a nest; but none did.

More than once I heard low, sharp, unaccustomed calls in an arbour above a shrubbery, and spotted Mahratta Woodpeckers hunting for grubs.

Baya Weaver-birds were other pleasing visitors. For some unexplained reason the species chooses to breed near water, almost invariably building their colonies of fantastic, dangling, bottle-shaped nests in trees overhanging wayside pools. So they were not tempted to exercise their remarkable talent in my pondless garden; but sometimes in June small parties paid fleeting calls on me. The males were in full courtship plumage, hooded in bright yellow, masked in near-black, and cloaked in brown and yellow.

Many river and marsh birds seemed to travel away from their customary haunts more frequently in summer than in winter, possibly because they resorted then to drier areas where suitable clumps of trees existed to accommodate their nests, and so had to journey further afield to fetch food. Whatever the explanation, one species or another appeared above my garden almost every morning during the hot months. Thus Paddy Birds or Pond Herons hurried overhead; Grey Herons napped majestically by; and all the four egrets found in Delhi—Lesser Egrets, Cattle Egrets, Little Egrets and Large Egrets—floated on leisurely wings across the blue, like white-sailed yachts on an infinite sea. Some of these species came singly and others travelled in trimly wavering, arrow-shaped formations. Night Herons sped past at dawn on their way to bed, sometimes halting for a while in a tree overlooking the garden.

Once or twice two other species gave me even bigger surprises by appearing over the lawn at sunrise; the long-necked, snakey-headed Darter and the bulky but none the less graceful Sarus Crane. They seemed amazed to find themselves high above King George's Avenue, for the parties of each that arrived circled aimlessly for a while, as if they had lost direction and wondered where they were. Then they took decisions about their destinations and flew away.

Two types of wild duck remain in Delhi through the summer as well as the winter, and they, too, sometimes sped through the sky in full view of my house. The Nuktas were recognizable by their long, goose-like necks as well as by the knob jutting on the drakes' beaks, while the Spotbills had normal ducky figures. They added refreshing virile, sportive touches to the sweltering scene.

TEN

WHITE-EYES

I

One of my favourite birds is the White-eye. It is a dapper little creature measuring only four inches long from the tip of its beak to the end of its tail, and its colouring is pleasing. Its upper body is golden-yellow tinged with green, parts of its wings are dark brown, its chin and throat are bright yellow, its breast is light grey, and the yellow motif is repeated on its abdomen. But its most distinguishing mark is a white ring round each eye, which gives it the appearance of wearing a pair of white horn-rimmed spectacles.

I caught my first glimpse of this good-looking character when it was having a bath. One hot afternoon in July a hose-pipe on my lawn had sprung a leak, and from it a thin, sparkling fountain of water spouted into the air. A pair of White-eyes had discovered this and were using it as a shower. Each in turn would fly towards it, hover for a few moments like a hesitant butterfly before daring to dash among its drops, and then dive through them and alight where the spray gushed from the pipe. There the bird dipped itself in the water, ducking, squirming and shaking its wings so that it got a thorough wetting. After a minute of this refreshing wash it would flit to a near-by shrub, where it dried itself with all the robust vigour of a man rubbing himself down with a towel after a swim. Ruffling its feathers, vibrating its wings, wriggling its body, flurrying its tail, turning its head this way and that to peck at different parts of its plumage, and making various other contortions, it gradually shook itself dry and clean—while its companion took a turn in the shower-bath. Both birds repeated this performance several times with evident gusto and enjoyment.

Like some other species, White-eyes seem to be enthusiastic

bathers. One morning I watched a pair engaged in some extraordinary rites which at first I took to be courtship display. Both crouched on the lawn close beside each other, dipping forwards until their breasts touched the ground, quivering their wings rapidly, and occasionally bowing their heads so that these swept the grass. I presumed that this was a demonstration of sexual excitement, and that each was expressing a powerful yearning for the other; and their mutual invitations seemed so eloquent that I wondered why they protracted their sensuous exhibition without proceeding to the act of mating. Then I noticed that when they bent their heads they also turned them sideways so that a cheek brushed the lawn, which was sprinkled with dew-drops. The birds were merely scrubbing their faces! First they wetted one cheek, and then the other. The wing-quiverings, too, were performed low among the grass-blades, and had the result of splashing beads of water over the birds' whole bodies. When they had displaced all the dew from one small area of ground they hopped a pace or two forwards to another damp spot and repeated their antics; and by crouching close beside one another each helped in spraying the other. Every now and then they flew to a bougainvillaea bush, where they shook and preened their feathers among the purple blossoms. Then they hopped down to the lawn again to continue their morning baths.

II

In the winter White-eyes usually congregate in small parties and travel together through the shrubberies, feeding energetically and maintaining an almost continuous whispering twitter of conversation among themselves. But before April they separate into distinct couples for the purpose of producing a new generation of their tribe.

It always gives me a small thrill of excitement to catch the first sight of a bird flying into a clump of foliage carrying what looks like nesting material in its beak, and to go and inspect the site and find, sure enough, a nest in the making. And the satisfaction of the discovery is never greater than when the unfinished structure belongs to White-eyes, for the birds' actions when building are exceedingly pretty, and their home when finished has singular charm.

Once I saw two White-eyes select the spot where they would build, and then lay the very foundation-stone of a nest. One bird was fluttering inquisitively from branch to branch and twig to twig in a rusty-shieldbearer tree; and the other White-eye followed almost on its tail wherever it went. The first explorer held a morsel of silvery fluff in its beak, gripping it purposefully while it inspected carefully each possible site. The second bird carried nothing, but was obviously keenly interested in the success which might attend its partner's searches. For more than ten minutes the pair examined every likely nook and cranny in the tree, until eventually the first White-eye felt satisfied with a place in the fork of a leafy twig and laid the little bit of fluff on a prong of the fork. Soon afterwards both birds flew away, leaving this mote of building material stuck securely there as if it were fixed with glue. It must have had a dab of adhesive fluid, and was a folded length of cobweb, or some similar extremely light yet strong strand, which could later be unfolded to form a link in a nest. Whatever its substance, it was the first 'brick' of those White-eyes' home.

Three hours later two strings of fine yet quite tough-looking material were loosely looped between the prongs of the forking twig—and when I looked two days later several more twists of what appeared to be fluffy cotton thread had been added. The collection of them seemed rather shapeless and purposeless, as if they had been dropped there by accident; but gradually afterwards the miniature edifice grew. On the third morning I watched both birds on the job. Each in turn came frequently to the site, bringing fresh building material every time and alighting on the twig to thrust quickly and deftly with its beak as it poked or wove the new strand into the right position. Sometimes it perched above the nest-to-be, working downwards with its bill; and at other times it perched at the side or below the nest and toiled from varying angles. All its movements were swift, dainty, precise and efficient.

That day the structure began to take a form recognizable to human eyes, appearing like the embryo of a tiny cup suspended hammock-wise below the twig, being attached to the stems above by numerous cobwebby cables along its edges. By the fourth afternoon the cup was completely formed, but its walls were as thin and transparent as a bag of gauze. Next morning I saw a bird sitting in the nest and skilfully poking, plucking and sewing with its beak as it wove fresh threads of material into place. The skeleton of the cradle was now finished, and the builders were adding an inner lining to increase its strength and comfort. But even when, several days later, the structure was complete it was still extremely thin, with the fragile fineness of a cup of Chinese egg-shell porcelain made in the reign of the Emperor Chien-Lung.

Though many other birds' nests are more complicated, and therefore cleverer, constructions—such as the Sunbird's dangling grass globe, the Tailor Bird's stitched-together leaves, and the Weaver Bird's bottle-shaped residence—no more enchanting example of avian architecture exists than the home of a White-eye family. It is an almost perfectly formed half-sphere, about the size of a golf ball cut in half, suspended beneath a cluster of twigs and leaf stems, and tied to these by slim threads varying in thickness from gossamer to fine cotton. Its wall and floor are made of slightly coarser grasses or fibres, upholstered here and there with cushiony scraps of down. The whole tiny edifice appears so skimpily formed and so precariously slung that one wonders how it can support for long its burden of eggs, chicks and adult birds. Indeed, its mesh is so fine that it is translucent, and from below you can see the shadow of eggs or chicks against the sky above.

That it survives is one of the countless examples of the uncanny, intuitive skill of birds as construction engineers. For three weeks it stands the strain of a lively family. The sample which I have described soon contained two delicate, faintly blue eggs. For ten days the parents took turns at sitting on them, and at the end of that lengthy vigil triumphantly hatched a pair of tiny chicks.

For the next week the mother and father were busy hopping in and out of the nest, bringing food, keeping the cradle clean, and in other ways caring solicitously for their twins. During the first few days, when the youngsters were still almost naked and the midday sunshine was too strong for their tender skins, I often saw an adult White-eye standing over them with wings outspread to act as a sunshade. Gradually they waxed more robust; their bare bodies became covered with down; their wing stumps sprouted quills; the quills then burst into feathers; their hitherto blind eyes opened; and their beaks gaped ever larger to receive nourishment. They began to look like small images of their pretty parents. All was progressing well.

Then, on the eighth afternoon of their lives as chicks, they were missing from home. I might have assumed they had flown to freedom if the nest had not been wrenched sideways and badly torn. Evidently an enemy had raided it, slain its young inmates and, presumably, eaten them. Such tragic endings to promising beginnings are all too common in bird society. In the world of wild Nature there are no edicts against robbery and murder, no commandments declaring 'Thou shalt not steal' and 'Thou shalt not kill' (though there seems to be one saying 'Thou shalt not commit adultery'), no moral code forbidding the coveting of your neighbour's property or the taking of life. On the contrary, such acts are parts of the Law of Nature itself—inevitable, essential means of attaining Nature's end of preserving her innumerable species. Almost all birds and beasts depend to a greater or lesser extent for their own healthy, lusty life on destroying smaller creatures than themselves, and Nature therefore arranges that these shall be reproduced in such immoderate multitudes that they provide sustenance for various other species at the same time as maintaining a sufficient surplus to preserve their own kind. The White-eye parents of the slaughtered chicks, for example, had fed their youngsters for seven days on many hundreds of minute, defenceless insects—and several other similar pairs of White-eyes were doing likewise in my garden at the same time.

I do not know what particular assassin made a meal of the two young White-eyes. Several times the same fate befell the chicks in other White-eye nests that I watched. Suddenly, when fledglings seemed almost ready to spread their wings and fly, they were liquidated by some greedy marauder. But that was not the conclusion of every story. Sometimes there was a happy ending.

III

It is pleasing to watch a family of young birds in their nursery grow up under their parents' tutelage and arrive at last at the fateful moment when they leave their home and venture into the outer world. One afternoon I watched that scene enacted on the small stage of a White-eyes' nest. Two chicks occupied the place. They had broken from their egg-shells ten days earlier, and one of them now sat passively on the nest-floor while the other stood gazing inquisitively over its wall. Suddenly this latter bird grew restless, shifted from side to side of the tiny apartment, peered over its edge with ever-increasing curiosity, stretched its wings experimentally and flapped them in a tentative, ambitious sort of way. Then it climbed half-way up the side of the nest and pecked at some overhanging foliage, as if it wished to collect its own food. Its juvenile plumage, awkward gestures and seemingly feeble wings all appeared to indicate that it was too infantile to fly; and I assumed its movements were just a few preliminary exercises for departure two or three days later. But the youngster did not share this judgment, and suddenly started heaving itself about rather boisterously. I realized it proposed to take its leave forthwith. Summoning all its strength, it ascended to the top of the nest-wall, stood poised there uncertainly for a few moments like a dizzy tight-rope walker on a loose rope, and then lost its balance and fell back into the nest-cup.

At the first sign that the youngster proposed to break away from its confinement a parent flew into the tree, perched on a near-by branch and watched with unconcealed interest these goings-on. It uttered soft White-eyeish mutterings which attracted its mate; and soon both adults were flitting excitedly from bough to bough round the nest, twittering ceaselessly with solicitude, evidently mightily concerned. Whether they were nervous about their chick's prospects of making a safe getaway, or felt perfect confidence in its capacity to achieve this revolutionary step, I do not know; but they did not seem to make any attempt to prevent it. On the contrary, perhaps their dartings hither and thither in the tree, and their constant chattering exclamations, were positive encouragement.

Back in the nest, the fledgling stumbled around for a while, spurred now by a keenly awakened vigour, a fresh, burgeoning energy. Before long it made another supreme effort, struggled to the nest's lip again, and stood poised there as it pecked at leaves in the vicinity. Suddenly it overbalanced and tumbled headlong from the nest. My heart was in my mouth, for I thought the youngster was about to commit suicide while of unsound mind. However, a bouquet of foliage just below the nest broke its fall, where it lay upside-down for a moment; and then it jerked itself into an erect position—and clambered back into the nest!

Presumably it was startled, if not frightened, by the experience. Nevertheless, after a brief period of reflection it decided that nothing had really gone amiss in its adventuring, that its escapade was amusing, and that a repetition of it would do no harm. At once it scaled the nest-wall again, this time with increased determination. After a few moments' hesitation on the summit it opened its wings, flapped them with wild abandon, and leaped to a leafy twig an inch away. At once it began nibbling at the surrounding greenery as naturally as if it had been accustomed for years to hunt its own food. As it did so, however, it reached too far, swayed dubiously on its legs, and in an attempt to correct its balance spread its wings, flapped them ineffectually, and half hopped and half fluttered another inch along a branch away from its original home. The foliage around grew thick, and faithfully supported it.

The fledgling seemed pleased with itself. Glancing first in this direction and then in that to see where it could proceed next, it waved its wings in a rapid series of experimental flutterings, and then made another desperate forward jump of a further inch. To me the bird looked as deplorably inefficient as it was recklessly courageous, with its small, almost tail-less body, juvenile feathers and general air of innocent inexperience. I feared again that disaster would befall it; but no serious trouble ensued. The youngster's instinct was sound. Though entirely unaccustomed to travel, and awkward in all its movements, it had been provided by Nature with two sets of implements which made its capacity for stumbling progress reliable. Certain parts of its anatomy were still far from fully developed; its beak was inadequate for feeding itself, its tail was almost non-existent, and several of its other members were incompletely formed; but it did not yet require perfection in those particular details; they could grow later as need arose. Nature is severely practical; it deals with first things first, and therefore arranges that during their days in the nest chicks shall develop adequately the two sets of limbs which are essential in their preliminary excursions into the outside world—wings and legs. Though the young White-eye's wings appeared undersized, they were in fact well and strongly made, so that they could bear their owner competently on short flights; and its legs and clawed feet were almost grotesquely large in proportion to the rest of its body, so that they could grip a branch with vice-like firmness and give the bird safe footholds wherever it perched.

As soon as the youngster made its successful escape from the nest both parents flew enthusiastically round it, as if offering congratulations. The second chick, too, who had hitherto squatted motionless and apparently indifferent in the nest, now became animated and gazed inquisitively and perhaps enviously at its twin. The scene was vivacious, with the hero standing amid its admiring relatives, displaying sublime self-assurance, bursting enterprise and obvious determination to achieve more. In fact it soon made several further short leaps, including one sustained, hectically wing-flapping flight of several inches which carried it beyond the clusters of foliage immediately surrounding its birthplace.

Then the second youngster became active, and during the

next ten minutes went through a similar succession of experiences. At the end of them it also was clear of the nest, fluttering in short hops, skips and jumps from twig to twig. The parents came to felicitate it. Yet there was a difference between its performance and that of the first chick. Its movements were less energetic, less impetuous, less adventuresome than those of its young relation, suggesting a notable contrast in their characters. The first fledgling was excitable, daring and ambitious, with the temperament of a pioneer; the second was calm, lacking initiative, behaving in conformity with what it saw others do—a mere copy-cat. Possibly the parents influenced its conduct, finding their other offspring such a problem child that they asked this second one in some emphatic White-eye phraseology to stay still while they looked after its almost uncontrollable companion. In any case, whatever the explanation, after advancing a short way from the nest the lazier youngster assumed a statuesque pose on a comfortable bough and settled there—stolid, imperturbable and immobile.

Meanwhile the other did not remain still for a moment, but kept progressing by a series of short stumbles, jumps and flutters from small branch to small branch while its mother and father darted from perch to perch in the surrounding foliage. They now constituted themselves its tutors in the art of flight. Six feet away from the home-tree stood a wall covered with thick creeper. The adult birds kept alighting beside their enterprising youngster, and then hurling themselves across the intervening space to the creeper, settling there for a moment, and immediately afterwards flying back to the chick's side. Were they deliberately showing the way, setting an example, encouraging their pupil to essay a flight across the yawning gulf of a few feet from the tree to the creeper? I think so. Anyway, the fledgling eventually cocked its head in the direction which they indicated, spread its wings, leaped into the air and crossed the chasm with all the brave dash of a Lindbergh flying the Atlantic. It landed clumsily but securely on the other side.

The older White-eyes seemed delighted with this triumphant feat and once more fussed excitedly round their infant, uttering paeans of praise. That went to the youngster's head. It made a jump towards another stem of the creeper, missed its target, and fell towards the ground; but with the inborn skill inherited from hundreds of generations of ancestors it somehow righted itself and alighted safely on a lower stalk.

I wanted to wait and see what happened next in this interesting crisis in the lives of young White-eyes—but at that tantalizing moment official diplomatic duty intervened. Looking at my watch, I saw it was time for me to join a flock of ambassadors and other envoys migrating towards Palam Airport to meet the Prime Minister of Japan, who would arrive soon afterwards as an honoured guest of the Indian Government. So I turned tail and fled.

When I visited my garden on the way to my office an hour later, I found one White-eye chick stumbling about in the creeper and the other still perching passively exactly where I had left it in the tree. The parents constantly passed between the two.

During the next few days I followed the family's fortunes. That first evening I saw both parents guiding the chick who had stayed in the tree to a roosting place near the nest; and on the next several mornings and afternoons I watched them sedulously attending it. Frequently they brought it food, for it was as yet incapable of foraging for itself. But I never saw the other young White-eye again. Its parents did not carry food to a second chick; they had completely forgotten they ever had another offspring, and were wholly engrossed in the welfare of their now solitary fledgling. Had the reckless adventuresomeness of the first bird brought it to a bad end on its very first day of liberty?

IV

During their earliest sojourns away from the nest young White-eyes—like fledglings of numerous other species—face many hazards. Indeed, through all their juvenile weeks they are surrounded by various perils, to one or another of which a large proportion of them succumb. In their eggs they are apt to be stolen and swallowed by enemies with a taste for omelets, as chicks they are liable to be murdered and consumed by unfriendly meat-eaters, and when they escape from their native heaths other dangers immediately surround them.

I realized this at another White-eyes' nest which I watched. On the eighth afternoon of its three young inmates' existence outside their eggs the place was empty, and I searched anxiously for them in the home tree. Had they been slaughtered to make a feast for some hungry raider, or had they for some reason left their nursery prematurely?

By observing the parents, and noticing that they flew with food to a certain branch of the tree, I soon discovered one youngster perched on a bough some distance from the nest, looking like a minute ball of fluff with an undersized beak protruding from one end and a pair of oversized feet extending from the other. The afternoon was getting late, and while I watched, the fledgling's head nodded and it fell asleep. For the next two hours it dozed, and it was still slumbering in precisely the same position on exactly the same spot when darkness fell.

My most careful searches, however, did not reveal the whereabouts of either of the other youngsters. The parents had now stopped fetching food, and so did not give me a clue to their positions—if they were still in the land of the living at all. I wondered whether they were alive or dead.

Next morning the White-eye chick was still in the same posture on the same bough as on the previous evening, and it remained there for several hours, unstirring except when its beak opened periodically to accept a bite of food from an elder. It either possessed a particularly phlegmatic disposition, or else had left the nest so prematurely that it was not strong enough to move about.

At first I could see no sign of the other two triplets; but by studying the adult birds' movements I later discovered them. Both were crouching with the same statuesque immobility on stems of a low shrub near the nest-tree. From their situation it seemed likely that when they left their cradle they proved incompetent at fluttering along the surrounding twigs, that they had tumbled out of the tree and crash-landed on the lawn below, and that then they made their ways (under their parents' guidance, no doubt) to the shrub. This appeared further evidence that they had perhaps been frightened out of their nest too early, and that they were incapable of even the modest, amateur movements of self-protection customary in young novices in the world.

Their defencelessness was illustrated by an incident which occurred immediately afterwards. One of them sat in an exposed position on a shrub stem, where a Jungle Babbler spied it. The characteristically inquisitive, fussy babbler—always ready to poke its nose into other creatures' business—promptly perched beside it to investigate this extraordinarily diminutive fledgling, the like of which it had possibly never seen before. At once both parent White-eyes appeared as if from nowhere, dashing at the intruder and uttering loud alarm calls. The babbler was obstinate and refused to leave; indeed, its curiosity seemed to be further stimulated, and it edged nearer the chick. At that the adult birds fluttered more threateningly over its head, and in retort the babbler flapped its wings angrily and raised its hoarse voice in protest. This attracted a second babbler, who joined noisily in the argument, which could hardly have been more abusive if the participants had been irate Billingsgate fishwives. In the middle of it all the young White-eye got dislodged from its now violently swaying perch, and plummeted to the ground.

A babbler at once jumped down beside it. Fearful that in the confusion this monster might do hurt to the youngster, I intervened to drive it away; but as soon as I withdrew again the babbler returned to the scene and hung around like a loafer, glowering through its pale eyes, sometimes at me and sometimes at the fledgling.

A White-eye parent darted to the ground where its chick lay, halted there for a fraction of a second, and afterwards flew swiftly into a near-by shrubbery. I thought it had perhaps performed a smart piece of rescue work, picking up the youngster and carrying it to safety; but then I saw the fledgling still lying motionless on the grass, as if it were dead. Possibly its parent had advised it to lie doggo, betraying no sign of life.

Again I chased the babbler away, and then watched from a distance through field-glasses the end of the White-eyes' little act. Both parents disappeared to fetch food, and when they returned fed their other two chicks. They did this many times, ignoring the bird that had collapsed on the ground. Then one of them again visited the spot where it lay, alighted momentarily there, and immediately flew away once more. For several minutes they continued feeding the other members of the family, quietly and efficiently, as if they had no other concern in the world. I wondered whether the comatose chick had died of fright—but at last, after quarter of an hour, I noticed a feeble wing-flapping in the grass where it had fallen. Slowly the youngster picked itself up, crouched cautiously, and then crawled low over the ground to a bush, where it hid beneath overhanging branches. Shortly afterwards it jumped on the bottom stem of the bush, and then with reviving confidence ascended in a series of half leaps, half flights from branch to branch until it perched securely two feet above the lawn. As soon as it settled there a parent brought it a reward of food.

V

A White-eye family stays together for the first few weeks of the fledglings' journeys through the world. In many ways the youngsters still depend on their parents, but gradually under tuition they learn to take care of themselves. During that period their bodies steadily mature. When they leave the nest they possess almost no tails, and so are incapable of efficient long flights, like rudderless aircraft. But their tail-feathers grow quickly in the first two weeks of emancipation, and the old birds coax them to try ever bolder sorties in the air. Their beaks also rapidly strengthen; and, mostly no doubt from instinct, but partly perhaps by watching their elders' example, they learn to find their own food. Nevertheless, for a considerable while they rely on their guardians for the larger proportion of their supplies; and it is presumably this vital commissariat requirement which keeps the family together so long.

The older White-eyes take care of their chicks in various other ways. They afford protection against possible enemies, and stand sentinel beside them at nights. Possibly on the first two or three evenings after fledglings leave a nest they are not sufficiently expert at even short flights to be easily mustered at dusk on the same perch for roosting, and their parents then have to keep an eye on them in different spots. But later the family sleeps every night together, composing a charming little White-eye dormitory.

One evening I watched such a party going to bed. The hour was about seven o'clock on a mid August evening, and the sun had just set. Light faded slowly. As I approached a shrubbery I heard two White-eyes twittering with concern, and caught sight of them with a third member of the species who was very small and tailless, obviously an almost brand-new fledgling. All the same, it was self-confident and dashed competently from branch to branch after its parents. They fed it now and then, and seemed to be deliberately leading it higher and higher in a tall shrub.

When they reached a lofty branch they halted. One parent stayed with the youngster there; but the other immediately flew away. A few moments later this bird reappeared, followed closely by a second fledgling. Again, the older White-eye guided the youngster stage by stage to the branch occupied by the other two members of the family. The actions of the parents were reminiscent of a shepherd and his dog in a sheep-dog trial persuading sheep into a pen. They fussed around their chicks, apparently telling them to settle close beside each other—which the pair obediently did. Then both elders flew away; but the juniors remained stock-still. Soon an adult bird returned with food which it gave to one of the youngsters; and shortly afterwards the other arrived and fed the second chick. They did this several times, both fledglings remaining still all the time except when they opened their beaks to receive their suppers.

Light was now fading rapidly, and the young White-eyes had evidently been settled by their mother and father for the night, just as human parents would tuck a couple of infants into bed.

Eventually the old birds roosted beside their twins. It was almost dark, and the quartet were little more than a shadowy group silhouetted among black twigs and foliage. There I left them.

Next morning I revisited the shrubbery a few minutes after six o'clock. The young White-eyes were still perched motionless, wing to wing and cheek to cheek, on exactly the same spot as the previous evening. Both parents were absent; but soon afterwards they returned, bringing breakfast for their dependants. Then the two youngsters shifted a pace or two apart, shook themselves, preened a few feathers, and began to flutter away on short jaunts of their own. The night's rest was over.

On another occasion I saw a White-eye family containing three fledglings perform a similar operation. Again, the parents settled their charges side by side at dusk so close together that each touched its neighbour; but instead of all facing the same way, the outer chicks looked in one direction while the middle one faced their tails in the opposite direction. It was a neat, compact arrangement; and when I visited the trio at crack of dawn nearly twelve hours later they were still precisely so regimented.

Birds are very energetic most of the day, and it is little wonder that by nightfall they are so exhausted that they sleep almost round the clock.

ELEVEN

CROWS AND KOELS

I

Once upon a time—but only once—I saw a Jungle Crow on the lawn. Entirely black from the tip of its beak to the end of its tail, it was easily distinguishable from its grey-and-black cousin, the House Crow. The species does not often come to town, being (as its name implies) a bird of the forest rather than the city; but occasionally it drops into Delhi on a scavenging expedition. I have once or twice noticed a member of the tribe strutting importantly in the Mogul garden at the Red Fort.

The House Crow is as common in the capital as the Jungle Crow is uncommon. All day and every day in every month of every year it frequented my trees. There was no escaping it. Before sunrise in the early mornings it was one of the first birds to wing overhead, and at dusk in the evenings it was among the last to go to roost. At any hour of day its raucous voice might be heard giving expression to its boisterous feelings.

Its light ashy mantle stretching from its nape, along its upper back, round its neck and down its breast, relieving its otherwise glossy black plumage, would lend the bird dignity if its character supported that appearance. But it is an extrovert, a bully and a thief, and these qualities detract from any claim it might otherwise have to irreproachable respectability. Like many rascals, it has an impertinent, lively charm, and so it makes itself thoroughly at home on the properties of the Generals, Admirals, Air Marshals and other dignitaries who live along King George's Avenue.

Sometimes House Crows visited me in large flocks, but usually they came in small parties of at most half a dozen. They are rather late nesters. The earliest I ever saw one carrying building material into foliage was in mid May. Each year two pairs built their unsightly piles of twigs near the tops of tall trees such as mangoes and Australian silver oaks. The male and female both joined in the labour, but they went about it in a somewhat casual manner, taking quite a long time to finish the structure. Although it always looked a rough and ready work, with its countless separate sticks apparently thrown together loosely, these must in fact have been skilfully interlocked, for I saw not only completed nests but also skimpy-looking embryonic efforts survive severe wind-storms without a single twig getting blown out of place. During the final stages of the work the crows fetched softer, more pliable materials, like fine rootlets, to make the inmost lining of the lodgment where their ugly offspring were to spend the first tender days of their lives.

A nest completed, the hen bird laid in it anything up to half a dozen slightly glossy, sparsely brown-spotted, whitish eggs.

II

These eggs are liable to interference in a brusque manner. Perhaps the crows deserve that indignity. They are themselves incorrigible stealers of eggs of other species; so no one need shed tears of sympathy if they in their turn are victims of similar depredations. Although Nature recognizes no criminal class, and awards no legal penalties for malefactors, it has its own laws and a system of what might, by human standards, be regarded as rough justice. House Crows' eggs are regularly filched by another pirate. The character responsible for this iniquity is also a common resident in my garden, the Koel.

To come to the point at once, however devoted a pair of Koels may be to each other, they never build a nest, lay eggs in it, or rear their own family. Instead they mate in the entirely proper, orthodox manner—and then do everything else with scant respect for orthodoxy. They deposit their eggs in other birds' nests and shift all the subsequent responsibilities of parenthood to those stooges. In fact, they have acquired the bad habits of cuckoos; and their favourite dupes are House Crows.

Koels are quite large birds measuring seventeen inches long, which is only an inch shorter than the crow itself, though nearly half this dimension is a lengthy, handsomely graduated tail. The male is all black with a bluish-green gloss, while the female wears a brown costume smartly spotted and barred with white. Like some shady characters in the human world, they advertise themselves rather shamelessly, calling aloud and roistering not only during the day but also through much of the night, when reputable citizens should be fast asleep. This is wholly in the hot months, however, when love is in season. During the winter they fall almost completely silent.

I have seen a cock Koel chasing a hen amorously as early as April 21st, which seemed premature, since House Crows are not supposed to start building nests until about a month later. Possibly a few pioneering crows get to work ahead of schedule, and a few precocious Koels likewise beat the gun. Their courtship is a blatant affair. Without any attempt at delicacy, finesse or romantic sentimentalities, a male Koel makes a pounce at a female, she flees with shrieks of outraged virtue, and he gives chase within a foot of her tail, yelling improper proposals to her all the way. More than once I have seen two males pursuing the same female with licentious gusto.

These lewd carryings-on became more frequent in May and reached a crescendo of noisy wantonness in June—about the time when the crows' building activities were reaching a conclusion. One afternoon then I witnessed a typical sample of Koel courtship. A hen bird, and two cocks who were contesting for her favours, stood together in a tree, making quite a musical shindy as they hurled a verbal mixture of compliments and insults at each other. Suddenly the female flew from her bough, and one of the males sped after her, leaving the other behind. She fled frantically, shrieking like an innocent virgin in danger of being raped by a sex maniac.

Her pursuer also cried aloud as he followed her, but he did not succeed in catching up with the lady. Frustrated, he returned to the tree whence they had started, to vent his spleen on his masculine rival. Alighting near him, he gave the other Koel a vituperative piece of his mind. The second bird retorted in kind. Thereupon the first began to advance on the other, hop by hop from twig to twig, with a threatening demeanour. His opponent stood his ground, and before long they were facing each other at close quarters like two duellers. Both struck impressive pugilistic postures, jerking their heads, flicking their tails, and making sparring motions with their wings. Every now and then the challenger uttered a defiant cry, and the challenged replied in a lower but by no means less offensive voice. Staring into each other's eyes with intense mutual disapproval, they poised their beaks like two antagonistic poignards. Their rather mechanical jerkings of heads, flippings of wings and wavings of tails were periodically repeated, and every once in a while the aggressor jabbed his opponent with his bill, scoring a hit. The defender struck back, and at that they both gave bloodcurdling yells.

This contest, which appeared more mock than actual, lasted ten minutes. Then the attacker's anger cooled off, and he gradually moved away from his rival. The other also forgot his retaliatory fury and calmed down. Indeed, he turned and fluttered into another tree; but as he left he made the mistake of emitting a final self-assertive exclamation which at once revived the first bird's resentment. This Koel promptly followed his rival, alighted near him and advanced upon him once more. When they came within striking distance of one another the duel started again, but this time more violently. The antagonists lashed out as if really to inflict wounds, flapping their wings wildly, securing momentarily beak-holds on each other and shouting at the top of their voices. They were well matched, and the combat continued so long that in the end I got bored and left them to it.

Two days later I saw a conclusive affair between a pair of Koels. A hen bird called from a tree, and a cock answered from another tree. Apparently she had made a certain suggestion, for he flew to join her, alighting first on a branch close beside her and then jumping on her back. She crouched compliantly, and they indulged in an unhurried, deliberate act of copulation. As soon as he hopped off her, he flew away. She shook her feathers into place and lingered on the spot where she had surrendered herself to her lover, as if expecting something further to happen. Soon it did. A male Koel flew to her side with berries carried in his beak. She seized them greedily from him and swallowed them. Presumably he was her pick-up, and the fruits were (so to speak) the wages of sin. As soon as he had delivered them he departed, no longer interested.

Or am I being unjust? Are Koels promiscuous, or do they marry monogamously for their brief, irresponsible encounters in the mating season? The heroine of the incident I have just related certainly seemed to behave like a streetwalker calling 'Hullo, dearie', receiving a willing response from a passer-by, and submitting to him in return for payment. But perhaps this is a libel, and her companion was a faithful husband whom she happened to see while he was out for a stroll.

Whatever the truth may be, that embrace between two Koels was the beginning of a sad story for some pair of House Crows.

Just as certain other species of birds customarily mate near their still unfinished nests, so I have seen Koels making love beside an uncompleted crows' nest. This may have been a coincidence. Two crows had recently begun constructing a home in a high tree, and its foundations were well and truly laid in the form of a dozen large, interlaced twigs. During an interval in their labours a cock and a hen Koel alighted within a few feet of it. The male presented his companion with a berry, which she accepted; and then he mounted her and flapped his wings vigorously as they mated. Immediately afterwards he flew away, and soon she departed in the opposite direction. A House Crow returned with a new bit of building material, and a moment later the male Koel arrived back, carrying another berry in his beak. Alighting on the very spot where his little romance had occurred a few minutes earlier, he called aloud inquiringly and looked round for his girlfriend. He stayed there quite a while, shouting repeatedly. The crow was too busy to notice the uninvited visitor, being preoccupied with chewing the bit of stick, trying to soften and bend it into a convenient shape for insertion in the nest. At last the Koel flew away in further search of his enchantress, still gripping the berry.

No doubt Koels keep a watchful, sympathetic eye on a pair of House Crows as they progress with the heavy labour of building a cradle for eggs.

III

On June 6th one year a pair of crows started carrying building materials into the top branches of a mango tree on the lawn. For the next few days they made little progress, seeming lackadaisical and uninterested; but on the 9th they began to work in earnest. I watched one of them exercising great care in the choice of sticks in the grass below the tree, where a lot of broken twigs happened to be strewn. The bird would pick up a bit in its beak, test its feel, decide that it was too light or otherwise impracticable, throw it down again and select another. Sometimes it rejected a dozen pieces for everyone it accepted. I have often seen other builders of stick nests, like pigeons, doves and egrets, show the same pernicketiness in choosing materials for their works. This helps to explain why birds' nests are such efficient constructions, able to survive storms and various other hazards.

For a few days the crows' nest remained a thin, wide-open mesh of strong twigs interlaced across forking branches; but slowly it assumed the form of a quite substantial platform. Then fresh layers of sticks got woven on it, the structure assumed greater solidity, and it gradually grew to be a bulky pile. Although partially concealed among foliage, its mass was apparent to any casual observer; nevertheless, its owners were cautious about approaching it when I stood near the tree, lest they should betray what they hoped was still a well-kept secret.

Their building activities continued for three weeks. One morning towards the end of that period I noticed a crow on the lawn with a bit of soft building material in its bill. It seemed on the point of taking off and carrying its find to the nest; but instead it squatted, half opened its wings and started fluttering them, as if it were offering itself for ravishment. A moment later its mate, which I had not noticed, flew down from the tree, mounted the hen and pleasured her. As it did so its wings flapped excitedly, and it lowered its head until its beak rested on the tilted brow of the female. Throughout the performance she kept her grip on her scrap of building material, and when they had successfully achieved coition she flew to the nest and fitted it neatly into place. Then I knew that eggs were on the way.

I first observed a crow sitting quietly and patiently in the nest, unconcerned with building and bent on another purpose, on June 27th. Both birds now became nervous if I approached the tree. They would caw loudly and drop defensively into the tree's lower branches, making grimaces at me in attempts to shoo me away.

One or two more justly suspect characters also loafed around the place. Several times I saw a hen Koel in the vicinity, and I watched her in the hope that she would fly to the mango tree and sneak on to the nest. But the crows kept a sharp look-out for potential marauders. Their instinctive repugnance to Koels in the breeding season had now become strongly developed, and as soon as one of those flashy creatures appeared, a crow would launch itself into the air and chase the intruder out of the garden, like an Air Force plane in hot pursuit of an enemy craft trespassing on national air space.

Whenever I looked during the next several days a crow was sitting tight in the nest. No doubt eggs were being laid. The male crow—which I could recognize because its beak was more hooked than the female's—became an ever more trigger-happy sentinel, giving chase to any hawk, kite or even eagle that happened to pass by. But the chief targets for its offensive actions remained the Koels. On July 14th I saw it fly with particular venom in pursuit of a hen Koel which had ventured much too near the mango tree. Both crows appeared to be very agitated and excited that morning.

Then I noticed an empty, half egg-shell lying beneath the tree. It looked like a remnant of a boiled hen's egg left by a picnicker, and I assumed that men mowing the lawn had breakfasted there.

Two days later, however, I saw other, smaller fragments of egg-shell scattered in the grass. Some looked like scraps of a hen's product, but on careful examination others proved to have a glossy surface with small brown blotches such as sometimes characterize a House Crow's egg. I wondered whether a Koel had managed to slip through the nest-owners' defences, destroy one of their eggs, and substitute a creation of its own.

Ten days later I suspected that chicks had hatched, for the parent birds began making frequent visits to their stately pile of twigs; but as it was located twenty feet up in the air I could have no notion of its contents. Not wishing to frighten the family by climbing to their retreat, I watched patiently from the ground for the first evidence of the identity of the new-born birds.

For many days they lay doggo in the rough, deep cup of their home, and I did not catch a glimpse of them until August 5th. Then I saw a youngster's head protrude above the nest-rim. It was a fleeting glance, for the little bird quickly bobbed down again at a warning croak from a parent; and I could not be sure whether it was a House Crow or a Koel. But it looked like the former, and I felt disappointed. I had hoped for the drama of a cuckoo-like changeling being foisted on its gullible elders.

Forty-eight hours later two nestlings squatted in full view on branches near the nest; so they already had sufficient strength and energy to climb over their nursery wall. Rather restless, they kept shifting their positions, sometimes hopping back into the nest and then climbing again on to a bough. They looked very juvenile, and I studied their figures and plumage carefully. I realized that I had been mistaken two days earlier. One fledgling was undoubtedly a hen Koel with white streaks already apparent on her brown plumage; and the other looked like a cock of the same species, for its beak was trimmer than one would expect in a crow. So the parent birds had been doubly cheated!

The young female seemed more precocious than her brother, frequently stretching her wings and occasionally shaking them as if to exercise or test them. Both looked extremely youthful and inexperienced, and neither ventured more than a few inches beyond the nest.

Their foster-parents became very concerned whenever I went near the mango tree during the next several days. They would fly to boughs close above my head and utter frightful curses at me. Sometimes they seemed on the point of choking with noisy excitement, and I feared they might suffer apoplectic fits. Their protective affection for their two counterfeit charges was evidently as highly developed as if the little brats had been their true kith and kin.

Most of the time the chicks stayed silent. I never saw them betray the slightest sign of conspiratorial recognition when an adult Koel in the neighbourhood started calling loud greetings to everyone in earshot. They were aware only of their foster-parents as fellow occupants of their tiny world. At the crows' approach they uttered faint, wheezy squawks of hunger which they maintained until they were fed.

The House Crows, on the other hand, were sensitive about the approach of strange Koels. They resented this with a heartfelt bitterness which made them give chase to any Koel that appeared within fifty yards of their nest; and they were not content until the intruder had retreated out of sight beyond the garden's boundaries. Obviously they regarded the Koel tribe as a crowd of wicked beings—with the exception of the two small samples of Koel spawn whom they nourished with such solicitous care! Was there ever a more absurd case of trying to close stable doors after the horses have been stolen?

No additional nestlings ever appeared. The crows' sole charges were the two impostors. Their own clutch of eggs must have been entirely destroyed, however numerous it was.

Gradually the young Koels grew in strength, fluttering further and further from their home on expeditions of exploration in the large mango tree, but always hastening back to the nest at the slightest unexpected incident. I think they roosted there every night for another fortnight. Their figures and plumage grew ever more mature, until there could be no mistaking their almost exact identities with the adult representatives of the species who frequented the garden. Yet their foster-parents continued to be blind to the obvious.

It was an extraordinary situation. The crows would become enraged at the sight of a strange Koel and launch themselves in vicious assault at it, only to return immediately afterwards to coddle its very images in the nest. Primitive parental instinct can sometimes be as pathetically misguided as it is admirably strong.

The fledglings waxed steadily more robust, constantly exercising their wings by flying from bough to bough. For two weeks after they first stepped from the nest, however, they never, even on their widest-ranging excursions, ventured outside the spacious mango tree, staying within its confines like pets held captive in a large cage. The reason for this was that they still depended on their guardians for nourishment. One would peck or nibble at a leaf, as if it were trying an experiment at feeding itself; but for long the results were unsatisfying. The youngsters' hunger was evident when a House Crow arrived in the tree; at once they would emit subdued yet desperate-sounding cries for food, and would quiver their wings in a paroxysm of greed. The foster-parents fed them by regurgitation.

On August 18th the female Koel—the elder and stronger of the pair—suddenly flew into a rusty-shieldbearer tree a few feet away. The foliage there was thinner, and so the young bird had more freedom for exercise and manoeuvre. It spread its wings, fanned its tail and stretched its legs frequently, hopping and fluttering round and round from branch to branch in the tree. It was still a trifle clumsy, alighting sometimes with imperfect balance and staggering to keep itself upright. It needed a lot of practice yet to make its movements self-assured.

Soon it flew back to the mango tree and perched beside the nest. Its flight across the space between the two trees was swift, smooth and purposeful—exactly like that of an adult Koel. The foster-parents were watching, and one would have supposed they would be unpleasantly struck by the similarity in form and motion between their young ward and their inveterate enemies; but apparently no such thought entered their thick heads. When the second Koel flew later into the next tree, both crows followed close on its tail, affording it the honour and protection of a double escort; and when I walked near they tried with special vigour to frighten me away.

Perching just above my head, they swore like troopers, stabbed their beaks furiously into the bough on which they stood, and in fits of angry concern broke off small twigs and hurled them to the ground.

For another week after that the young Koels confined themselves to the two trees. Then they took a further step towards emancipation from dependence on elders of a strange breed. One evening I saw them perched side by side on a branch in the rusty-shieldbearer tree, looking settled for the night. Of a sudden an adult Koel started calling with typical ringing insistence from the next-door garden. Whether in instinctive awakening response to this, or from some other natural impulse, the older fledgling at once became restless. It hopped for a while from bough to bough, and then returned to its roosting companion and pecked at him gently, as if to stir him also into action. But the second bird seemed sleepy, and stayed phlegmatically unmoved. The other then leapt to a higher branch, its movements became quicker and more nervous, and it flew about widely in the tree, aroused by some mysterious discontent. It was possessed by a confusing split-personality, partly young crow and partly adolescent Koel. One of its foster-parents arrived, aware somehow of its mood, and cawed encouragingly to it. The youngster flew to the outer edge of the tree, hesitated there uncertainly, then suddenly mustered its resolution, spread its wings and flew across a wide lawn to a tall shrub alongside the garden whence the adult Koel's voice had sounded. Both House Crows followed in its wake, like two cruisers escorting a gallant little destroyer. They kept calling, in felicitation rather than concern. The fledgling halted in the shrub for a while and then took off again, speeding into a tree in the middle of the next-door lawn. For a while I saw it silhouetted in the dusk among some foliage, but then darkness descended too thickly for me to watch it any more.

Perhaps my imagination was too vivid, or possibly I was too inclined to attribute human motives to birds; but it seemed to me that when the young Koel went and nudged its fellow fledgling, it was attempting to say, 'Come on, little brother, let's leave. It's time we went adventuring in the world,' and that when its less enterprising relative did not respond, it decided to 'go it alone'. I presumed it had left its original home for ever.

However, when I visited the rusty-shieldbearer early the next morning the young cock Koel was on the same perch where it roosted the previous night—and beside it was its sister. The wanderer had returned! Probably she felt lonely in the next garden. Before long a crow flew to them, and both youngsters immediately quivered their wings and wheezed aloud in a violent demonstration of hunger. This elementary dependence on the crows for being fed still kept them from flying away and becoming unqualified, unashamed, honest-to-god Koels.

As I watched, the female youngster became restless again, flying round and round inside the tree like a goldfish circling inside a vast bowl. Then she broke out of the tree and sped with unmistakably Koel-ish action to a distant shrubbery. If the crows had seen an adult Koel do exactly the same they would have raced instantaneously after it with every mark of hostility; and one crow did indeed speed after the young Koel—but with signs of most gentle, friendly solicitude! Alighting beside its ward, it croaked approvingly while the fledgling fluttered its wings and opened its beak in a shameless request for food. Then the second youngster joined them, attended by the second foster-parent, and both crows broke into a chorus of congratulatory cries at their adopted family's achievement.

During the next several days this incongruous quartet of 'parents' and 'children' travelled freely from tree to tree in my and my neighbour's gardens, steadily extending their area of travels. The principal vocal expression of the young birds was still a juvenile, hoarse grunting of hunger; but occasionally they would emit a rather more musical, high-pitched shriek with a faint suggestion of a Koel's ringing call. Their character as Koels was gradually becoming more pronouncedly revealed. Yet still the fond, dense crows were deceived.

By now at least two sets of other fledgling Koels, slavishly attended by crow guardians, were paying visits to the garden. Evidently several pairs of mating Koels had duped several pairs of nesting House Crows in the neighbourhood. I could not always distinguish between one family party and another; but the crows felt no such difficulty. The stubborn refusal of my pair of crows to recognize the similarity between the young Koels whom they protected and the old Koels whom they assaulted became an even odder quirk in their characters when they at once distinguished between their own fledgling Koels and all other, apparently identical, fledgling Koels. If one of those other Koel youngsters came near them, they adopted towards it an attitude almost (though not quite) as unfriendly as if it had been an adult.

More frequently now I saw young Koels pecking at foliage in attempts to feed themselves. Indeed, one morning I caught sight of the older of the pair born in my garden gripping proudly in its beak a berry, which it had just succeeded in plucking. But when it tried to swallow the fruit, it fumbled and dropped the morsel by mistake—like an inexperienced user of chopsticks losing hold of some delicacy as he sought to pop it in his mouth.

Gradually the youngsters' skill in gathering their own provisions developed, and the transition from dependence to independence was complete. So far as I could observe, the moment of this final emancipation did not arrive for my two Koels until the end of the first week in September, a whole month after their initial stepping from the nest. Sometime after that they waved a final farewell to the House Crows who had been for so long their devoted nursemaids.

Had their true parents been keeping an eye on them all this time? And did the youngsters receive a cordial welcome from the older generation of Koels when they were at last free to acknowledge their kinship? I do not know.

IV

The hatching of Koel chicks in that House Crows' nest was no isolated, unique event in the garden. During my three years of bird-watching, six pairs of crows built nests there, and only in three of them were their own chicks born. In the other three Koels' eggs were foisted on the unwitting crows, and the old birds lavished their maternal and paternal affection on Koel changelings.

When no Koel intrudes on the scene to add a touch of villainy to the act, conjugal life between House Crows lacks drama. It is a prosaic affair. Let me sketch the main events in the experience of a pair who nested one June about forty feet high in an Australian silver oak. Both birds helped in building their formidable pile of sticks, and both took a share in the labour of incubating eggs. One bird would often bring food to the other as it sat in the nest, producing the meal by regurgitation with all the bland aplomb of a conjurer picking a boiled egg out of his empty mouth.

Their youngsters hatched about the middle of July, and I caught my first glimpse of them towards the end of the month. They were ugly, scruffy, large-beaked, pop-eyed little crows, an unpleasant contrast to sleek young Koels. When they begged for food they made a louder, more raucous noise than Koel chicks would have done.

Whenever I saw them I was struck afresh by their monstrous ugliness. In the first few days of August they left their nest from time to time to perch on surrounding branches; but periodically they returned to the nursery, and they always slept there at night. As the days passed their looks gradually improved, their heads growing into better proportion with their oversized beaks, their necks appearing less scrawny as their feathers filled out, the plumage on their bodies acquiring a smart gloss, and its mixture of black and grey presenting a distinguished pattern.

Like young Koels, they did not venture from their home tree for more than a fortnight after first stepping from the nest. Then they flew into a mango tree thirty yards away, escorted by jubilant parents. They landed a trifle awkwardly, but recovered their sangfroid quickly and soon made themselves at home in the new surroundings. When I went to take a close look at them their guardians became extremely agitated, cawing wild protests at me. One dive-bombed me three or four times in attempts to frighten me away.

Shortly afterwards I watched one of the young crows enjoy its first experience of sustained flight. Mounting uncertainly into the air, it steadied itself on outstretched wings low above the treetop, and then began circling round and round in a confined space of sky, with no apparent purpose except to experiment with its pinions. Its wing-beats were slower than those of a practised crow aviator, its face and body looked tensely held, and its style was more amateur than professional. It remained thus aloft for several minutes; and occasionally one of the adult birds rose on stronger wings, with swifter, surer flight, to accompany it over a short space. This mature companion wore a distinctly protective air towards the young adventurer.

For another two weeks the youngsters stayed in the garden with their parents, dependent on them for food; but they became steadily more independent, and by the end of August their voices had developed a deep-throated caw scarcely distinguishable from that of their elders and betters. The family then merged with small flocks of other old and young House Crows. The sweet, innocent days of childhood were over.

TWELVE

THE MONSOON—JULY, AUGUST AND SEPTEMBER

I

The monsoon breaks in Delhi in early July. Sending a few cloud-heralds ahead to proclaim its coming, it then occupies the city with a sudden sopping onslaught of rain and dismisses the very dry, very hot summer into banishment for a year. During the next ten weeks the temperature remains high—hovering between 90 and 100 °F—but the atmosphere becomes exceedingly moist and sticky. Periodically, fresh torrential rain-storms descend. Roads and gardens are flooded, electricity and other public services get temporarily damaged, and the citizens' comfort and tempers suffer. It is the only climatically unpleasant period in a capital whose weather throughout the rest of the twelve months has much to commend it, despite its occasional fierce moods.

II

The loveliest of all Delhi's winged inhabitants, the Golden Orioles, arrived for their annual sojourn in northern India at the beginning of April. They sang melodious catches of song to each other throughout the next few weeks; and many were paired and nest-building by the end of that month. These quick workers were the proud parents of chicks in May, and in June fledglings recently out of nests appeared with their parents in my garden. But the nests that I found there were still laden with family cares in July.

It was enchanting to see a flash of golden-green followed closely by a flash of pure gold dart above the lawn—a hen Golden Oriole brightly shadowed by her male escort. On earlier such journeys they flew to the accompaniment of their own mellifluous music, for he was courting her and sang the orioles' equivalent of the Kashmiri love-song—Golden Orioles being partial to summering in Kashmir. But now they were building a nest and did not wish to draw unnecessary attention to themselves; so they travelled in silence. She did all the work, and he merely gave her devoted moral support. Among other nesting materials they favoured the fine, plumed stem-tops of a tall reed which grew in my shrubbery, and many times a female would alight in that reed-bed to examine the stems for a sample of the right length, texture and lightness. As she hopped from plant to plant, the stalks bent and swayed gracefully beneath her weight, and she would consider their comparative merits with all the careful deliberation of a lady choosing the most becoming silk for a dress. When she made up her mind, she gripped the chosen stem in her beak, snapped its top off (plume and all) and then adjusted her hold on it to balance it conveniently across her bill. Sometimes she selected three or four specimens at one visit to the shrubbery and carried them all together in her beak. Her gorgeous-looking mate watched her with approving eyes from a near-by perch, and when she left to carry her load to their nest he also took off and followed her, like an elegant, gaudily uniformed A.D.C. escorting a Governor's consort home from a shopping expedition.

The nest was a loose though closely-woven bag of grasses slung beneath a drooping, forking branch near the outer edge of a tree. It was roomy, comfortable and well sprung on its flexible bough, swaying gently in every breeze. Usually it was concealed in foliage, a very necessary precaution, for otherwise the brilliant plumage of its owners as they visited the site would betray its whereabouts. Like other birds, whether plain or beautiful, they had enemies; and when they owned nests they acquired a fine quality of courageous pugnacity in their defence. I often saw a hen oriole chasing a House Crow from her home tree.

Even more frequent quarrels arose between hen Golden Orioles and hen Green Parakeets. These tiffs always ended in a vicious, sustained pursuit of the parakeet by the oriole, the former flying panic-stricken and squealing in protest as she swerved swiftly this way and that to escape the latter, who followed closely on her tail repeating exactly her every manoeuvre. I was never sure what caused their bickerings. The two species cannot have been rivals for nesting sites, since they occupied entirely different types of premises; and so far as I know neither was a stealer of the other's eggs, a kidnapper of the other's young, or a seducer of the other's mate. The reason for their conflict seemed more trifling. Once, for example, I saw a hen parakeet and a hen oriole perched near each other on the same branch. They were quiet and passive until the parakeet suddenly pecked disapprovingly at the oriole's tail. The oriole at once flew into a rage, snapped back, and launched herself in impetuous assault on her neighbour, who promptly fled with loud shrieks. At other times the oriole seemed to be the original picker of the quarrel. Could it be that both birds recognized the exceeding loveliness of the other, that a feminine sense of rivalry filled the two famous beauties' breasts, and that every now and then it so enraged them that they fell out in violent quarrels?

Just as the hen oriole receives little effective assistance from the male in the building of their nest, so also (I think) she performs all, or almost all, the duties of incubating their eggs. When their chicks hatch he recovers a more proper sense of his parental duties and helps to feed them. But he is less assiduous than she, and also much shyer about approaching the nest if some unusual, suspicious presence is around. We raised 'hides' near two Golden Orioles' nests to take photographs of them. After some initial surprise at the appearance of the hide, and considerable hesitation about approaching the vicinity, the hen in each case later accustomed herself to the new monstrosity and brought food regularly to her youngsters. But the cock was so disturbed that for twenty-four hours after the hide's erection he absented himself entirely, and for another day or two after that his visits were rare. If the nestlings had depended on him for nourishment, they would have starved before he recovered his confidence. The same was true of the males and females of various other species whom we photographed. It was an interesting illustration of the comparative strengths of the maternal and the paternal instincts in birds.

Thanks to the loving care of their mothers, the oriole chicks in all the nests in the garden survived the hazards of infancy, grew in vigour day by day, and in due course added their beautiful personages to the bird population of Delhi.

III

We wished to get pictures of the Spotted Owlets occupying a hole in the house wall; and so we built a hide against the Australian silver oak where they invariably perched for a while before entering and after leaving their dwelling. The birds, however, felt disturbed by this structure, and began to follow another route for their entrances and exits. So photography was impracticable. Nevertheless, the owlets were not deterred altogether, and continued to live in their retreat.

It was the end of July, and for some weeks past a pair of Common Mynahs had attempted (as in the previous year) to cajole and bully the owlets out of their hole, so that the mynahs themselves might nest there. But the owlets stubbornly stood their ground. One morning I saw the usual scuffle between the contending species. A mynah kept perching on the threshold of the passage leading into the hole, as if to enter; but it merely fluttered its wings and screeched frustratedly while the two owlets—both of whom I could see indoors—glared scornfully back at it. They were so sure of their right of ownership by long usage that they did not even bother to make verbal protest at the would-be gate-crasher's ruderies.

It was remarkable that the mynahs never accepted defeat. Month after month, right through the breeding season, they maintained their efforts to eject the owlets; and with equal resolution the owlets refused to budge.

After the mynah left that morning I watched one owlet affectionately scratch the other's head with its beak inside their home—a charming picture of established contentment. Later in the day some workmen removed the hide—and when I visited the place that afternoon the scene had completely changed. A Common Mynah was flying into the owlets' private property, carrying building material! Gazing astonished through my field-glasses into the hole in the wall, I discerned a massive, untidy foundation for a mynah's nest piled within.

The owlets must have taken fright while the workmen were demolishing the hide, and deserted. Characteristically, the mynahs lost no time in moving in as their successors. After dark that evening I heard an owlet's voice raised in protest in the silver oak; but in vain. Next morning the mynahs were carrying more building material into the wall.

For the next six weeks they remained in occupation of the place. Sometimes in the evenings and early mornings I heard the owlets expostulating in the tree a few feet away; but they failed to reassert effectively their landlordly rights. In due course the mynahs produced eggs and hatched chicks.

Yet the owlets never lost interest in their old abode. One morning, just over a month after their rivals had turned the tables on them, I happened to look from my bathroom window. It was half an hour before sunrise, and an almost full moon rode in a dark sky. At that moment a silhouette of a bird flew into the silver oak; and I saw that it was a Spotted Owlet. Immediately both Common Mynahs issued from their nest-hole breathing sound and fury; and at once the owlet retreated to another tree twenty yards away. The mynahs pursued it there, and for the next ten minutes the trio fought a violent battle of words. By now the mynahs had youngsters to protect, and they suspected the visitor's intentions. They were not happy to let it perch even a score of yards distant, and sought to persuade it by threats—or was it really sweet avian reason?—to leave the vicinity altogether. In the end the owlet meekly did so.

That was an interesting, significant incident. In the previous year the owlets had been in occupation of the hole, and without difficulty they frustrated all the mynahs' efforts to gain admission. Now the mynahs were in occupation, and with equal ease they prevented the very same owlets from forcing a re-entry. Those facts seemed to establish the principle that in bird society, as in human society, possession is eleven points of the law. But it established more than that. The owlets, and very likely the mynahs too, were the same combatants as twelve months earlier, each endowed with exactly the same qualities. So why did the owlets prove the stronger pair one year, and the mynahs prove the stronger pair the next? It must be because, whereas the owlets were protecting a home with nestlings on the first occasion, the mynahs were now the defenders of a young family. This seemed to show that the relative power of different species does not depend solely on their comparative physical strengths, but also on their comparative emotional states. The decisive element settling the issue between the owlets and the mynahs in each conflict was the extent to which the birds' emotions, indeed passions, were aroused at any given moment. Parenthood lent a species added zeal, determination and power.

The same principle is illustrated when nesting bulbuls chase Tree Pies, nesting drongos chase kites, nesting crows chase eagles, and other nesting species strive against enemies much larger than themselves.

The Spotted Owlets enjoyed a sort of revenge, for another pair of Common Mynahs were accustomed each year to rear a family in a second, exactly similar hole further along the same stretch of house wall; and I discovered that when the owlets left their own resort on the day that workmen disturbed them, they found this other resort empty, and commandeered it. There they snoozed all day—and when two mynahs appeared with nesting material, expecting to occupy the place as usual, the new tenants shoo'd them off! Every morning for the next few weeks skirmishes between them took place; but in this instance the law of possession operated in the owlets' favour.

Eventually the fledgling mynahs left the first nest-hole, and their parents departed with them. Next morning I saw a Spotted Owlet perched in the tree just outside its entrance—and the other owlet crouching indoors. The second bird's head protruded from behind the heap of the mynahs' recent nest, like the face of a rebel peering over a street barricade on a day of revolution. At the very same moment a pair of Common Mynahs were carrying building material into the other hole, now vacated by the owlets. So the interruption caused by the erection of a futile bird hide was ended, and avian affairs had reverted to normal.

IV

One evening I saw a very unusual bird feeding amid a flock of sparrows outside the kitchen door. It was a blue sparrow. The markings on its plumage seemed similar to those of the vulgar crowd with whom it condescendingly associated, except for that wondrous, heavenly indigo hue. Among its drab, brown plebeian cousins it appeared a scion of royalty—or even some fairy-like apparition from another world, such as the Blue Bird of Happiness.

At my first glimpse of it I got excited, studied it carefully to memorize its features, and then ran indoors to consult the erudite pundits marshalled on my library bookshelves. Apparently, for some astonishing reason, neither Whistler, Stuart-Baker, Salim Ali, nor any of half a dozen other authorities had ever heard of this magical creature. In all their roll-calls of the sparrow tribe there was no species which could by any remote stretch of the imagination be described as blue. Yet I could not have been mistaken, and I hurried out of doors again to glean new, irrefutable facts about my great discovery. Sure enough, in the middle of the throng of lesser beings, feeding on seeds thrown by my servants through the kitchen doorway, was the lovely vision—the Ultramarine Sparrow (as I called it tentatively, until those learned in the mysteries of scientific ornithological nomenclature could attach a proper name to it).

Examining it more carefully, I was struck by another strange feature of the bird. Its blue feathers did not shine with the natural gloss of more ordinary plumes, their texture seeming dull. Then I noticed a further odd circumstance in the landscape. My bearers were all peeping surreptitiously through the kitchen windows, watching my excited perplexity with grins on their faces.

The truth dawned on me. My discovery was a House Sparrow which they had captured, dipped in indigo dye, and released when they saw me stroll towards their corner of the garden on my morning round of observations!

On another occasion I was intrigued at the sight of a rare munia in a vegetable patch. Its small round head, blunt beak and slim, tapering body were familiar from my acquaintance with the earthy-brown Whitethroated Munias common in Delhi, as well as from other munias scattered through South-East Asia. But this specimen was bright green. It was solitary, like a stranger wandering into a strange land, though it hopped around trustfully, and gave me good opportunities to study its features.

When I consulted the reference books afterwards I concluded that it must be a Green Munia. No tome contained a picture of the species, so I could not feel absolutely certain; yet it seemed to answer to the verbal descriptions, or at least to come nearer them than to the account of any other type of munia. Only one point of doubt left me somewhat sceptical. All the authorities agreed that the extreme northern limit of the Green Munia's migrations is Jhansi. I knew Jhansi well, for it is the railway junction from which one motors to view the glorious temples at Khajuraho—and the place is situated 200 miles south of Delhi!

However, I recollected my impression that the munia in my garden seemed conscious of being a little out of place, a sojourner in a strange land; and I hoped that this solitary bird might be the forerunner, the lone pioneer, the pathfinder of a fresh spirit of enterprise, a new adventuresomeness among Green Munias which would bring them trekking as far north as India's capital.

I went out of doors again, and lo and behold, the bird was still busily feeding in the same vegetable patch. It had now been joined by half a dozen other creatures who flitted around it in lively fashion as they, too, searched for food. They were all Whitethroated Munias, and I realized that except for its different hue the green vision was their exact replica.

The Monsoon—July, August and September

Like the blue sparrow, it was a fake—a dyed doll! In this case I did not suspect my servants, but some anonymous disciple of Salim Ali conducting a scientific experiment to observe the foibles of these gay, lightsome Whitethroated Munias.

V

Pairs of Magpie Robins nested in the garden from May onwards. They were discreet householders, selecting unobtrusive holes in tree trunks in which to hide their eggs. Sometimes they quarrelled with Common and Brahminy Mynahs about possession of a property, and on those occasions they usually admitted defeat in the face of the others' ruder forcefulness of purpose. Magpie Robins have genteel manners. But once they had established proprietary rights to a crevice, the cock defended the place with knightly valour. He would post himself outside its entrance while his mate sat within, and dash furiously at any intruder, including the boldest of mynahs.

The hen seemed to do all the nest-building, though the male dutifully escorted her as she flew to and fro fetching bits of grass for upholstering the interior of their apartment. Like most female Magpie Robins, those in my garden invariably added a piece of a snake's cast-off skin as decoration to their homes, as if the species harboured a superstition that this odd talisman would keep away evil spirits. Her eggs safely laid, the hen incubated them without any assistance from her mate beyond his almost perpetual guardianship outside their doorway. When the chicks hatched he became more active, sharing the labour of feeding them. But like a male oriole, he was shyer, more easily discouraged than she. When we built a hide from which to take photographs at a nest last July, the cock bird became terrified and virtually went on strike. Only rarely in the next few days did he visit the home tree. Then he would flutter nervously on to every branch in the tree in turn except the one containing his young family, though he carried food for them in his beak. When he finally plucked up courage to perch at the entry to the nest, he instantly turned and fled in fright when the flashlamps flashed—with the food still gripped in his bill.

The hen bird was at first also greatly alarmed, and acted similarly; but after a while the heartrending buzzes for nourishment from her famished youngsters proved more compelling than her fear of the flashlamps, and she resumed her regular visits with rations of food.

VI

One morning in early August I almost trod on an Indian Nightjar squatting asleep on an obscure path winding through a shrubbery. The bird woke with a start, and immediately rose and fluttered silently for about a dozen yards, weaving a tortuous course low among the bushes, and then settling once more on the ground. When I walked forward and disturbed it again, it repeated exactly the same performance, alighting once more a score of yards further on, where it hoped to remain invisible. Four times I flushed it, and four times it went through the same brief succession of actions, almost as if it were a piece of automatic mechanism set in motion by my approach. I had excellent opportunities to observe its cunningly camouflaged plumage, which would have concealed it from me even at very close quarters if I had not known precisely where to look. Its instinctive confidence in the efficacy of that camouflage was remarkable; for when disturbed it never troubled to shift more than a short distance away.

On the following day I disturbed it again on the same spot, and once more we both played our parts exactly as before. But the nightjar must have found this tedious, for I never found it on any later morning. Probably it merely moved slightly off the path and snoozed through the daylight hours a few feet away, where I could not distinguish it from its surroundings.

Quite often at dusk, and later on moonlight nights, I caught glimpses of the silhouette of a nightjar flitting, silent but purposeful, above the lawn and flower-beds.

VII

Vultures of various kinds often soared majestically in the blue above my garden, but only one type ever deigned to alight on its lawn. That, of course, was my own fault. If I had chosen to turn the place into a morgue for dead dogs, donkeys, bullocks and other carrion, the grand scavengers would have descended in multitudes to entertain me endlessly with their disgusting orgies.

The only representative of the clan who visited my precincts a few times was the Neophron, alias the Egyptian Vulture, alias Pharaoh's Chicken. Occasionally one perched in a tree above my shrubbery and surveyed the scene in the hope of spying a tempting piece of offal lying around. The bird is a scruffy, unbecoming creature somewhat smaller than other vultures, measuring twenty-four inches long as compared with the Whitebacked Vulture's thirty-five inches. A few white, hair-like plumes project from its head as if it were a mangy albino golliwog; its face is a fleshy, wrinkled yellow mask through which gaze small, mean eyes; its beak is murderous; and its body is dirtily patterned in off-white and black.

Early one morning a Neophron flew low over the garden, circled round two or three times with sinister mien above the lawn, and then to my astonishment landed in the grass. It walked cautiously—with much peering around to make sure no unfriendly eyes observed it—to a shapeless dark heap which I noticed lying at the edge of a flower-bed. Arrived beside this object, the bird jabbed and pecked at it as if testing its substance, and then caught hold of it and dragged it across the ground to a more convenient position. I went to examine the scavenger's treasure-trove. The vulture was holding it down with one clawed foot while stabbing and tearing at it with an avid beak. So preoccupied was it that it did not see me until I drew quite close. Then it glanced up at me, stepped reluctantly off its quarry, spread its wings and flew thirty yards away. There it stayed looking at me resentfully while I inspected the corpse.

The dead animal was a rat-like creature about the size of a mongoose, but with a long hairless tail.

As soon as I moved away the bird returned to the body and resumed its greedy work of dismemberment. Gratified though I was to get such a close-up view of Pharaoh's Chicken, I could not feel flattered by its visit. Later a Common Pariah Kite alighted beside it and looked enviously at the feast, but did not dare to attempt to join in. A House Crow proved more impertinent. Landing near the Neophron, it strutted round it several times, every now and then edging close to the carrion, stabbing at it swiftly with its beak, and stealing each time a small scrap of offal. Once it managed to drag away a stringy length of entrails, which it proceeded to swallow with the zest of an Italian gourmet savouring spaghetti. The Neophron was too obsessed with its own gobbling to prevent these petty thefts; but it would not have allowed greater liberties. With one foot planted possessively on the dead rodent, it kept tearing voraciously at the flesh.

When I revisited the scene an hour later the Neophron had departed, and almost all the deceased beast had gone with it. Nothing of it was left except some clean-picked bones and a few tufts of fur.

VIII

Except for a small goldfish pool there was no splash of water in the garden. No pond or stream tempted water birds to alight and loiter there. Only once did such a creature stray into the precincts, as if by mistake. One mid July morning I was astonished to see a Whitebreasted Waterhen stalk across the lawn, its gawky grey-and-white figure and nervous strut lending an exotic touch to the smooth, cultivated garden. The bird itself seemed rather surprised at being in such unaccustomed surroundings; yet the explanation of its presence was simple. The monsoon had broken during the previous night, rain had descended in torrents for hours, and the lawn looked like a miniature model of a lake district, with small green isles emerging here and there where the ground was uneven. All the world that morning seemed to be a playground for Whitebreasted Waterhens.

Except for that incident, aquatic birds contented themselves with flights above the garden. Quite often they came. In addition to egrets and herons, Little Cormorants and Common Cormorants put in occasional appearances during the rains. Several times in the monsoon months small parties of River Terns also sped overhead on sharp-pointed, gracefully-curving wings, and sometimes Blackbellied Terns did likewise. I do not know why they only arrived at that moment of the year, for they are residents in Delhi. It may have been coincidence that I caught no glimpses of them at other seasons.

Some intriguing marsh birds also flew over between July and September more often than in the other nine months. They included the White Ibis, unmistakable with its swan-white body, black neck and head, and long, down-curving beak. The grotesque-faced Black Ibis also put in several appearances then. Other monsoon acquaintances were a quartet of storks: the Painted Stork, the Blacknecked Stork, the Whitenecked Stork and the Openbilled Stork. All these were handsome on the wing, and it was exciting to see small companies of them make a fly-past. It never entered their heads to nest in the garden or elsewhere in the city. For breeding they resorted to high tree-tops in remote villages or open country where rustic quietude surrounded them. There we followed them to secure their solemn, dignified family portraits.

IX

A Common Kingfisher once scooted within a few inches of my nose as I stood on the lawn; and it got as big a fright as I did when I jumped with surprise. Until I moved it must have presumed I was an immovable natural object in the landscape. I never saw it or any of its kind in the garden again.

Three or four times a Pied Kingfisher flew overhead, very handsome in its black-and-white livery.

Its relative, the Whitebreasted Kingfisher, was a fairly frequent visitor to the garden. Quite often its excitable cackle made all other sounds in the neighbourhood seem insignificant, and its brilliant blue wings brought flashes of gem-like beauty to the scene. One of the larger kingfishers, it measures eleven inches long from the tip of its formidable red beak to the end of its stunted brown tail, and its plumage is a striking combination of sapphire, chestnut, white and sable. To some extent its name is misleading, for unlike other members of its tribe, this sporting creature is more a hunter than a fisher.

One August a Whitebreasted Kingfisher came every morning, and again every late afternoon, to the garden, engaged on 'safari'. Using a low branch in a mango tree as its 'machan', it perched there for an hour or two at a time as it watched wild game creep through the grassy lawn five feet below. That jungle was alive with creatures like beetles, grasshoppers and other insects; but most of these were too small to attract the hunter. It was searching for big game like lizards, frogs and the fattest, longest, juiciest worms. The latter especially were plentiful after downpours of rain, and the sportsman's bag was then very gratifying. Every few minutes he would pounce from his perch, extract a worm from the ground and lift it captive in his beak. Always the catch wriggled in protest, and sometimes its size and strength were so considerable that for a while it defied successfully the bird's efforts to subdue it. Twisting and turning vigorously, it sought to escape its captor's clutch; and the kingfisher had to bash it several times on the earth or on a tree branch before its resistance was finally overcome. Then the bird swallowed with relish this latest fruit of the chase.

The machan happened to be near my lily pond, and I sometimes suspected the hunter of turning poacher and stealing my goldfish; for periodically Whitebreasted Kingfishers resort to a fish diet. My suspicions were first aroused one afternoon when I caught sight of the bird perched in a high tree, soaking wet, as if it had just been immersed in water. It was preening and shaking its feathers to dry them. Five minutes later my apprehensions were sharpened when it flew to a bougainvillaea beside the goldfish pond and settled on a stem overlooking the pool. I thought I would now catch the thief red-handed, and for half an hour I spied on it from afar through field-glasses. All that time the kingfisher stayed on its perch, gazing down at the water every now and then, and sometimes crouching as if it were about to dive. But for long it did no more than that. Then suddenly it half opened its wings, dropped from its stance and shot towards the pool. I watched its line of flight critically—but it passed low over the pool, landed on the ground just beyond, extracted a worm from the grass and flew with it back to the bougainvillaea. Several times in the next ten minutes it repeated the performance, each time swallowing its unfishy meat with obvious pleasure. I granted it a temporary reprieve.

But I did not feel satisfied that this act was not a clever ruse to relieve me unjustifiably of my suspicion. How, otherwise, could the bird explain its sopping wetness earlier that afternoon?

Often in the next few weeks I saw it perched on the bougainvillaea, with its eyes peering down keenly at the pond and its beak poised sharply like a harpoon ready for hurling into the water. Yet every time that it dived earthwards it skimmed over the pool, alighted on the lawn beyond, and captured another land-lubber worm... Except on one occasion. Then its body plummeted suddenly from its perch and plunged straight into the water. At last, I thought, the criminal had, in a careless moment, given itself away. It remained hidden by a splash of water for a fraction of a second, and then emerged triumphantly gripping its catch in its beak. The captive was—a frog.

To this day I do not know whether the kingfisher ever stole any of my goldfish.

x

Towards the end of August this year several Large Grey Babblers built a nest in a rusty shieldbearer tree on the lawn. Many strange events occurred round their home which completely bamboozled me. I had no idea of the precise significance of some of them, and the story became a mystery tale to which I never discovered most of the solutions. The only feature that seemed clearly established was that it was a murder mystery; and—to add to the novelty of the incident—though the identity of the murderer was quite apparent, what remained in doubt was the identity of the victim.

My attention was first drawn to the situation on August 25th, when I noticed three Large Grey Babblers taking a hand (or rather, a beak) in laying the foundation twigs of a nest. It transpired later that four birds in all—presumably two pairs—were concerned in the work; which seemed to prove that these babblers, like their cousins the Jungle Babblers and unlike their other relatives the Yelloweyed Babblers, cooperate in the running of communal nurseries. Often the whole quartet were gathered together near the nest as its construction proceeded, and more often than not they were chattering in the raucous tones typical of these incorrigibly garrulous birds. They made no attempt to keep the existence of their nest a secret; on the contrary, they frequently advertised its whereabouts by their loud-mouthed gossipings on its very doorstep. This seemed to be inviting trouble for beings with so many potential enemies.

On the second day of the nest's existence the few interlocked sticks composing its embryo looked like the beginnings of a dove's nest. Apparently this idea struck a pair of Ring Doves even more forcibly than it did me, for I was astonished to see a cock dove fly into the tree with a piece of building material in its bill, give the twig to a hen dove sitting right on the babblers' nest, and then speed away to fetch another stick! When a babbler returned, this rightful owner shoo'd the illegal squatter away; but the misunderstanding between the doves and babblers about their respective claims to the property continued for two days, causing a sporadic feud between them. After that the Ring Doves admitted their mistake and flew away.

The structure was skied twenty feet from the ground on a branch too thin and brittle for me to reach by climbing either on my own feet or up the steps of a ladder—an unfortunate circumstance which prevented me from observing at any stage precisely what was happening in the nest. Otherwise I could have unravelled some of its attendant mysteries by straightforward ocular evidence.

The babblers were casual builders. They seemed in no hurry to complete their construction, on some days toiling hard and regularly at the task, and on other days appearing to forget it altogether. I was never quite sure when they finally completed the work. Several times during the second, third and fourth weeks of their effort I thought the job was finished, only to see the birds bring fresh building material to the site a day or two later. Long before the end of that period the nest looked a formidable pile, large and untidy enough to satisfy the taste of the most punctilious babbler. It was built of dry, tough sticks on top of a branch where upward-sprouting twigs buttressed its walls, which were cleverly fitted among them. Its texture and form appeared like a slightly smaller edition of a House Crows' nest.

Again, this similarity apparently struck another species of bird besides myself. From the early stages of its growth the nest exerted a fascination over certain Koels. On the second day of its building two male Koels flew into the tree and gazed interestedly at it from close quarters. Characteristically, at that moment all the babblers were conspicuous by their absence. Five minutes later a female Koel flew not only into the tree, but right on to the unfinished nest. Peering down at the structure, she bent her head and touched its twigs appraisingly with her bill. Disturbed by my arrival, she hopped out and perched a few feet away; but soon afterwards she returned to the nest and once more nuzzled its floor with her beak.

Eight days later, when the nest had grown quite large, I again saw a hen Koel in the tree. She stood a few feet above the babblers' work of construction, staring inquisitively at it. Three babblers arrived on the scene, and so long as they dallied there she did not move; but as soon as they left she hopped towards the nest. Then a House Crow alighted in the tree, cawing threateningly, and at the appearance of this hereditary foe the Koel turned tail and retreated to the nearest shrubbery. Perching on a branch where she could keep an eye on the nest, she stayed for a long time watchful there. The return of the babblers made her remain discreetly on that look-out post.

Two days later I caught sight of the hen Koel again standing right in the nest. She stayed motionless for several minutes, not squatting—perhaps disturbed by my arrival. Then two babblers flew into the tree, and she immediately stepped out of the nest and departed. No doubt the babblers saw the trespasser, and when they landed beside the nest they betrayed every sign of wild agitation, bowing their heads concernedly towards it, gazing fixedly into it and making a louder outcry than I had ever heard even from Grey Babblers before. After a considerable time they fell silent, and one bird hopped away while the second jumped into the nest and settled there as if to incubate eggs. Later evidence seemed to indicate, however, that as yet no eggs were in it, and I doubt whether the Koel deposited an offspring on that occasion. But it very likely did so on a later secret visit.

On another day I saw a babbler proprietor angrily chasing a Pied Crested Cuckoo away from the nest's vicinity. These cuckoos often pay Large Grey Babblers, as well as Jungle Babblers, the indelicate compliment of using them as foster-parents for their youngsters; and I wondered whether, either then or later, this bird added a contribution to the local collection of eggs. It would be intriguing if the nest contained an assortment of babblers', koels' and cuckoos' youngsters!

So the situation became rather confusing. I was not even sure when the babblers laid their own eggs in their popular cradle. Often when two or more of them were at the nest they quivered their wings suggestively, and once I saw a pair mate inside it. On September 20th I thought I detected the shadows of eggs through its thick network floor, and by that date a babbler was often sitting tight and businesslike there.

On the next afternoon the curtain rose on the last act of the drama. I saw a House Crow fly into the tree and hop to the unguarded nest. At once two babblers sped shrieking to the defence of their home; but in spite of their clamour the crow stayed deliberately for several moments at the nest edge. It dipped its head into the cup. Then it flew away, with one babbler hot on its heels. Unfortunately the crow's back was turned towards me as it left, so I could not see whether its beak held an egg or any other evidence of highway robbery; but when it alighted on a distant branch it stooped and wiped each side of its bill several times on the bough, as a human diner might wipe his lips with a table napkin after a meal. Many birds do that after swallowing a delicacy; and I could only conclude that the crow had helped itself to an egg from the babblers' nest.

Through the next three days a babbler was often sitting on the remainder of the clutch; but during that period the other eggs must have been stolen one by one, for on the 25th the nest was empty and deserted. I could not tell whether the loot was a koel's, a cuckoo's or a babbler's eggs, or a mixture of all three. To a hungry House Crow one omelet is as good as another.

XI

Birds were not the only animals who built nests in the garden. One creature who emulated their example was a four-footed beast—the little Striped Squirrel. An expectant female squirrel would gather heaps of moss, cotton wool, frayed rope and other soft materials and shape them into a large hollow ball planted among branches in a shrub or tree. Into this cosy chamber she would then retire for her accouchement, and there she gave birth to her cubs.

Several such nests were built in my garden every year. One August day I saw a mother and her youngsters at home shortly after the latter were born. She sat inside the nest peering anxiously at me from its entrance, while her two infant squirrels lay at full length on a branch just outside it, absolutely motionless in the hope of avoiding my attention. Later I saw the cubs cleansing each other of fleas or other vermin. Squatting on a branch, they scratched with their forepaws and nibbled with their teeth at each other's fur, with evident mutual satisfaction.

Soon they left their nest and scampered across the lawn and up tree trunks with the effortless grace of their elders, of whom they were exact miniature replicas with fluffy tails and three white stripes down dark-brown backs. One day I watched a mother squirrel washing a pair of small twins. She employed the technique of a cat cleansing its kittens. One youngster lay stretched on its back in the grass with its four paws held up in the air, while she gently licked its tummy and thighs. The other youngster stood beside them, and it too received an occasional lick on its head and along its back. Both were docile and obedient under their parent's care; but as soon as the toilet was finished and she released them, they became very lively. Running, skipping and jumping with charming agility, they played what appeared to be a game of touch-last.

Mongooses also begat and reared their young in the garden. On August 9th this year I watched a pair of these agile, feline creatures mate on the lawn. Three times the male mounted the female from the rear and clutched her convulsively to himself for quite a while before they seemed satisfied. Each time she crouched submissively while he gripped her round her waist with his forepaws and hunched his hind-quarters to effect an entry. In that posture he jerked his body convulsively every now and then, and she responded with gentle flicks of her tail. Throughout the action they both gazed around them with a matter-of-fact, unexcited, unemotional air, no doubt on guard against interrupters. When they finished their third spasm of love-making, they separated. He twisted himself to sniff at his hind-quarters, then extended his sharp nose to hers; and after that they trotted into a shrubbery together, she leading and he following.

Each year the parent beasts paraded the fruits of such unions at various periods between the beginning of July and the end of October. Sometimes two sets of parents and youngsters inhabited the garden at the same time, residing in different shrubberies. It was charming to see the adults escorting two or three graceful miniature models of themselves across sunlit spaces of lawn. The young mongooses were as lively as young squirrels, and their elders were also sometimes very skittish. In that mood they would dart at each other, become locked in playful embraces like puppies enjoying a mock wrestle, biting each other harmlessly and rolling over and over in one another's arms on the ground. When they broke apart they continued to gambol, each stretching itself on its back in the grass and wriggling first to this side and then to that, and quite often turning head over heels. The purpose of these somersaults seemed to be to enable the animals to take bites at their own tails. At other times their high spirits made them leap into the air, and then chase each other in a game of touch-last in, out, under and around small shrubs.

When they had worked off their excess energy by such antics, they would lie restfully in a family group of adults and youngsters together, sunning themselves on the lawn. They especially liked to do this in the early mornings and evenings of the winter months, when the sunlight was bright but cool. They reclined with relaxed bodies, their tails stretched out behind them, their forepaws extended in front, and their heads held erect as they calmly and proudly surveyed the surroundings—as if they were pretending to be the lions in Trafalgar Square.

XII

One day a small party of Yellowthroated Sparrows spent a brief while in the garden. They were light and airy on the wing, behaving like flycatchers as they chased insect prey from the boughs of a tree. Another unusual bird who paid a solitary visit was a Redheaded Bunting. Occasionally a Rufousbacked Shrike appeared; Baybacked Shrikes tarried on the premises rather more often; and every now and then a Great Grey Shrike paid me a visit. Common Wood Shrikes came frequently at any and every time of year. The deceptively sweet song—a mere phrase—of these little butcher-birds could often be heard. One summer a pair began to build a nest across a forking branch of a jacaranda tree, but for some reason they soon abandoned the attempt.

Redrumped Swallows and Indian Swifts were regular residents in the sky above the garden. Except during the summer months—when they were nesting elsewhere In the neighbourhood—they could be seen almost any day. Absolutely tireless, they flitted, swerved and glided ceaselessly overhead, rarely coming to land except to roost at nights. I never saw an Indian Swift at closer quarters than about thirty feet up in the air, though at that height, and above it, they were common. Sometimes they gambolled in large, close-packed, twittering parties like swarms of gigantic bees.

Redrumped Swallows sometimes descended much lower, chasing a coveted fly a foot or two above the lawn, or dipping prettily in full flight to the surface of the goldfish pool to snatch a sip of water. With steel-blue backs, pale rufous breasts and chestnut rumps, they had the finely streamlined grace of all swallows.

Additional creatures of similar habits whom I sometimes saw join their aerial manoeuvres during the monsoon were Common Swallows (who are winter visitors to Delhi), Alpine Swifts (who are unusual birds of passage) and Indian Sand Martins (who are residents). Once in September I saw a bird which at first sight I took to be a Redrumped Swallow; but on looking at it through field-glasses I spied the two long outer shafts of the tail which revealed it as a Wiretailed Swallow. On another occasion I held in my hand a Dusky Crag Martin which flew into a veranda and fell on the floor one evening, dazzled by the electric lights.

XIII

When the temperature falls after the onset of the rains, grand migrations of birds commence. The first waves of mighty travellers reach Delhi about mid August—flock after flock of Rosy Pastors arriving, halting for a while, and then journeying onwards; all birds of passage returning from their summer resorts. Among the adults are many youngsters in immature plumage, fruits of the sunny holidays. For a month the procession of countless thousands of these colourful starlings continues, companies of them scurrying above the garden morning, noon and night.

In September White Wagtails arrive to take up their winter quarters in the capital. It is pleasant to wake one morning and find these engaging little harbingers of cooler weather running across the lawn, as much at home as if they had not absented themselves for the last six months. Comparatively fearless, they often came close to me as I sat on the grass. Their movements were always elegant. Sometimes a wagtail walked, picking its feet carefully as it strolled over the lawn; and then it would spy a morsel of food ahead of it, and dart forward in a swift, short sprint to capture its prize. At other times the bird would flutter briefly into the air, skipping an inch or two from the ground to catch a flying insect. Periodically it bobbed its tail several times in quick succession, and every now and then its small voice uttered a high-pitched twittering. All the wagtails were very industrious in their search for prey.

At about the same time another pretty winter visitor returned to Delhi, the Black Redstart. Usually the hens preceded the cocks by a few days, but by the end of September both sexes resumed their occupation of the garden. Whitethroats, Blyth's Reed Warblers, Chiffchaffs, Tree-pipits and other travellers also reappeared.

Even more eloquent of winter's approach was the return of various migrant wildfowl. Some species did not reach Delhi until October or November; but others came earlier. In September I saw a flock of Garganey, which are birds of passage in the autumn and again in the early summer; and also a few parties of Common Teal, which are regular winter residents around the capital. The pioneers of multitudes of duck who would settle on our jheels throughout the cold months, they brought a now welcome promise of cool, refreshing, bracing weather.

THIRTEEN

ASHY WREN-WARBLERS

I

The Ashy Wren-Warbler is an engaging creature. Measuring five inches long, it is half trim body and half a long, rather decorative tail. Its markings are pretty; an ashy-grey head and back, rufous wings, pale buff flanks, white underparts, and a brown tail speckled dark and light at its feather-tips.

It is a permanent resident in Delhi, and two or three pairs built nests in my garden every year. One of the birds' captivating qualities is their lack of shyness. They pursue their various activities unperturbed by the presence of a human stranger, continuing to feed, sing or flirt even when he is standing close by. It is true that they conceal their nests rather cunningly, and approach them as secretively as they can; but if you discover a nest's exact location and watch it quietly from a few feet away, its owners seem to become accustomed to you, and they carry on their domestic activities more or less regardless of your prying.

Through the winter the birds roam about solitary, and their plumage then is in moult; but by February cocks and hens begin to show an interest in each other, and to join in partnerships. Their dress recovers its full courtship smartness, and their shapely, colourful tails have then grown an inch longer than they were in the off-season. The birds start gay, abandoned, passionate flirtations, and soon afterwards build nests.

Their architectural styles vary, but the most favoured type is not unlike a Tailor Birds' nest, consisting of a purse-shaped structure either sewn between two or three leaves or else slung beneath one large leaf. These creations need a great deal of painstaking engineering skill; and quite often, for one reason or another, the builders do not succeed in their task. Their judgment can err in various ways. I have seen a nest in my garden collapse because the leaves to which it was attached turned out to be diseased, and disintegrated; and three others come to grief because the foliage on which they depended was too weak to bear the load of growing chicks, and broke; and another split into fragments because it was inefficiently constructed. Sometimes the wren-warblers themselves become dissatisfied with their work as it progresses, and abandon it.

The most remarkable case of that concerned a pair of birds whom Christina Loke photographed while they were building. Some friends reported that an Ashy Wren-Warbler was sitting on a nest in their garden; but before we could construct a hide from which to take shots, some accident occurred which caused the couple to desert. About a week later our friends announced that the wren-warblers were making a second nest; so we raised a hide and installed the camera, flashlamps and other paraphernalia for photography four feet away from the busy birds. For a while they were timid and ceased their labours, but then they became reconciled to the new landscape, and resumed work. During that morning Mrs Loke secured many attractive pictures of the pair building their home; and she returned in the afternoon for more. But instead of a further series of studies of Ashy Wren-Warblers creating a nest, she got a set of snapshots of them destroying the very same structure! In the middle of the afternoon one of the birds changed its mind. Whether the bulky hide overshadowing the nest irritated it, or the periodic lightning strokes of the flashlamps frightened it, or some other circumstance made it lose its nerve, or grow angry, or just become temperamental, was impossible to say; but suddenly it began pulling to pieces its and its mate's own careful, painstaking handiwork. One strange detail of the little drama was that for a while after this bird decided to break up their unfinished home, its partner continued the work of construction; so one wren-warbler kept adding new materials to, while the other kept subtracting them from their effort. Eventually the first bird persuaded the second to join in demolishing the place, and both then engaged in an orgy of destruction. Steadily the nest dwindled in size; and with the same building material the pair started to make a third nest in the next-door garden.

Before the third nest was finished some untoward event—I know not what—occurred to make the wren-warblers reverse their decision; and they started to build a fourth nest in the very same shrub which had supported their second. This time they finished the job, and in it the hen laid four eggs. Three weeks later a lusty quartet of fledglings hopped merrily from their home to begin life in the wider world.

II

In the summer of 1958 a pair of Ashy Wren-Warblers decided to build in my kitchen garden. I first saw them together there on May 15th; and during the next two weeks I often caught sight of them feeding among rows of dahlias, snapdragons and other flowers grown for cutting for decoration in the house. Sometimes they chased each other in a mildly flirtatious way in and out of pumpkin, celery and other vegetable patches. They seemed to be at an early stage of their wooing, though towards the end of the period I noticed an incubation patch on one of the birds' breasts, which may have indicated that they had already owned a nest. If that was the case, I had no means of telling its fate.

Whatever their previous history, on May 31st I found the beginnings of a new nest which they were building. It was slung beneath a pumpkin leaf. The large leaf's opposite edges had been pulled downwards, curled inwards, and fixed in that position by stitches of cobweb; and within the semi-tunnel so formed the skeleton of a cradle of more cobwebs, horsehairs, cotton threads and similar thin fibres was being fashioned. The structure was at a very early stage of its making. Observations of the building of several Ashy Wren-Warblers' nests had shown me that there are three successive stages in their construction. The first is the laying of the nest's foundations in the form of a complex criss-cross system of cobwebby cables sewing a leaf or leaves together in the right position to support the cradle-to-be. This is a work of immense industry and cunning. On one nest that I examined the enfolding leaf was punctured in more than 200 places, and in another in more than 150 places to receive stitches. The second stage of the nest's construction is the weaving into this base of a cup of fine grasses and rootlets—the cradle proper. And the third stage is the padding of the cup with thistledown, cotton wool and other soft upholstery to make the couch comfortable.

It took the wren-warblers in my garden ten days to complete these processes after I first discovered their embryonic nest. Both birds joined with great energy in the labour, on some days working round the clock. The nest was secreted in the middle of a large pumpkin patch, and when a bird came with building material it would plunge into the vegetation at a distance, approach their home by devious hidden routes beneath the thick foliage and only reappear (like a submarine resurfacing) close beside the chosen leaf, where it at once disappeared again into the well-concealed nest-structure. At busy periods of their work one or the other would arrive every few minutes with a fresh supply of grass or down for the construction, and each would usually stay on the site weaving this new addition into place until its partner appeared with another contribution. Then it would depart in search of more material while the second bird took a turn on the job.

A few days after I discovered the nest, when it was still not more than half completed, I saw a tree-lizard—scaly and ugly like a miniature model of a prehistoric monster—run across the ground beside the pumpkin patch. It struck fear into my heart, for I had reason to believe that these cold-blooded beasts were fond of eating wren-warblers' eggs and chicks. I wondered whether the drama of the nest which I was about to witness would be a comedy or a tragedy. Perhaps the villain of the piece had now entered the scenes. Two or three times in the next few days I noticed the lizard exploring the pumpkin patch.

As the nest neared completion its two makers engaged in other acts of creation. Their courtship flights became extravagant, and they repeated them several times each day. Early on the morning of June 11th their first egg was laid. With a dentist's mirror which I used for exploring otherwise unobservable nest interiors, I caught sight of its brick-red shell beneath the protectively overhanging pumpkin leaf.

When I passed that way the same afternoon, both wren-warblers stood on top of near-by pumpkin plants murmuring plaintive cries of alarm. I moved away quickly, supposing they were feeling unusually sensitive about my presence on this day of the laying of their first egg.

When I returned later I could see no sign of them, and somehow that corner of the garden seemed ominously silent and deserted. I went to the nest. It was empty.

Its sheltering leaf with the cradle slung beneath appeared unaltered, untouched. The thief must have picked the egg very deftly from its surroundings. I suppose the lizard had climbed the stalk and committed the robbery at the time that afternoon when the Ashy Wren-Warblers were so agitated.

III

Next morning the birds were in the usual place in the kitchen garden, feeding and slightly flirtatious. Occasionally they passed near their bereft, abandoned nest; but they never gave a glance in its direction. They had lost interest in it.

On the following morning I noticed them diving into the pumpkin patch suspiciously often at about the same spot, and I discovered that they had begun to build a new nest beneath another large leaf. For a few moments I watched the hen bird at work. One of her feet gripped the plant-stalk while the other held part of the leaf-edge in position as she punctured this edge with her beak, thrust a cobweb through the hole, and sewed the edge to a lower leaf. It was a charming glimpse of a skilful seamstress at work. There were three or four gossamer-fine threads stitched through other pairs of holes along the two leaf-edges—so few that the construction can have started only that morning.

Work on the nest proceeded steadily for eight days. It was another ingenious and neat wren-warblers' home, fixed this time between an upper and a lower leaf. Then inclement weather brought strong gusts of wind blowing skittishly through the garden, and they wrought havoc among the cobwebby cables binding the structure. Many of them snapped, the two leaves shifted apart, and the unfinished nest was wrenched badly out of shape. The birds decided that it was beyond repair, and deserted it.

IV

Next day the Ashy Wren-Warblers started to build another nest under yet another pumpkin leaf. I watched one of them lay the very foundation of their home-to-be. Standing beneath the leaf, it made a sudden swift stab with its fine, sharp beak which punctured a small hole near the leaf-edge. Then the bird gripped the leaf in its bill, and tugged it downwards to fix it in a desired position; and when the warbler flew away the leaf stayed thus fixed. I noticed a solitary thin strand of cobweb stretching from this upper leaf to another below.

That afternoon a fresh wind-storm blew, and when I inspected the spot later I found the cobweb broken, the leaves separated once more, and four tiny holes punctured along the edge of one leaf as the only evidence of the wren-warblers' third attempt to build a nest.

V

Undismayed, on the following morning the birds began a fourth nest, and their work made steady progress for five days. Then for some unaccountable reason they changed their minds, abandoned this attempt, and started another a few feet away. No amount of discouragement shook their confidence that they could build a successful cradle in the pumpkin patch, for their five endeavours so far had all been situated within two yards of each other in the middle of that thick mass of vegetation. The birds' persistent, unperturbed and apparently imperturbable resolve to build nests—a whole series of them, one after the other—regardless of every difficulty, was a notable example of the strength of the urge in animals to reproduce their species.

That day I had a fascinating glimpse of an Ashy Wren-Warbler on the job. The construction had scarcely begun, and the nest as a nest was still non-existent except somewhere vaguely in the imagination, or the intuition, of the pair of birds. On the pumpkin leaf the translation of their idea into practice consisted, so far, simply of a few rows of tiny holes bored along opposite leaf-edges, with two strands of cobweb connecting two of the holes. I had watched a wren-warbler bring these cobwebs to the leaf, each length of the stuff being folded up in a neat packet in its beak and unfolded for use after the bird's arrival on the building site.

The new nest was to be built beneath a single leaf, with a protective roof formed by the centre of the leaf, outer walls fashioned by the leaf-edges being forced downwards and inwards to make a sort of tunnel, and a floor provided by the nest itself, which would be lodged inside the tunnel.

The first stage of building had been the boring of holes along certain parts of the leaf-edges. This boring was done by a succession of stabs of the bird's stiletto-sharp beak. It had been accomplished with remarkable precision. There were three rows of holes in separate places, with about half a dozen holes in each row. The punctures in every group were more or less equidistant from each other, and also equidistant from the leaf-edge, to which they were close.

The second stage of the work was to draw the leaf-edges together by sewing threads through pairs of the holes along opposite sides. Already this had been done in the case of the cobwebs connecting them in two places, and I watched the bird proceed with the task. To achieve it the wren-warbler showed considerable talent as an acrobat. First it stood on a lower leaf which acted as a scaffolding platform for the worker. Then it seized an edge of the upper leaf with one foot, gripped the opposite edge with its other foot, and forced the two edges downwards as it raised itself into position between the two. It was now standing on nothing substantial but was balanced in mid air by the holds of its two awkwardly splayed legs on the leaf-edges, like a trapezist poised with his feet inserted in two high-altitude rings suspended on loose ropes. Gradually the bird brought its legs closer together, thus pulling the two leaf-edges nearer to each other. Then it got to work with its beak, using this as a needle to stitch the curving foliage into place. In this instance its thread was a bit of cotton which I had seen gripped in the bird's bill, trailing across one shoulder like a scarf, as it flew into the pumpkin patch. The wren-warbler first threaded the cotton through a hole from inside the leaf, then swiftly popped its head outside the leaf, pulled the thread through and tied it somehow into a knot or an equivalent of a knot to secure it firmly. This performance it afterwards repeated with the other end of the cotton on the opposite leaf-edge. The work was tricky, and the bird stayed for quite a long time delicately balanced in mid air, pushing, tugging and otherwise manipulating the thread so that it should be properly fixed. All its movements were quick and deft, and it worked with a busy, concentrated air; but every now and then it stopped sewing for a few moments to examine the situation critically and make sure that things were going according to its instinctive plan. When it flew away the leaf-edges were curled downwards and inwards, much nearer than they had been two minutes earlier.

Time and again a bird repeated this operation, until the leaf appeared bound into place by almost as many silken cords as gripped Gulliver when the Lilliputians tied him to the ground.

Often in the next few days I watched both birds perform various similar feats as their work progressed, securing the steadily growing nest ever more firmly by piercing countless additional holes and sewing countless extra stitches through the leaf. Eventually the bit of foliage enveloped the nest like a firmly pegged tent protecting it from hot sun, strong winds and (when the monsoon broke a little later) drenching rain. Often the builders raided their old, deserted nests in the vicinity to get fresh building material for this latest effort. Through their earliest attempts they had acquired much expertise. They were now professional, not amateur, builders; and they completed their task more speedily than before. By the end of the fifth day the job was done.

Often, after a bout of building, the cock bird would fly to a tall shrub overlooking the pumpkin patch, perch on a twig and give vent to his joyful feelings in a sweet, loud song. At other times, when both wren-warblers were resting for a while from their labours and feeding at different spots among the flowers and vegetables, he would call a briefer phrase to her, and she would answer in a low, contented tone of voice. Often the Ashy Wren-Warblers seemed extremely exhilarated. As I have said, they usually approached their nest surreptitiously, moving to it for the last several yards beneath the concealment of the forest of pumpkin leaves. Yet at other times they advanced on it openly and rashly, walking and sometimes running, skipping or fluttering very prettily across the top surfaces of the leaves, like water-hens stalking across lilypads floating in a pond.

Shortly before each nest was completed their joy would reach its climax. I remember one such instance. The hen bird flew to a branch protruding from a shrubbery beside the pumpkin patch and began flickering her wings excitedly. Then I became aware of the cock making a wildly abandoned flight in the air above her, rising, side-slipping and falling as he manoeuvred to and fro, and making sounds as if he were clapping his quills. She became more excited, shifted to a nearer branch and continued her wing-quiverings even more vehemently. The infatuated bird overhead promptly dropped to her, alighted on her back and mated instantaneously with her. In a few seconds the act was over, and the birds sped away in different directions.

Three hours later I saw the pair repeat the encounter. This time the male took the initiative by calling from a shrub-top an inviting challenge to a love-bout. She at once responded by flying from a flower-bed, where she was feeding, to a lower branch in the same shrub. There she crouched her body and started vibrating her wings. The cock bird rose into the air in his fluttering, climbing and tumbling courtship flight, clapping his wings with delighted anticipation. He remained aloft in this gay, ecstatic mood for about a minute while his spouse remained on her perch flickering slightly outstretched wings. Of a sudden he swooped down at great velocity, alighted on her back, twisted his hind-quarters below hers and pleasured her. Again the act was completed in a few seconds, after which the male took off in one direction while the hen flew away in another.

Nature's timing in such affairs is exact and efficient. As a pair of birds' nest-building approaches completion they take the necessary steps to enable the hen to lay their first egg at the right moment.

When I went into the garden at six o'clock on the morning of July 4th the female was sitting in the nest as quiet as a little mouse. She seemed relaxed, and gazed calmly through the narrow entrance between the nest below and the pumpkin leaf above. But after a few minutes her manner changed. She became restless and even agitated. First she half stood up, then she settled down again, and soon afterwards she half rose once more. She jerked her small body three or four times, and then stood erect, stepped a short pace backwards and peered at the nest floor. Bending her head, she touched some object there several times with her beak, and then squatted again deep in the cup with only her eyes, beak and tail appearing above the nest-wall. After five minutes she hopped out of the nest and flew away.

She had just laid an egg. The intense period of the operation had lasted only a few minutes.

Next morning I rose before six o'clock in the hope of seeing the Ashy Wren-Warbler lay her second egg. When I arrived in the garden she was perched in a shrub, calling loudly and insistently in a tone, I thought, more eloquent of distress than I had heard from a wren-warbler before. I feared that she had just visited the nest to lay her egg and found the place robbed. After a while, however, she calmed down, fell silent and flew to a flower-bed, where she started feeding unconcernedly. Her mate joined her. Perhaps I had mistaken the significance of her cries. Her exclamations might have been shouts of pride that she had just delivered herself of a second youngster. Since the birds showed no intention of visiting the nest, I went and felt carefully in it.

It was empty.

So a killer had struck again. The murderer must have been slinky and soft-footed, able to insert its jaw easily through the narrow entry to its prize, for the pumpkin leaf and nest looked intact and completely undisturbed. Was the villain the same watchful, voracious, cold-blooded lizard as before?

VI

During the next few days the pair of wren-warblers reverted to their behaviour in the earliest stages of courtship, starting all over again to flirt in a mild way. As if automatically, they shed the feelings and conduct of a married couple who had already built their home, enjoyed their honeymoon and begun to produce progeny, and resumed once more the feelings and conduct of a fresh young couple with no experience of those matters, who were betrothed but not yet wedded, with their home still to build and their love-making still in the future. It is remarkable, that power of Nature to force such sudden backward transitions in her creatures.

For their sixth nest the pair deserted the pumpkin patch. At last the fact dawned on them that success was impossible there. Instead they built a nest beneath a leaf on a brinjal plant about ten yards away. Whereas all their earlier lodgings had been suspended only a foot or two above the ground, this one hung nearly five feet high. I discovered it on July 24th, when it appeared to be just completed.

It was destroyed in an extraordinary manner. A pair of White-eyes were building a nest in a near-by shrubbery, and they took it into their heads to use the wren-warblers' home as a quarry for getting fresh material. Unfortunately the wren-warblers were absent at the time, and for a while the White-eyes kept raiding their nest and extracting from it bits and pieces of grass and down.

Ten minutes later a wren-warbler returned and caught one of the robbers red-handed. It became infuriated and chased the White-eye with awful vigour. I have never seen an Ashy Wren-Warbler look so angry.

But the damage was done. The nest had been despoiled by a stranger, and I suppose the Ashy Wren-Warblers lost confidence in its security. They never visited the place again, and it remained deserted—except by the White-eyes, who continued to steal an occasional fragment from it.

VII

Nearly four weeks later, on August 19th, the Ashy Wren-Warblers built their seventh and final nest in the kitchen garden. It was situated beneath a leaf three feet from the ground in the same group of brinjal plants as the previous effort. Possibly in the interval they had attempted to build a home which I did not discover in the surrounding shrubbery, or somewhere just over the garden wall, for occasionally during that time I heard the familiar voice of the cock bird singing a joyful ditty from a high branch in the vicinity. Whether that were the case or not, I believe it was a reasonable assumption that the couple whom I found building a nest on August 19th were my old acquaintances. They were putting the finishing touches to the structure, which meant that they had already been on the job for several days.

Early on the morning of August 21st their first egg was laid; at dawn on the 22nd the hen was delivered of a second egg; and on the 23rd she added a third to the clutch. Then she began to incubate them, sitting tight on her precious treasures day and night except when she left them briefly to fetch food. Almost always when I visited the place I found her sitting cosily there. At my approach she would sink her body into the nest and draw down her head until only her eyes appeared above its edge, in the hope that I would not observe her. Evidently she did not realize that her whole tail protruded at the back, giving her presence away!

So far as I could observe, she bore the entire burden of

incubation. I never saw the cock on the nest during that period, though he often stood guard in a shrub close by. Sometimes he uttered a few notes of warning to her when a suspicious-looking character like a crow or a cat approached; at which she would lower herself in the nest for concealment in the manner I have described.

The monsoon was now in full spate, and sometimes torrents of rain descended; but the overhanging leaf acted as an effective umbrella shielding the nest and its occupants. The lash of rain, however, put a strain on it, and during one particularly heavy storm the leaf got torn at one edge. Afterwards the birds did a skilful repair job, pulling down a higher leaf and sewing it against the nest to provide extra cover for this partial breach.

On the morning of September 3rd the hen bird did not leave the nest as usual to get her breakfast. Moreover, she appeared uncomfortable and kept shifting her position. I concluded that a commotion had started inside the eggs which was the beginning of hatching. Sure enough, when she flew off the nest later, and I peered inside, two eggs and one naked chick sprawled there.

When I returned for another inspection that afternoon the mother bird was sitting contentedly in the nest. She stayed until I went very close, and then slipped quietly away. The cradle bore one egg and two chicks. This was the thirteenth day since the laying of the first egg, and the eleventh after the completion of the clutch. The third chick emerged safely from its shell about thirty-six hours later.

In the meantime I had to do some artificial repairs to the nest to save the family from disaster. Presumably because the overhanging leaf, beneath which the nest was sewn, was too weak to carry its burden of eggs growing ever heavier, its stalk had snapped from the plant's main stem. As a consequence it sagged sideways and remained held partially in place only by a score of cobwebs with which the birds had attached it to lower, supporting foliage. This anchor would soon have got cut adrift; so with as little disturbance as possible to the leaf's natural position I rebound its broken stalk with Scotch tape to the plant. But for that salvage the edifice would have crashed to the ground in the next gusty shower of rain.

Usually when I visited the place in the next day or two the hen was sitting on her brood. She showed no undue alarm as I approached, continuing to squat there almost until I touched the nest with a finger to put her off. Then she rose, hopped silently over its side and alighted on a perch a foot away. Eyeing me dubiously, she then retreated further by a series of short jumps and flights, still quiet and apparently unruffled. It was a charming example of her tranquil character.

Whenever I looked into the nest the three chicks, sensing a presence and presuming it must be a parent, craned their necks and opened their beaks for food. They looked pathetically helpless, with bare bodies and blind eyes. For a day or two their mother scarcely ever left them, not even going in search of grubs for them. At that time the father was the sole breadwinner. He used to bring tiny, almost invisibly small, insects for their consumption; and he gave these to the hen as she sat in the nest. She would then rise, climb on to the nest-edge, turn round, and from there feed her youngsters while he flew away to fetch more rations.

Later she helped him in the search for nourishing morsels. The parents would arrive in turns at the nest with insects which grew larger and meatier as the days passed. Every few minutes one would appear. The hen seemed undisturbed by my presence, even when I stood very close to her nursery, flying calmly to and fro and feeding the chicks as I watched, almost as if she were my tame pet. The cock was more nervous and did not visit the nest while I stood near. Instead he waited at the edge of the shrubbery several feet away, with some tasty winged insect jutting from his beak, until I withdrew. Then he went and presented the fare to his offspring.

By September 9th the youngsters were able to enjoy large insects which must have been for them the equivalent of juicy steaks—no mean feat for creatures less than a week old! Under the stimulus of constant guzzling they waxed rapidly in size and strength. Their bodies grew, their skins became down-covered, their quills burst into feathers, their eyes opened, and they began to look like pretty little images of their elders. They heaved themselves about in the nest with powerfully awakening energy.

This put a great strain on the Scotch-taped leaf which was their nursery's main support, and which had now faded and shrivelled, since no sap nourished its broken stalk. The situation became desperate on September 11th after many hours of continuous rain. That evening I found the nest tilted sideways with its entrance almost closed by a wetly adhering neighbouring spray of foliage. Access to the youngsters by their parents must have been extremely difficult. In addition, the nest-leaf was soaked by rain, and hung damp and soft, with the result that the weight of its chick-filled bag had caused more tears to open in the nest wall. I had to perform a major operation with additional Scotch tape, being careful when binding the sodden, flabby stalk and leaf not to put strains upon them in places which would cause more rips. When the nest was restored to a firm, upright position, I removed the obstruction from its entrance, so that the adult wren-warblers could once more gain admittance to their family.

All the time that I worked the trio of chicks maintained a constant demand for food from me. They positively begged for it, opening their beaks wide, swaying their heads as if they were swooning, and buzzing ravenously. Evidently they were seriously undernourished, even starved. Perhaps they had been completely inaccessible to their parents for several hours. So as soon as I finished my salvage duty I stood aside. Within a few moments the mother bird flew to the nest and perched on its lip. Even from a few feet away I could hear the chicks' loud, eager exclamations of gratitude.

All was well again.

The nest held securely during that night. When I arrived to check the next morning, its three young occupants buzzed greedily again, mistaking me for a fairy godfather. Their hunger was evidently far from appeased, and for a considerable while I watched both their parents busily bringing them lashings of food. They succeeded in making up for the neglect of the previous day, for when I looked into the nursery after lunch the chicks did not buzz at me at all. They opened their mouths instinctively, but made no noise—satisfied.

I peered into the nest early the following morning—and my heart sank. The grass cup was empty. Yet the Scotch tape still held the leaf in place, and the nest stayed firmly upright. The young family could not have tumbled out. To make sure, I searched the ground below and found no sign of any of the chicks. At first I wondered whether they could have departed of their own volition, fluttering like children on a spree into the surrounding foliage; but I reckoned they were still two or three days too underdeveloped for that. To check up, I gazed everywhere in the neighbourhood and caught no glimpse of the missing trio.

As I stood speculating on what might have happened, I heard worried murmurings from an Ashy Wren-Warbler in the shrubbery, and a moment later the hen bird appeared. She perched first on a twig where she often halted briefly on her way to the nest, with a large fly gripped in her beak. Then she flew to the nest, alighted on its threshold and peered inside. She stayed there for quite a while, uttering soft, perplexed, agitated notes. Afterwards she flew back into the shrubbery and disappeared.

Then I heard a gentle, bird-like buzzing in a near-by bush, not unlike the hunger call of a nestling wren-warbler; and my hopes rose. Perhaps I had been wrong in thinking the chicks too juvenile to fly from home. But on investigation I found that the sound issued from an Indian Robin alarmed by a cat beside its near-by nest and expressing its apprehension.

Two minutes later the cock wren-warbler perched in a tree overlooking the nest, called loudly, and sallied into the air with a spasm of butterfly-swoops and wing-clappings such as it demonstrates in courtship flights. Not long afterwards I saw the hen on the ground below the nest. She moved about unconcernedly, picking up morsels of food and swallowing them. She was feeding herself, already forgetful that she should have been feeding a family. Both birds had snapped back into normal, family-less existence.

If their chicks had been alive that would not have happened, for the fledglings would have stayed for several days in the surrounding flower-beds and shrubberies, entirely dependent on their parents for nourishment. The adults' conduct was the surest proof of all that the youngsters were dead.

I felt little doubt who the murderer was. The villain had clearly been sure-footed and deft-mouthed, for once more it had ravished the delicate nest without disturbing a single grass of its make-up. I suspected a lizard.

VIII

Next morning there was no sign of the Ashy Wren-Warblers in the kitchen garden; but on the following day I heard one calling and saw it hopping and fluttering along the very row of brinjal plants where the empty nest still hung. It was the male bird, and I realized from his behaviour that he was looking for a site to build a new nest! Alighting on a number of leaves in turn, he performed little antics on each to test their suitability. At first he found every one unsatisfactory, and rejected them all; but eventually he landed on a broad leaf with another leaf drooping overhead. Sometimes with his beak and at other times with his claws, he began pulling the edges of the upper leaf this way and that, apparently examining how they could be either drawn together or fitted to the lower leaf to make an aperture for a nest. He stayed there a whole minute, tugging and twisting and shaping the leaves. Then he flew into a high tree and sang a challenging song. Thence he disappeared out of the garden; but a few minutes later he returned and sped back to the two leaves. Tugging and pushing at them energetically for quite a while, he tested them once more. After that he flew away to fetch his mate and show her his discovery. She came with him soon afterwards and together they surveyed the prospect.

That was the last I ever saw of them—unless they were the same as a pair who came to the kitchen garden in the following summer and built a succession of four nests which suffered a similar series of unhappy fates. For some reason they decided that day against the new site. No doubt it is too fanciful to suppose that when the cock took the hen to inspect the proposed property, she said: 'No; I don't like this district. We've had seven homes here, and every one of them has come to grief. On the last occasion our children were murdered in their nursery. It's a nasty area; there are lots of bad characters around. Let's move elsewhere.'

If she had spoken like that she would have been justified. For four months, from mid May until mid September, the pair had ceaselessly, but vainly, striven to rear a family. During that time they started to build seven nests to my knowledge, and they might have built one or two others before mid May and yet another in mid August. In two cases their eggs were stolen and in a third their chicks were slaughtered.

I could not tell for certain who was their persistent persecutor, or whether it was, indeed, any one particular creature. Possibly a variety of thugs lived in the kitchen garden. Two days after the Ashy Wren-Warblers' final departure a Great Grey Shrike visited the place several times and gave a fright to a pair of Tailor Birds with a young family there. The Tailor Birds twittered loudly with nervousness so long as the shrike stayed around. But I am not aware that these butcher-birds kill fledglings; and in any case I believe the wren-warblers' enemy was the lizard (or lizards) which I sometimes saw exploring furtively in the pumpkin patch. If that were the case, it was an ironical trick of Nature so to arrange matters that all the breeding efforts of this pair of Ashy Wren-Warblers were dedicated to the preservation, not of the species of Ashy Wren-Warblers but of—lizards.

IX

One reason why I suspected a lizard was that in the previous year a family of four young Ashy Wren-Warblers in their nest was almost certainly massacred by a gang of those reptiles. The nest was sewn beneath a drooping leaf on a tobacco plant. Its creators spent the last week of April and the first few days of May making it; between May 6th and 9th four eggs were laid in it; from May 19th to 22nd four chicks broke out of their shells; and by the 26th they were waxing lustily. The eyes of most of them opened that day, and they began to stumble about quite energetically in their tight-packed little apartment.

On the next day I found that a tragedy had occurred. Only two chicks occupied the nest. A careful search revealed no trace of the missing pair, either on the ground below or anywhere else. They had been spirited away, vanished into thin air—or rather (no doubt) into the fat paunch of some gourmet. Was the culprit a bird or a beast?

Five minutes later I looked into the nest again—and saw only one chick within! In the interval I had not wandered more than a few feet away, hunting for the lost nestlings; and I was sure that no Tree Pie or other winged murderer had visited the place. The attacker must be some small, silent-footed slayer who approached its prey furtively, killed quietly, and then withdrew with noiseless unobtrusiveness. My suspicions fastened on a sly tree lizard that I had sometimes seen prowling through the flower-bed where the nest was built.

The solitary youngster in the nest-cup was very restless and kept trying to climb out, as if it were frightened. One of its parents fluttered unhappily around it, apparently trying to urge it to calm down. But this plea went unheeded, and soon afterwards the chick struggled to the nest-edge, climbed over, hung for a few moments by one claw to the outer wall, and then fell helpless to the ground. The mother bird at once visited it there, touching it solicitously several times with her beak, as if to comfort it. Then the cock joined them, and both parents fussed around their offspring. They brought food, but it did not seem interested in eating. Its elders were very perplexed; they kept going away and returning, wondering what to make of the situation.

After watching for a few minutes I lifted the youngster and put it back in the nest. At first it lay unmoving, but soon began heaving about again very restlessly. I wondered whether the nest had become infested with bugs which made all the chicks desperate to jump from it; but careful examination revealed no signs of this. Later the chick settled down and fell asleep.

At 5.30 the next morning I was relieved to find it snoozing quietly. I felt that, with great care, its parents and I could perhaps keep it safe until it grew sufficiently robust to flutter from the nest and make its debut in the world. In a few days its wings would have developed the necessary strength for that.

When I looked again five minutes later the youngster had gone! There was no clue that I could detect anywhere of the kidnapper. But when I visited the place a few hours later one tree lizard was climbing a flower stalk beside the empty nest and two other tree lizards lolled on stems five yards away.

X

The stories of other Ashy Wren-Warblers who nested in my garden had happy endings. A family group was photographed one day before its three chicks flew gaily from home. For the next two weeks they hopped and fluttered in the surrounding flower-beds, entirely dependent on their parents for nourishment. After leaving their nests, parties of fledglings of various species stay thus near their birthplace for long periods. For example, a trio of young Redvented Bulbuls whom I watched through birth, childhood and adolescence remained in a shrubbery containing their nest for more than three weeks after they took to their wings, being fed many times each day by their parents. Gradually they learnt how to feed themselves, and only when they had gained sufficient proficiency in that necessary function did the family at last disperse.

FOURTEEN

JUNGLE BABBLERS

I

In spite of some amusing traits in their characters and some dramatic episodes in their lives, I cannot feel any enthusiasm for Jungle Babblers. Their dull earth-brown plumage looks dowdy, their voices sound strident, and their manners are deplorable. Many people who do not know their proper name are familiar with them by the nickname of 'The Seven Sisters', a description which presumably flows from the facts that they usually move about in companies of seven or more birds, and that invariably they all talk at once like a party of chattering women. The analogy is perhaps strengthened by the further circumstance that these conversations frequently end in a quarrel, and even a brawl.

When a fight breaks out among them it is an unedifying spectacle. They yell at each other at the tops of their voices, and then indulge in indiscriminate mutual physical assault, grappling with each other, standing on each other, jumping over each other and striking at each other with all the ferocious zeal of Siamese wrestlers. Yet none of them ever seems to get hurt. No doubt it is mostly done in a spirit of playful cameraderie.

One of their favourite pastimes is holding a party to delouse each other. Gatherings for this hygienic purpose are a regular feature of babbler social life. Sometimes the participants are only a few in number, but at other times the company is considerably larger, and they go about their business with a wholehearted zest. I remember watching a quartet of Jungle Babblers thus engaged. They were huddled together so compactly that it was sometimes difficult to tell which head and which tail belonged to which bird, and they were busily occupied giving each other what seemed to be vigorous massages. Every babbler appeared to play the parts of a masseuse and a client in turn, and they did a thorough job. Once, for example, a client lay stretched on the ground while one companion stood on its back and a second planted a foot on its neck as both these operators pecked delicately but determinedly all over its face. Its body was comfortably relaxed to accept the treatment, and its eyes were dreamily closed, as if it were experiencing some physical ecstasy. At another moment two birds were standing firmly on the backs of the other two, and each of the upper birds scratched and nibbled with its beak at various parts of its client's anatomy. The purpose of these exercises must be to search out and remove uninvited vermin who have become squatters in the babblers' plumage.

Babblers stay in the garden all the year round, and throughout the twelve months they engage in these noisy, energetic, gregarious activities. Nor do their groups become appreciably smaller during the nesting season, which lasts through the hot summer months and the monsoon. They then reveal another extraordinary social custom.

I often watched them building untidy nests in shrubs and trees at any height from eight to fifteen feet from the ground, sometimes progressing with the task in a careless, casual, almost absent-minded sort of way which resulted in its taking an inordinate number of days to complete. They seemed inquisitive about each other's efforts, several of them fussing around in the foliage beside an unfinished structure. When at length the nest got completed, a clutch of beautiful, glossy, turquoise-blue eggs was laid in it. They are lovely creations—one of the redeeming features of Jungle Babblers' otherwise rather drab appearances and inelegant demeanours.

In the first nest that I observed the hen always sat very close on the eggs. The edifice was nine feet from the ground, and periodically I climbed to it to see how its contents were faring. When I arrived below the nest the sitting bird would peer suspiciously at me, her pale yellowish-white eyes expressing hostility; but only when I actually set foot on a low fork in the tree and began to ascend did she fly off the eggs, uttering protesting swear words. She settled on a branch near by, and from there continued vehement, noisy criticisms of me. At once several other babblers congregated in the surrounding leafage, hopping about agitatedly and adding their rude comments to hers—as if they, too, had proprietary rights in the nest.

In due course the eggs were hatched, and the parents began to feed youngsters. Again, several other babblers in the neighbourhood showed as much concern for the well-being of the chicks as did the pair whom I judged to be the mother and father. Often four or more birds fluttered in the vicinity, all joining in a chorus of unseemly vituperation whenever I came near. Sometimes a bird other than a parent flew to the nest-edge and peered inside to assure itself that the occupants were safe.

One morning I was surprised to see three different adult Jungle Babblers in quick succession carry food to the young family. I could scarcely believe my eyes, and watched carefully to see whether this strange event occurred again. Before long it did.

The truth—or what I think is likely to be the truth—began to dawn on me. There were not two parents of the chicks, but four, or even more. The nest was the home not of one family, but of at least a couple of families. It was a communal nursery in which two, or possibly three, hens laid their eggs, where (if the theory be correct) they all presumably shared the duties of incubation, and where a group of fond parents cared collectively for their hungry spawn. So the gregarious habits of babblers extended through every phase of their lives, even causing a party to share a nest and rear their offspring together. Again, I emphasize that this is a theory: more intensive and accurate observation will be necessary before it can be accepted as proved.

Many times afterwards at other Jungle Babblers' nests I watched more than two parents feed the same unfledged family. Several times I saw four adult birds, all with insects in their beaks, queue up on branches beside a nest and await their turn to feed the young. One after another they went to the nest-edge, bent their heads to

Jungle Babblers

deposit a viand in some chick's wide-open mouth, and then flew away to make room for the next supplier—like a line of waiters bringing a succession of dishes to a party of banqueters. One day in July this year I saw an even more impressive concourse of babbler waiters than that—five adult birds coming in quick succession with food for youngsters in a nest.

Periodically when a parent comes to the nest it performs an additional duty besides feeding the chicks. Having thrust some succulent morsel into a young babbler's beak at one end of its body, the elder then touches with its own beak the rear-quarters at the other end of a youngster's body. This is to stimulate the nestling to eject its excrement, which at once emerges as a neat parcel enclosed in a transparent envelope known to ornithologists as a 'faecal sac'. The old babbler takes this in its bill, flies away with it, and drops it at a distance from the nest. By this means the parents of many other species as well as Jungle Babblers keep their nurseries from being fouled.

The babbler parents, or apparent parents, stay with the fledglings long after they leave the nest; and remain in attendance even when the chicks are very few. I have seen five or six adult birds waiting hand-and-foot on two youngsters, following them like obsequious slaves wherever they went, for several days after they left their nursery. I cannot vouch that all of them carried food to the juveniles and therefore laid claim to parenthood. It may be that, say, two of the half dozen were mere hangers-on who had attached themselves to the family in accordance with clannish babbler tradition. I have never for certain seen more than five adults bring food to the same brood of youngsters.

II

On August 17th, 1957, I found a Jungle Babblers' nest containing four bluey-green eggs and one naked chick so small that it must have just hatched. A fragment of broken egg-shell lay beside the baby bird, seeming a slightly paler bluey-green than the other eggs.

When I visited the nest next morning a parent babbler stood

beside it, keeping careful guard over its precious cargo. The adult stayed motionless and silent even when I went close to peer at the nest—a strange and seemingly significant quietness on the part of the usually lively, rowdy bird. I thought another chick might be on the point of hatching, and so withdrew in order not to disturb the family at such a vital moment.

When I returned and looked into the nest before lunch, however, and again before tea, and finally before dusk, there was never any change in the situation: four eggs and one chick lay in the cradle. The youngster was now at least thirty-six hours old, and growing fast. It seemed odd that none of its brothers or sisters had yet appeared, and I began to wonder what was the explanation of this mystery. Could all the four eggs be addled—or was the chick some sort of impostor?

When I inspected the nest next day it contained two chicks and three eggs. One youngster was so tiny that it must have hatched that morning. Its companion was much lustier.

On the following morning a large chick, two tiny chicks and only one egg lay in the nest. The older bird was twice the size of its companions. Those other two looked exact twins, and I doubted whether one of them could be the second chick I had seen the previous day. In any case, either a youngster or an egg was missing—and once more I wondered if the more stalwart infant in the company was perhaps a cuckoo who had already ejected from the nest its first-born rival. Though its eyes were still blindly closed, it began to look rather formidable. I searched the ground below the tree for any trace of a victim and found none; but that was not necessarily conclusive proof against my suspicion, for a helpless chick lying in the grass would probably soon be carried off by some predatory animal. I awaited curiously and eagerly my next inspection of the nest.

That evening it contained a large chick, a smaller chick and a single egg—no more! So the tale of the young babblers was beginning to resemble the story of the ten little nigger boys who disappeared one by one. The larger bird's eyes were now open;

but beyond its size (which could be explained by its greater age) there was no physical indication that it was anything more sinister than a precocious young babbler; and I suspended judgment on its identity. The disappearance of its two mates might be due to raids by House Crows, Tree Pies or other piratical characters.

On the following morning a large chick and a small one were still side by side in the nest, but I could see no egg. The smaller babbler could be the youngster which I had seen before, or else a new baby bird hatched from yesterday's egg-shell. In any event, either another chick or an egg seemed to have disappeared in the last few hours. The circumstantial evidence against the older inmate as the villain in this intriguing murder mystery now appeared too consistent to be rejected.

But I had made a mistake. When I looked again next day there were two chicks and one unhatched egg in the nest! During my last inspection the egg must have lain concealed beneath the other occupants; and its presence now made me feel I had been over-hasty and unfair in my condemnation of an innocent young bird.

The situation remained precisely the same for the next forty-eight hours, except that the quills on the large bird were now growing thick and dark. But none of these had yet burst into feathers—which would probably be the revealing occasion when I could pronounce a decisive verdict on the issue.

A group of older babblers always gathered in the surrounding foliage when I climbed to look into the nest, making a protesting shindy. They did not appear troubled by the problem which bothered me. Between my visits they busied themselves fetching food for their incongruous pair of charges, apparently entertaining no doubts about the legitimacy of either of their supposed offspring.

During the first few days the youngsters had always craned their necks at me for food when I climbed the tree, as if they thought I was yet another parent bringing them gifts. But now this rash action ceased; at initial warning cries from their elders at my approach both chicks lay motionless in the nest and remained unstirring until I left, having doubtless been advised by their guardians that I was a potential enemy in a hostile world, and that they should make every effort to conceal their existence from me.

The larger youngster was now eight days old. It looked at me guilelessly out of its dark eyes whenever we exchanged glances, and I inclined again to think I was over-dramatizing the situation, and that it was probably a youthful babbler after all.

When I arrived on the scene on the following morning a parent babbler was sitting contentedly on both chicks, keeping them dry in a drizzle of rain; and I only saw the face of the larger one peering from beneath its protector's tail. It was a charming, peaceful family group; but I still could not help retaining a slight suspicion that all was not quite so innocent as it appeared.

My hopes of ever resolving the riddle were dashed, however, when I visited the nest next morning—and found only the smaller chick in occupation. The bigger fledgling and the unhatched egg had both gone. The solitary youngster looked forlorn; and I, too, felt dejected, for now I should never know whether its rather overgrown companion had in truth been an honest-to-god Jungle Babbler, or a parasitic Pied Crested Cuckoo. This sudden, inexplicable and disappointing turn of events was frustrating.

But shortly afterwards affairs took an opposite turn. Imagine my surprise when I glanced at the nest at dusk that evening, and saw protruding from it the silhouetted head of a bird with what appeared to be a half-grown crest on its topknot! Was I suffering from hallucinations, or was this the chick which had done a complete disappearing trick from the same nest that morning? And did the crest mean it was definitely a cuckoo? Once or twice earlier in the day I had surmised that the missing youngster might be somewhere in the shrubs near by, for the usual group of mature babblers seemed to become particularly fussed, and to utter even louder exclamations of disapproval than were customary, when I stood at a spot a few feet along the shrubbery away from the nest. Yet I could scarcely believe this really possible, because twenty-four hours earlier the nestling had seemed much too immature for voluntary departure from home, and too defenceless to survive any involuntary departure.

It was too dark for further reliable investigation that evening, and in any case I did not wish to frighten the errant from the nest by climbing to view it more closely. I went indoors and waited patiently for daylight.

Dawn broke fresh and clear the next morning, and at six o'clock I very cautiously climbed a step-ladder beside the nest, trying not to disturb whatever birds might be in residence; and my care was handsomely rewarded. The larger chick lay sprawling in the nest-cup like a young giant, and beside it crouched its companion like a pigmy. As soon as it saw me, the monster rose and leaped to a branch alongside its home. At once I withdrew, so as not to scare it further away.

It had thrown off its mask; its feathers had burst from their quills, and they were not the dull-brown tint proper for a respectable young babbler, but a bizarre piebald design. On the bird's head rose a distinct crest; its plumage was dark along the back and whitish on its breast; and its tail-feathers, which were just beginning to sprout, were half black and half white. In fact it was an indubitable Pied Crested Cuckoo.

The unhesitating way in which it stepped from the nest on my arrival indicated a strong, precocious character, and the brightness of its eyes as it stared hostilely at me showed admirable resolution and self-confidence. It was a very different creature from its helpless, feeble-looking foster-brother remaining in the nest.

Four adult babblers were in attendance on this ill-assorted pair, and they made an excited hullabaloo as long as I stayed in the vicinity. The young cuckoo quickly became less apprehensive of me than attracted by them. Ceasing to look in my direction, it gazed instead at them, with its wings quivering and its beak wide open, begging for food.

When I visited the nest at six o'clock the following morning only the young babbler was inside, lying flat and unmoving as if dead—trying to evade my attention. The cuckoo was nowhere in sight. Had it flown for ever? Two hours later this question was

Birds in my Indian Garden

answered when I returned and found it sitting plumb in the middle of the nest, with the infant babbler crouching beside it, the two looking like a study of Dignity and Impudence. A group of five parents, foster-parents or adopted parents fussed solicitously around them.

Thereafter for several days the cuckoo played a game of hide-and-seek with me. At my approach it would take fright, hop from the nest, and conceal itself somewhere among the surrounding leaves. There it waited until I wandered elsewhere, when it promptly returned home. Thus, at one time it would be squatting serenely in the nest; a few minutes later it would be absent and invisible; and a quarter of an hour afterwards it would be back in the nest! These appearances and disappearances had the air of inexplicable and marvellous mystery attaching to a conjurer's tricks. One afternoon, for instance, only the young babbler was at home. I searched the surrounding shrubbery in vain for its outsized companion, and—deciding it had gone far away—turned to depart; but when I happened to glance back a few minutes later the cuckoo was fluttering quickly from branch to branch towards the nest. It jumped into the cup beside the other chick, and both immediately started clamouring for food. Again, on the next day I found the tiny babbler alone in the nest. Determined not to be fooled this time, I conducted a thorough search of the shrubbery for several yards around. The cuckoo was not there. My suspicion that it sat concealed somewhere was aroused by the fact that four adult babblers protested lustily throughout my hunt, but was allayed by the counter-fact that my search had really been very painstaking—and fruitless. No doubt, I thought, the guardian elders were concerned only about the safety of their genuine young babbler in the nursery; and I let my attention stray after another species of bird in another direction. But when I looked at the nest again less than a minute later, the cuckoo was sitting coolly in it as if it had been there all the time! I was nonplussed. No magician producing a rabbit out of a hat could achieve a more unexpected, triumphant surprise. I had (so to speak) searched the hat a few moments earlier, and done the job so conscientiously that it was as if I had searched the conjurer's sleeves and pockets as well. They were all empty—and yet here, an instant later, was the rabbit protruding from the hat—or rather, the cuckoo jutting from the nest.

The explanation of the cuckoo's strange behaviour was, of course, that it was much more sophisticated than its babbler colleague. Filled with energy and enterprise, it felt eager to go exploring in the world beyond the nest. If its youthful family life had been like that of other types—if it had been born and bred in a nest built by cuckoo parents and shared by cuckoo brothers and sisters—it could have left home and adventured with them outside as soon as it grew strong enough to do so. But the circumstances of its childhood were different; they were, to say the least, unorthodox by most avian standards. It was an impostor, a sponger, an interloper in a nursery of babblers, and so it was dependent on the timetable which governs babbler existence. The young cuckoo was more than ready to leave the nest; but the young babbler was not. The young cuckoo could have flown away and never returned to its birthplace; but the young babbler could not fly at all and so was still bound to their nursery. That meant the cuckoo was also bound to the nursery, for it was still dependent on being fed by its adopted parents—who must stay beside the nursery nourishing also their own babbler chick. They were not free, as they would otherwise have been, to depart with their cuckoo protege, attending it wherever it went in its earliest days of liberty. So although the cuckoo could roam at will through the surrounding shrubs, it had to keep returning to the nest to receive fresh rations of food. I think it roosted there every night in addition to making periodic visits during the daytime.

Sometimes the old babblers fed the cuckoo inside the nest, and at other times outside. On several occasions I saw it perched on twigs with its wings quivering and its beak open in greedy demand for food while an adopted parent brought delicacies to appease its hunger. The babbler youngster was naturally always fed in the nest.

This state of affairs lasted for five days.

Then the childhood partnership between the cuckoo chick and the babbler chick advanced a stage further. At six o'clock one morning I saw them sitting together in the nest; but when I visited the place four hours later the nest was empty, and the two young birds were perched side by side on a bough a few feet away.

It was an affecting sight. The small babbler and the large cuckoo sat closely wing to wing. No demonstration of affection could be more touching than this fond comradeship between a murderer and the solitary survivor of a young family every other member of which it had foully done to death. The cuckoo had certainly got away with its crime; and to complete the picture of sorry deception, an adult babbler was fussing around it, anxious for its well-being.

The small babbler was cuddling close to the cuckoo, evidently for comfort and protection. It looked pathetically helpless, with fluffy juvenile plumage and no tail beyond the tiniest tips of embryonic feathers sprouting from its rear. I felt sure it had left home prematurely, induced to do so a day or two earlier than should have been the case by the energetic, infectious example of its prodigious foster-brother.

Once the young babbler had broken away from the nest, the family never returned there. The cuckoo now began to wander further afield. That afternoon I found it perched self-assuredly in a bush more than fifty yards from its birthplace, making short, expert flights from branch to branch, but still halting every now and then to quiver its wings and open its mouth in request for food from three old babblers attending it. Its figure was more or less mature, though its crest and tail were both shorter than they would later become, and its piebald markings were less clearly black and white than they are in a full-grown Pied Crested Cuckoo.

The babbler chick was not there, being left behind on a perch much nearer the nest. But by the next morning it had caught up with the cuckoo and was once more settled cosily at its side. They looked even more incongruous in size and colouring than before, and yet as companionable as ever. The cuckoo appeared like an older child looking after an infant brother or sister entrusted to its care. Now their voices, in addition to everything else about them, betrayed that they belonged to different breeds, for the young babbler emitted a single harsh chirp at frequent intervals while the cuckoo uttered a soft, sweet, melodious double whistle. Yet four mature babblers in attendance—who should long ago have reached years of discretion—made no distinction between the two, feeding them impartially, first one and then the other.

The young babbler still appeared a tail-less, fluffy nestling; and yet it had made the immense journey of more than fifty yards from home—a veritable Christopher Columbus effort for one so inexperienced. That illustrated how powerful, inspiring and compelling was the example of its playmate! Its admiration for the cuckoo knew no bounds, and the next day it still kept edging up to its companion on whatever branch they occupied, seeking close, little-brother contact with its elder, as if they still shared a nest. The babbler entirely lacked the initiative and energy of the other bird—and the cuckoo now seemed to me to betray an occasional hint of boredom and impatience at its juvenile behaviour.

Three days had passed since their joint departure from their cradle. The group of four (and sometimes five) adult babblers, one immature babbler and one adolescent cuckoo remained together for at least another four days, travelling as a party here and there through the shrubbery. During that time the young babbler developed rapidly in figure and character, becoming independent of the cuckoo. It ceased to follow its colleague like a shadow. But it was not yet independent of its parents and foster-parents; and several times in the following week I watched them feeding it.

But I never saw the young cuckoo again. Had it grown capable of looking wholly after itself—twenty-three days after emerging from its egg and thirteen days after first hopping from the nest (if my calculations were correct)? Had it therefore become independent of its guardians? Had it waved farewell for ever to this family of Jungle Babbler dupes? Or was it fluttering unobtrusively somewhere in the shrubbery, still occasionally coming to them to beg a bite of food?

I do not know; I was not sure. Pied Crested Cuckoos have a genius for keeping secrets.

III

Pied Crested Cuckoos are summer visitors to Delhi, and indeed to most of India, arriving in the capital in early June and departing again about mid October. Many of them are believed to spend the rest of the year in Africa. So the parents of the youngster described above had perhaps flown several thousand miles to deposit their egg in a nest in my garden—as well, no doubt, as other eggs in other nests in other gardens in the vicinity.

I often saw a pair of adult Pied Crested Cuckoos flying together above the lawn, one closely following the other. Their black-and-white plumage was very natty. They used to call to each other suggestively, and to lark together in the tree-tops, and occasionally to look about them as if they were searching for some hidden, secret treasure. Once I saw the hen bird inspecting an unoccupied Jungle Babblers' nest, clearly interested in it as a possible boarding-house for a youngster; and more than once I saw the pair copulating half hidden in foliage.

Sometimes a second pair of cuckoos appeared, and then the four parasites would scuffle and skirmish together until the two new arrivals beat a discreet retreat. Probably the first couple regarded my garden as their territory, and all the likely nests in it as their private property. They were the local cuckoo landlords, and any other cuckoos who intruded on it were trespassers who should be prosecuted. It was a fine instance of pots calling kettles black.

It takes all sorts to make the bird world.

FIFTEEN

OCTOBER, NOVEMBER AND DECEMBER

I

The monsoon ends about the end of September, and after that the weather in Delhi is wellnigh perfect for some months. The atmosphere becomes dry, the temperature drops to agreeable levels, and the sun shines all day long. Perhaps at first the heat is a trifle excessive, for at noon throughout October the mercury in the thermometer continues to ascend to the middle 90s F ; but that seems a relief after the much higher altitudes of the earlier summer and the much soppier humidity of the monsoon; and in November the temperature descends into the eighties, while in December it drops to the seventies or lower. In January, February and March this process is repeated in reverse.

Each day shines like one of those perfect English summer days which are so elusive in England. A glorious quality of this season in Delhi is its reliability. You can count on being able to lunch always out of doors on a veranda or in the shade of a well-foliaged mango tree; you can arrange parties for sipping tea in the afternoons and for imbibing stronger liquids in the early evenings with certainty that your friends can enjoy these pastimes in the garden; and most of the time you can also dine on the lawn beneath the stars, though in December and January there is too much chill in the air at nights for that pleasure. Then we indulge in the alternative enjoyment of dining and wining indoors in rooms warmed by blazing, crackling fires.

Before the end of September there is a revival of flowers in the garden. Rusty-shieldbearer trees are cascaded with golden blossoms which give them a very rich appearance. In the first week of October their petals fall and spread royal carpets on the lawn beneath the trees. A pink frangipani shows some flowers; the purple bougainvillaeas are covered with blooms; coral creepers are embossed with red blossoms; and along the shrubberies yellow-elders, peacock-flowers, moonbeams, heavenly-blues, tavourmantanas and yellow-oleanders are aflame with various bright hues. At nights trees-of-sorrow are palely adorned and faintly scented with ghostly white stars, which lie dead on the ground each morning.

One shrub was decorated beautifully this October, not with flowers but with beetles. There were several such bushes in the garden, and all were adorned with parties of this same insect. The little creatures' heads and wings were patterned like an Egyptian scarab, and the design's details were picked out in jet black and pure gold as vividly contrasting as the black silk and gold thread on Benares saris. So far as I could discover, the beetles patronized only one type of plant, which at the time happened to bear plentiful berries. On every such bush a score or more beetles were scattered among the foliage like small, glittering flowers, some settled motionless on leaves, others ambling slowly along stalks, and others nibbling at the fruits. I saw one hanging upside down from a stem by its hindlegs while its forelegs clasped a plucked berry. The animal was turning the berry round and round in its paws in front of its mouth—as a child might turn an apple round appraisingly in front of its teeth before deciding where it should take a first bite into the tempting food.

Throughout the summer water-lilies had bloomed in the goldfish pool, and in October pink, purple and white varieties still put forth a series of flowers, each opening voluptuously for two or three days and then withering to make way for a successor. And in the last week of September the gardeners planted new seeds in the flat, empty flower-beds. Under the stimulus of bright sunlight the infant plants grew quickly. By the first day of October many of them already protruded an inch or two above the ground, while clumps of lupins stood four inches tall like miniature plantations of palm trees. A fortnight later a group of young hollyhocks had outstripped the lupins, reaching about nine inches towards the sky as against the others' seven. Their rate of growth became phenomenal, the hollyhock stalks adding an inch to their height every day.

Before the end of October flowers appeared on lineria and caliopsis, and through November and December new types of blooms kept opening their bright faces to the sun, until the herbaceous borders were riots of brilliant colours. But they did not attain their finest glory until the New Year.

II

Bird society in the garden reverted to winter conditions. By October the breeding season for most species had ended. Creatures who, like cock Purple Sunbirds, donned fine courtship dresses in the spring and summer had discarded their gorgeous raiment and resumed more modest garb; and although the warm sunlight seemed to stimulate Hoopoes and Green Barbets to hoot and yodel with renewed melodiousness, in general the volume of song dwindled. The garden became quieter, and life among its inhabitants seemed less eventful. Most birds did little more than sleep, eat, fly around and occasionally talk.

Yet some still indulged in more romantic pastimes. House Sparrows mated, built nests and reared young families throughout October. Their coupling often seemed to be a casual, ill-coordinated, somewhat inconsequential affair. Usually the male took the initiative by uttering a soft, seductive chirp which was an invitation to his bride to submit to his advances; and a few moments later he would jump on her back. But as often as not he jumped off again immediately afterwards with nothing accomplished beyond that simple exercise. Frequently I noticed cock birds mount their hens nearly a dozen times before coition seemed successfully achieved, and once I saw a pair go through these motions fourteen times in quick succession without attaining their aim.

I watched a Turtle Dove gathering building material for a nest in mid October, and Ring Doves being amorous throughout the month—with the inevitable consequence of homes robbed of eggs in early November. Evidence of successful recent nestings strolled across the lawn in early October in the forms of youthful Magpie Robins, Common Mynahs, Brahminy Mynahs and Jungle Babblers, while young Koels were still being fed by House Crow foster-parents in numerous trees.

At the same time several Green Barbets and Coppersmiths were hard at work excavating tree-trunk tunnels for their next year's nests. Nature's cycle was perpetually revolving.

III

In October the last of the summer migrants left Delhi. Having had their annual fun at the expense of babblers, the Pied Crested Cuckoos betook themselves to Africa or wherever they spent the winter; and by the middle of the month the Golden Orioles also disappeared. The latest date when I ever glimpsed their bright glory in the garden was October 10th.

About the same time other migrants returned to Delhi. The White Wagtails were joined on the lawn by some equally elegant relations. Every year Grey Wagtails spent a few days there in the first week of October, and then departed as suddenly as they came, for they were birds of passage. Three different species of lovely Yellow Wagtails winter in Delhi; and two of them—Sykes' Yellow Wagtail and the Ashy-headed Yellow Wagtail—dropped now and then into my garden. Only once, on a November day, did I see a Pied Wagtail there, though these birds are all-the-year-round residents in the region.

Other cold-weather visitors reappeared at intervals in October and November, among them scores of thousands of quacking wild duck and honking wild geese streaming back to their winter quarters.

IV

At 6.30 one winter's morning a Shikra flew into the garden, dashed at a flock of Green Parakeets gossiping in a tree-top and dispersed them. They circled round excitably and re-alighted in another tree. In playful mood, the hawk repeated the action three times quite deliberately, though apparently only in fun. It never darted at its quarry with the fatal purposefulness of a murderer, but merely with the less serious persistence of a teaser.

Between these raiding sorties it would perch on a bough with its head held proudly erect, its fierce eyes gazing here and there, its hooked beak looking like a small tomahawk, and its striped front and banded tail handsomely displayed. Then it would relax for a while, tucking up one leg invisible among its breast feathers while the other gripped the branch; but suddenly it would leap into the air again, speed after a passing squadron of parakeets, scatter them noisily, and then settle once more in a tree, as quiet as a little mouse.

Twice it made more determined dives after an individual parakeet, separating the victim from a flock of comrades by chasing it in a different direction from theirs and pursuing it viciously. The parakeet swerved this way and that in swift retreat, twisting in and out among the trees, its fine turn of speed enabling it to keep always a few inches ahead of its pursuer. On these occasions the falcon seemed more earnest about the hunt. Was it really trying to bag a parakeet, or was it simply working off an excess of energy against a bird whose supercilious looks had irritated it? Probably the latter, for after a while it wearied of the sport and swung away to some near-by perch.

At other times the bird of prey settled near groups of smaller birds like Jungle Babblers and Redvented Bulbuls. The babblers in particular would promptly mob it, making an almighty shindy. But the hawk stayed unheeding, peering down at the ground, gazing sharply in this direction and that, obviously searching for an appetizing snack of breakfast running across the lawn. Shikras are partial to grasshoppers, lizards and frogs as well as small birds; but this hunter did not spy one that morning. It would spread its wings and swoop low over the grass, passing slowly a few feet above the ground as if it had sighted a meal and was about to pounce; but in the end it always veered upwards again, empty-beaked and empty-clawed. It must have been hungry; and it stayed restlessly in the garden for over an hour. Then it rose into the air and disappeared across a shrubbery—still, so far as I could see, with its hunger unappeased.

Redheaded Merlins are other small falcons which frequent Delhi through the year; and sometimes one visited my garden.

V

Grey Partridges were country bumpkins who customarily dwelt in rustic fastnesses outside the city; but a few came to town. Sometimes on winter mornings I was woken by the ringing salute to dawn yelled by one of these game-birds skulking in the undergrowth of a shrubbery outside my window; and occasionally I heard the same pleasant, wild cry issue from many feet up in the air, for Grey Partridges like to roost in trees. More than once I caught a fleeting glimpse of a member of the tribe scuttling across the lawn, hastening into cover in a flower-bed as soon as I appeared.

Crow Pheasants were more usual in the garden. At any time of year they might be seen or heard there. Larger than crows and smaller than pheasants, their black bodies with chestnut wings are handsome in a blatant sort of way, and were distinctive as the birds strutted sedately across the lawn, scratched for food on shrubbery floors, or sat watchful on low branches of trees. Perhaps their most distinguishing feature was their voice. Their deep hoots had a sepulchral quality, and the birds bowed their heads as if in solemn prayer at each series of notes they uttered. During the monsoon I saw Crow Pheasants carrying building material over a wall into a neighbouring garden; but none ever constructed its large, hollow, upright, egg-shaped nest of grasses on my property.

Most magnificent of all the birds inhabiting Delhi is the Peacock. When its long train is fully grown a bird can measure 90 inches from end to end, and its metallic-blue, bronze-green, purplish-black and other colours have regal brilliance. A sacred and therefore protected creature in the surrounding countryside, countless numbers of Peafowl stroll like princes and princesses through the villages and fields. A family periodically took up residence in one of the larger gardens on Delhi's outskirts; but, alas, none ever so patronized me. I would have liked to watch an infatuated, courting peacock spread his gorgeous train fanwise above his body and dance his fan dance to an audience of peahens; and later to see this polygamous rajah lead his harem of ranees across my sunlit lawn.

VI

Through much of the winter I slept on an upstairs veranda with a wide view of the garden below and the sky overhead. The earth was still dark when I woke soon after five o'clock. The scene was palely lit by the silvery light of a moon, and always a myriad stars sprinkled the black heavens. Occasionally a shooting star plunged with incredible velocity among them, blazing a fiery trail through space. As I lay watching the constellations, they gradually shifted their positions in response to the revolving world. I hardly needed a watch to tell me the time of my awakening, for I learned to know the hour by the situation of belted Orion, rampant Taurus and other inhabitants of the universe.

Gradually darkness faded and the stars twinkled ever dimmer, like lamps going slowly out. Nearer at hand forms of earthly life became visible or audible around me. Occasionally a shadowy Nightjar fluttered inquisitively close to my pillow; and I could hear my friends the Spotted Owlets utter gratified exclamations as they enjoyed the last forays of their hunting in the garden. Other nocturnal prowlers were also still abroad. Just before dawn hordes of flying-foxes streamed in countless hundreds across the sky, returning like an invasion of vampires from their nightly feeding grounds to their daytime dormitories. On a wall where an electric light made a small luminous area little lizards chased flying insects attracted by the glare; and toads hopped after their prey on a flagstone path below.

As darkness gradually dissolved, small bats began to frolic close above my head, swift-moving shadows coming and going in the twilight. They used some rolled-up blinds and a folded curtain hanging from the veranda ceiling as sleeping-quarters. For half an hour before daylight they kept flickering in and out of the veranda, their forms becoming more apparent as the darkness grew less intense. Their airy manoeuvres were amusing to watch. Never still for a moment, they flitted here and there, up and down, round and about in the vicinity of the blinds, taking final spasms of exercise before daylight drove them to bed. Mostly they sped in absolute silence, but sometimes when one suddenly changed direction within a few inches of my head I heard the rush of its swerving wings. They seemed reluctant to go to bed. One would glide to a rolled-up blind's end, hover for a few moments as if about to enter its folds, and then turn and flutter away again, unwilling to retire. Often the same bat did this three or four times in quick succession; or it would actually alight on a blind, crouch there for a second, and then drop from it and speed away again, unable to make up its mind. Perhaps it was examining the situation inside the blind, considering whether this or that crevice in the split-bamboo screen would be comfortable for resting during the next twelve hours. Now and then a bat found a chosen spot unsatisfactory, for it would alight on a blind, squeeze itself through a slit, remain within for a short while, and then suddenly spill itself out again, to take more turns round the veranda before selecting another sleeping place.

Gradually, one by one, a dozen bats would slip into the blinds or into loops of the drooping curtain and disappear from view. They tucked themselves in between folds of the screens like human beings tucking themselves in between sheets on a mattress. As one squeezed itself through a narrow entrance and crept along the shelf within, a tiny squeaking would issue from the blind—no doubt from another bat already settled there who thus expressed annoyance at being disturbed. By the time that light got the better of darkness in the world beyond the veranda the air was empty of these fluttering shadows. All the bats lay invisible in their dormitories, fast asleep.

Then birds awoke in the garden. First a few Koels broke the dawn hush with their loud calls, and then caws from House Crows further rent the quietude. The earliest creatures to appear overhead

October, November and December

were Common Pariah Kites, half a dozen of them flying over the lawn at intervals, each travelling by spasms of slow, strong wing-beats followed by periods of floating on motionless, outstretched pinions.

I rose and went downstairs. Out of doors the Green Barbets had already left their night's lodgings, and half a dozen Coppersmiths were peering from their holes in trees before jumping out of bed. A faint mist hung over the ground, and there was a nip in the wintry air.

VII

Shortly before dawn one late October morning I was watching the bats flitting to and fro in the air above my bed when an equally silent but much larger winged shadow joined them for a fleeting moment and then departed again into the darkness outside the veranda. I thought it must be an owl of sorts, for it seemed twice the size of an owlet. Sure enough, when my eyes searched the night whither it disappeared I suddenly saw it reappear, alighting on a bare branch of a tree where its figure stood dimly silhouetted in black against the blue-black sky. It was undoubtedly an owl about the size of a crow, with an untufted head and a rather slim body. In the then state of twilight I could distinguish no more. The bird kept turning its face in this direction and that, staring downwards much of the time, searching the ground for prey. Three times in the next few minutes it made sorties into the air, fluttering its wings silently as it swooped low towards the grass and then climbed higher to tree level, apparently chasing some victim, as a bee-eater or flycatcher might do. I was tempted to think it was hunting the bats, but I have read no records of such owls favouring that particular dubious delicacy. Sometimes it passed out of my sight round a corner of the house or behind a tree; but always it returned and settled back on its bare branch. As darkness gradually melted I could discern more of its features, and I saw that its breast and much of its long, pinched face were white. I think it was a Barn Owl.

I hoped it would tarry long enough for me to observe it in

precise detail; but a few minutes before the rapidly strengthening light became good enough it launched itself into the air again, fled quickly across the lawn, and disappeared beyond a line of trees.

I never saw any other kind of owl in the garden. But in the pitch blackness of one November night I heard an oft-repeated, subdued, mournful hoot from high in a silver oak which answered the description of a Collared Scops Owl's small talk. I stood beneath the tree for quite a long time, staring up into the darkness; but the bird never revealed more of itself than those intriguing fragments of its voice.

VIII

One November 25th I saw a pair of Whitethroated Munias building a nest in a thick creeper against the house wall. Both birds were very active. They carried trailing strands of dry, dead grass into the creeper, or soft, small feathers picked from the ground beneath the Fantail Pigeons' dovecote. I did not disturb their labour that day, but when they were absent on the following afternoon I discovered their home. It was a typical specimen of the hollow, oval globe which munias create, composed of woven grasses and cushioned inside with the pigeons' plumage.

The nest was almost complete, and somewhere in the neighbourhood its owners were presumably indulging periodically in the gay skipping and twirling act that accompanies their mating. When I visited the site on November 30th a munia flew out of the nest as I drew near, lingered for a while in the creeper whispering its concern, and then sped away. I inserted a finger carefully through the small round nest-entrance and felt one egg inside the chamber.

The structure lay on its side, and the eggs were deposited at its further extremity; so I was not able to tell exactly how many the clutch finally contained. Whitethroated Munias are particularly fruitful creatures, and a couple can produce as many as eight eggs. Sometimes more than one pair share a nursery; but in this case only a single family resided in the creeper. Nevertheless, the number of eggs must have come near the maximum, for after the chicks hatched and they waxed in strength a formidable twittering and chirruping used to issue from the bowels of the nest, as if from many lusty throats.

The youngsters left the nest on Christmas Eve; but on the following morning I saw them gathered again round their home in the creeper, some hopping about on stems outside and others sitting inside their comfortable dome of grasses. For the next week the whole family slept in the nest every night. They were ceaselessly talkative and vivacious, and I gained the impression that they celebrated a very Merry Christmas and a Happy New Year.

INDEX OF BIRDS

The English and Latin names of the birds in this index have been updated.

Species which nested in the garden at 2 King George's Avenue are denoted by an asterisk. The two species which laid their eggs only in other birds' nests are marked in bold.

English Name	New English Name	Latin Name (new Latin names in italics)	Hindi Name	Page
*Babbler, Jungle		Turdoides somervillei *Turdoides striatus*	Satbhai	
*Babbler, Large Grey		Argya malcolmi	Satbhai	
*Babbler, Yelloweyed		Argya malcolmi *Chrysomma sinense*	Satbhai	
*Barbet, Crimsonbreasted	Coppersmith Barbet	Megalaima haemacephala	Chota Basantha	
*Barbet, Green	Brownheaded Barbet	Megalaima zeylonicus *Megalaima zeylonica*	Basantha	
Bee-eater, Bluetailed		Merops superciliosus *Merops philippinus*	Bara Patringa	
Bee-eater, Green	Small Bee-eater	Merops orientalis	Patringa	
Bluethroat		Cyanosylvia suecica *Luscinia svecica*	Husseni Piddi	

English Name	New English Name	Latin Name (new Latin names in italics)	Hindi Name	Page
*Bulbul, Redvented		Molpastes cafer *Pycnonotus cafer*	Bulbul	
*Bulbul, Redwhiskered		Otocompsa jocose *Pycnonotus jocous*	Sipahi Bulbul	
Bulbul, Whitecheeked		Molpastes leucogenys	Bulbul	
Bunting, Redheaded		Emberiza bruniceps	Gandam	
Buzzard, Crested Honey	Oriental Honey Buzzard	Pernis ptilorhynchus	Shahutela	
Buzzard, Longlegged		Buteo rufinus	Chuhuma	
Buzzard, White-eyed		Butastur teesa	Tisa	
Chiffchaff		Phylloscopus collybila		
Cormorant, Common	Great Cormorant	Phalacrocorax carbo	Pan Kowwa	
Cormorant, Little		Phalacrocorax niger	Pan Kowwa	
Crane, Sarus		Antigone antigone *Grus antigone*	Sarus	
*Crow, House		Corvus splendens	Kowwa	
Crow, Jungle		Corvus macrorhynchos	Dhal Kowwa	
Crow, Pheasant	Greater Coucal	Centropus sinensis	Mahoka	
Cuckoo, Common-hawk	Brainfever Bird	Hierococcyx varius	Papiha	

English Name	New English Name	Latin Name (new Latin names in italics)	Hindi Name	Page
Cuckoo, Pied Crested		**Clamator jacobinus**	**Chatak**	
Darter or Snake Bird		Anhinga melanogaster	Pan-dubbi	
*Dove, Little Brown	Little Brown Dove	Streptopelia senegalensis	Chola Fakhta	
*Dove, Red Turtle	Red Collared Dove	Oenopopelia tranquebarica *Streptopelia tranquebarica*	Seroti Fakhta	
*Dove, Ring		Streotopelia decaocto	Dhor Fakhta	
Dove, Rufous Turtle	Oriental Turtle Dove	Streotopelia orientalis		
Dove, Spotted		Streotopelia chinensis	Chitroka Fakhta	
*Drongo, Black		Dierurus macrocercus	Kotwal	
Eagle, Bonelli's		Hieraoaetus fasciatus	Morangi	
Eagle, Pallas' Fishing	Pallas' Fish Eagle	Haliaeetus leucoryphus	Machrang	
Eagle, Short-toed	Short-toed Snake-eagle	Circaetus gallicus	Sampmar	
Eagle, Steppe		Aquila nipalensis	Jumiz	
Eagle, Tawny	Eastern Imperial Eagle	Aquila heliacal	Wokhab	
Egret, Cattle		Bubulcus ibis	Gai Bogla	
Egret, Large		Egretta alba *Casmerodius alba*	Bara Bogla	

Index of Birds

English Name	New English Name	Latin Name (new Latin names in italics)	Hindi Name	Page
Egret, Lesser	Median Egret	Egretta intermedia *Mesophoyx intermedia*		
Egret, Little		Egretta garzetta	Kilchia Bogla	
Falcon, Lugger	Laggar	Falco jugger	Lagger	
Flycatcher, Paradise	Asian Paradise Flycatcher	Tchitrea paradise *Terpsiphone paradisi*	Doodhraj	
Flycatcher, Whitebrowed Fantailed		Rhipidura aureola		
Garganey		Anas querquedula	Chaitwa	
Goose, Barheaded		Anser indicus	Rajhans	
Goose, Greylag		Anser anser	Rajhans	
Harrier, Pale	Pallid Harrier	Circus macrourus	Dastmal	
Heron, Common Grey	Grey Heron	Ardea cinera	Nari	
Heron, Night	Black-crowned Night Heron	Nycticorax nycticorax	Wak	
Heron, Pond	Indian Pond Heron	Ardeola grayii	Andha Bogla	
*Hoopoe	Common Hoopoe	Upupa epops	Hudhud	
Hornbill, Grey	Indian Grey Hornbill	Tockus birostris *Ocyceros birostris*	Dhanesh	
Ibis, Black		Pseudibis papillosa	Baza	
Ibis, White	Oriental White Ibis	Threskiornis melanocephalus	Safed Baza	

English Name	New English Name	Latin Name (new Latin names in italics)	Hindi Name	Page
Jay, Blue	Indian Roller	Coracius benghalensis	Nilkhant	
Kestrel	Common Kestrel	Falco tinnunculus	Koruttia	
Kingfisher, Common	Small Blue Kingfisher	Alcedo atthis	Chota Kilkila	
Kingfisher, Pied	Lesser Pied Kingfisher	Ceryle rudis	Koryala Kilkila	
Kingfisher, Whitebreasted		Halcyon smyrnensis	Kilkila	
Kite, Blackwinged	Blackshouldered Kite	Elanus caeruleus	Kapasi	
Kite, Brahminy		Haliastur indicus *Haliastur indus*	Brahmini Cheel	
Kite, Common Pariah	Black Kite	Milvus migrans	Cheel	
Koel	**Asian Koel**	**Eudynamis scolopaceus**	**Koel**	
Lapwing, Redwattled		Lobivanellus indicus *Vanellus indicus*	Titiri	
Martin, Dusky Crag		Riparia concolor *Hirundo concolor*	Chatan-Ababil	
Martin, Sand		Riparia paludicola		
Merlin, Redheaded	Redheaded Falcon	Falco chiquera	Turumti	
Minivet, Shortbilled		Pericrocotus brevirostris		
Minivet, Small		Pericrocotus peregrinus *Pericrocotus cinnamomeus*	Bulal Chashm	

Index of Birds

243

English Name	New English Name	Latin Name (new Latin names in italics)	Hindi Name	Page
*Munia, Whitethroated		Uroloncha malabarica *Lonchura malabarica*	Charchara	
*Mynah, Brahminy	Brahminy Starling	Temenuchus pagodarum *Sturnus pagodarum*	Brahmani Myna	
*Mynah, Common		Acridotheres tristis	Desi Myna	
Mynah, Pied	Asian Pied Starling	Sturnopastor contra *Sturnus contra*		
Neophron	Egyptian Vulture	Neophron percnopterus	Safed Gidh	
Nightjar	Common Indian Nightjar	Caprimulgus asiaticus	Chhipak	
Nukta	Common Duck	Sarkidiornis melanotos	Nukta	
*Oriole, Golden	Eurasian Golden Oriole	Oriolus oriolus	Peelak	
Owl, Barn		Tyto alba	Kuraya	
Owl, Collared Scops		Otus bakkamoena	Tarkhari Choghad	
*Owlet, Soptted		Athene brama	Khakusat	
Parakeet, Blossomheaded	Plumheaded Parakeet	Psittacula cyanocephala	Tiria Tota	
*Parakeet, Green	Roseringed Parakeet	Psittcula krameri	Tota	
Parakeet, Large Indian	Alexandrine Parakeet	Psittacula eupatria	Hiraman Tota	
Partridge, Grey	Grey Francolin	Francolinus pondicerianus	Teetur	

English Name	New English Name	Latin Name (new Latin names in italics)	Hindi Name	Page
Pastor, Rosy	Rosy Starling	Pastor roseus *Sturnus roseus*	Tilyer	
Pie, Tree	Indian Treepie	Dendrocitta vagabunda	Maha-lat	
Pigeon, Blue Rock		Columba iiaria *Columba livia*	Kabutar	
*Pigeon, Green		Crocopus phoenicopterus	Harial	
Pintail	Northern Pintail	Anas acuta	Seenkh-par	
Pipit, Tree	Oriental Tree Pipit	Anthus hodgsoni		
*Purple Sunbird		Cinnyrus asiatica *Nectarinia asiatica*		
Redstart, Black		Phoenicurus ochruros	Thirthira	
Reed-warbler, Blyth's		Acrocephalus dumetorumt	Podena	
*Robin, Indian		Saxicoloides fulicata	Kalchuri	
*Robin, Magpie	Oriental Magpie Robin	Copsychus saularis	Dhyal	
Rock Chat, Brown	Indian Chat	Cercomela fusca		
Rosefinch, Common		Carpodacus erythrinus	Lal Tuti	
Shikra		Astur badius *Accipiter badius*	Shikra	
Shoveller		Spatula clypeata *Anas clypeata*	Tidari	
Shrike, Baybacked		Lanius vittatus	Chota Latora	
*Shrike, Common Wood		Tephrodornis pondicerianus	Tarti Tuiya	

Index of Birds

245

English Name	New English Name	Latin Name (new Latin names in italics)	Hindi Name	Page
Shrike, Great Grey		Lanius excubitor	Safed Latora	
Shrike, Rufousbacked		Lanius schach	Kagala Latora	
*Sparrow, House		Passer domesticus	Gauriya	
Sparrow, Yellowthroated		Gymnorhis xanthocolis *Petronia xanthocollis*		
Spotbill	Spotbilled Duck	Anas poecilorhyncha	Gugral	
Stork, Blacknecked		Xenorhynchus asiaticus	Loharjang	
Stork, Openbilled	Asian Openbill Stork	Anastomus oscitans	Gungla	
Stork, Painted		Ibis leucocephalus *Mycteria leucocephalus*	Janghil	
Stork, Whitenecked		Dissoura episcopus *Ciconia episcopus*	Manik-jor	
Swallow, Common		Hirundo rustica	Ababail	
Swallow, Redrumped		Hirundo daurica	Masjid Ababil	
Swallow, Wiretailed		Hirundo smithii	Leishra	
Swift, Alpine		Apus melba *Tachymarptis melba*		

English Name	New English Name	Latin Name (new Latin names in italics)	Hindi Name	Page
Swift, House		Micropus affinis *Apus affinis*	Babila	
Tailor Bird	Common Tailorbird	Orthotomus sutorius	Darzi	
Teal, Common		Anas crecca	Chotti Murghabi	
Tern, Blackbellied		Sterna melanogaster *Sterna acuticauda*		
Tern, River		Sterna aurantia	Tehari	
Vulture, Indian Griffon	Eurasian Griffon	Gyps fulvus		
Vulture, King	Redheaded Vulture	Sarcogyps calvus	Rajgidh	
Vulture, Whitebacked		Pseudogyps bengalensis *Gyps bengalensis*	Gidh	
Wagtail, Ashyheaded Yellow		Motacilla flava thunbergi	Khanjah	
Wagtail, Grey		Motacilla cinera		
Wagtail, Pied	Large Pied Wagtail	Motacilla maderaspatensis	Khanjah	
Wagtail, Sykes' Yellow		Motacilla flava beema	Khanjah	
Wagtail, White		Motacilla alba	Dhoban	
Warbler, Hume's Leaf		Phylloscopus inornatus humii		
Waterhen, Whitebreasted		Amaurornis phoenicurus	Dauk	
Weaver-bird, Baya	Baya Weaver	Ploceus philippinus	Baya	

Index of Birds

English Name	New English Name	Latin Name (new Latin names in italics)	Hindi Name	Page
*White-eye	Oriental White-eye	Zoesterops palpebrosa *Zoesterops palpebrosus*		
Whitethroat, Lesser	Common Lesser Whitethroat	Sylvia curruca		
Woodpecker, Goldenbacked	Lesser Goldenbacked Woodpecker	Brachypternus benghalensis *Dinopium benghalense*	Katphora	
Woodpecker, Mahratta	Yellowfronted Pied Woodpecker	Dryobates mahrattensis *Dendrocopos mahrattensis*	Katphora	
*Wren-Warbler, Ashy	Ashy Prinia	Prinia socialis	Phutki	
Wren-Warbler, Indian	Plain Prinia	Prinia inornata		

Latin and Hindi names according to *Book of Indian Birds* by Salim Ali, and the *Reference List of the Birds of Delhi and District*.